WHAT ABOUT THE KIDS?

BOOKS BY JUDITH S. WALLERSTEIN, PH.D.

Surviving the Breakup
How Children and Parents Cope with Divorce
WITH JOAN BERLIN KELLY, PH.D.

Second Chances
Men, Women, and Children a Decade after Divorce
WITH SANDRA BLAKESLEE

The Good Marriage
How and Why Love Lasts
WITH SANDRA BLAKESLEE

The Unexpected Legacy of Divorce
A 25 Year Landmark Study
WITH JULIA M. LEWIS AND SANDRA BLAKESLEE

WHAT ABOUT THE KIDS?

Raising Your Children Before, During, and After Divorce

JUDITH S. WALLERSTEIN
SANDRA BLAKESLEE

NEW YORK

The Library of Congress has catalogued the hardcover edition of this book as follows:

Wallerstein, Judith S.
    What about the kids? : Raising your children before, during, and after divorce / Judith S. Wallerstein, Sandra Blakeslee.
        p.   cm.
     ISBN 0-7868-6865-1
     1. Children of divorced parents—United States.   2. Divorced parents—United States—Life skills guides.   3. Parenting—United States.   4. Divorce—United States.
I. Blakeslee, Sandra.   II. Title.

HQ777.5 .W355 2003
306.89—dc21

                                                                            2002038712

Paperback ISBN: 978-0-7868-8751-4

Hyperion books are available for special promotions and premiums. For details, contact the HarperCollins Special Markets Department in the New York office at 212-207-7528, fax 212-207-7222, or email spsales@harpercollins.com.

FIRST PAPERBACK EDITION

10   9   8   7   6

This book is dedicated to the hundreds of gallant children and parents who generously shared their intimate feelings and struggles with me so that those who came after would benefit from all that I have learned.

ACKNOWLEDGMENTS

We are indebted to Nordin F. Blacker, who as a certified specialist in family law brought his knowledge and experience to a careful reading of the chapters on custody and on the legal system. His comments were enormously helpful to us and we thank him. We also benefited from consultation with Pauline H. Tesler, J.D., who has written extensively and lectured widely on collaborative law and from consultation with psychologists Rodney Nurse, Ph.D., and Peggy Thompson, Ph.D., who contributed their experience with this model. We also want to express our gratitude to Jan Blakeslee for her helpful comments on reading the entire manuscript.

It has meant a great deal to us that Bob Miller, president of Hyperion, has had a serious interest in our work from the start. We have felt very supported by his understanding of our efforts and our goals. We also thank him for coming up with the book title. We want to express our sincere appreciation to our editor, Mary Ellen O'Neill, for her sensitivity, her respectful responsiveness to our concerns, and her ability to identify fully with the book as we envisioned it. We also want to thank our agent, Carol Mann, for the clarity of her thinking, her excellent advice, and her consistent availability.

Finally I want to thank my husband, Robert S. Wallerstein, for his critical reading of the manuscript at each stage, for his many, many helpful ideas, and his loving, generous support of my work throughout my entire career.

Judith Wallerstein

September 2002

CONTENTS

INTRODUCTION XI

PART ONE ● THE BREAKUP 1

Chapter 1: Take Care of Yourself 3

Chapter 2: Telling the Children 19

Chapter 3: The Developmental Ladder 31

Chapter 4: Zero to Three 43

Chapter 5: Three-, Four-, and Five-Year-Olds 51

Chapter 6: Six-, Seven-, and Eight-Year-Olds 63

Chapter 7: Nine- and Ten-Year-Olds 73

Chapter 8: Eleven-, Twelve-, and Thirteen-Year-Olds 87

Chapter 9: Fourteen-, Fifteen-, Sixteen-, and
            Seventeen-Year-Olds 99

Chapter 10: College-Age Children 113

Chapter 11: Vulnerable Children 121

Chapter 12: What Is the "Best" Time to Divorce? 127

Chapter 13: Setting Routines and Structure 133

Chapter 14: Supporting the New Family 141

PART TWO ● PARENT-TO-PARENT 155

Chapter 15: A New Kind of Parent 157

Chapter 16: You and the Law 163

Chapter 17: Laying the Foundation for Custody
and Coparenting 175

Chapter 18: Custody 185

Chapter 19: High-Conflict Divorce 203

Chapter 20: How to Choose the Right Custody
for Your Child 215

PART THREE ● THE POST-DIVORCE FAMILY 221

Chapter 21: Take Another Close Look at Your
Children and at Yourself 223

Chapter 22: The Overburdened Child 231

Chapter 23: Parent-Child Alignments 239

Chapter 24: A New Kind of Teenager 247

Chapter 25: A New Kind of Father 259

Chapter 26: A New Kind of Mother 269

PART FOUR ● SECOND MARRIAGE 275

Chapter 27: Dating and Sex 277

Chapter 28: Remarriage 289

Chapter 29: Insiders and the Remarried Family 299

Chapter 30: Stepparents 311

Chapter 31: Blending Two Families 323

Chapter 32: Holidays and Special Occasions 333

PART FIVE ● CONVERSATIONS FOR A LIFETIME 339

Chapter 33: How to Protect Children of Divorce in
Young Adulthood 341

EPILOGUE 363
INDEX 365

INTRODUCTION

When I was a young mother and my four-month-old daughter cried for an entire afternoon, I reached for *Dr. Spock's Baby and Child Care* for advice on what to do. I quickly learned that babies her age start teething, and on close inspection, her tiny swollen gums confirmed the diagnosis. I felt immediately reassured. Benjamin Spock's book, with its well-worn pages, guided me through many of her developmental milestones, well into her adolescence.

When my grandson turned two and wasn't speaking as well as other children his age, my daughter consulted Dr. T. Berry Brazelton's classic book *Infants and Mothers*. There she learned that all toddlers develop language according to their own pace and that her worries were misplaced. Dr. Brazelton's other books helped her find answers to many parenting questions as her children grew up. She, too, immediately felt reassured, as if the kindly doctor had just paid a house call.

But if you are among the millions of American parents who have decided to divorce and you subsequently hear your children tossing and turning long after you put them down to sleep, you won't find the special kind of advice you need from most experts on child development. Dr. Spock and Dr. Brazelton don't write books about the effects of divorce on children. And so you probably find yourself feeling alone, confused, and in a state of shock, struggling to get out of bed to face each new day, dealing with your whimpering, red-eyed children who haven't slept, and trying to calm your angry adolescents who yell, "What's the matter with both of you? How could you be so selfish? How could you not care about my needs?" Or you may feel freer and happier than you have felt in many years, but you're still facing distress in your children. How is it they don't understand? What do they want from you?

When you decided to divorce, you knew what you were trying to escape. You can describe it in Technicolor. But now you face a new problem—what lies ahead? Building a life after divorce is as demanding as building a marriage. Just as a marriage license makes any kind of marriage possible, a divorce sets into motion—but does not shape—the post-divorce family. Both you and your soon-to-be ex-partner will need to determine who lives where, who cares for the children on a day-to-day basis, and how your responsibilities as parents will be shared or not shared. Will the post-divorce family continue the disappointments that marked your marriage or will it be a fresh start? Will it add new pain or will it help you and your children to create a much happier family? How will you and your spouse get along after the breakup? How will your new lover get along with the children? Or with your soon-to-be ex? You're entering the divorce with far less information about what's ahead than you had when you entered your marriage. If you're to protect your children and yourself, you're going to have to learn a lot of things very fast.

As you read through these chapters, I hope you'll keep in mind the many facets of the job ahead. When you got married, you really faced only one major complex challenge—to build a marriage that worked for both of you. But now that you're getting a divorce, you are about to be challenged by three major, interlocking challenges. Moreover, you have to work on them all at the same time, here at the outset and in the years to come. The first challenge is to get your life under control, literally to restore yourself and rebuild your social supports. You must find your equilibrium and fashion a new identity that is strong enough to cope with the stressful years that lie ahead.

The second challenge involves you and your children. You need to prepare them for the breakup and to support them through the crisis. You'll need to choose the best custody arrangement for them and reevaluate it at regular intervals, as they grow older and have different needs.

The third challenge is to create a new relationship between you and your ex-partner. You need to define for yourself what it means to be a co-parent after divorce and how you will carry it off together. It's an entirely new family role.

All three of these challenges begin the day you decide to divorce and last, in many respects, until death do you part. This is why divorce is so complicated and why so many people don't benefit from their divorces. Just because you succeed at one challenge does not mean you'll do well at the other two. But if you succeed in meeting all three, I believe you can open up new opportunities in your life and put the disappointments of your marriage behind you, once and for all.

Because these challenges last many years, this book is a guide for parents who are thinking about divorce, who are in the process of getting a divorce, or who split up a few or even many years ago and are deeply concerned about how their children are doing in the post-divorce family. It describes the changes that you will experience in those first few days, weeks, and months after the decision is made and what you can do to take and stay in control of your life. I can tell you exactly what to say to your children and how, depending on their ages, they are likely to respond. I can lead you through those first crazy years after divorce and describe what you can do to protect your children from harm. I will help you decide how to choose the right kind of custody for your child and how to help each child settle into his or her new schedule without tears. Most of all, I can show you the changes that lie ahead once the dust settles. The turning points are numerous, the danger points are unexpected, but so are the opportunities. I will be your guide.

Why me? Why should you trust me? For starters, I have talked to more children and adolescents of divorce than anyone else in America. I have also spoken to parents all over the country and learned from what they had to say. As founder and director of the Center for the Family in Transition in Corte Madera, California, I have met and worked with thousands of divorced and remarried parents and their children from every economic background and culture that the California melting pot has thrown together. I've counseled them through every phase of the divorcing process, from separation through the post-divorce years, including second marriages and sometimes second divorces.

More than thirty years ago, I began a small study of sixty couples and their 131 children who were going through a divorce, and I have, through all these years, kept in close touch with three-quarters of the children and most of their parents. I interviewed them at the time of their parents' divorce, a year later, and then every five years up to twenty-five years after the event. I knew them when they were little and am still talking to them now that they're in their thirties and forties with children and stepchildren of their own. My research has always been based on a case method approach to understanding human behavior and motivation. This means I put my faith in the power of individual stories to shed light on crucially important themes in our contemporary culture. Instead of asking 1,000 people in a questionnaire how often they visited their father (every day, once a week, once a month, never), I like to say, "Tell me about your dad." If a young woman begins to cry or her body stiffens as she slowly responds to my request, I learn a great deal about her feelings and her relationship with her father that is not conveyed by tabulating the number of visits. This kind of face-to-face study has a power that can't be matched in large surveys. And it has enabled me to distill a message from children of divorce in their own words and to capture their voices as they grew up in the post-divorce family. I have written three best-selling books about these children of divorce whose childhood and adult lives, I submit, are emblematic of millions of young Americans.

Based on this knowledge, I believe that I can tell you what lies ahead for your own family. What should you fight for and what should you let go? Issues will arise related to when you move, find a new job, and find or lose a new love or spouse. Many things change when your children grow to adolescence and young adulthood, when you and your divorced spouse are invited to college graduations, weddings, and visits with new grandchildren. It's a long road ahead. You need to get ready for the journey.

Parenting is always a hazardous undertaking. Much of the time it's like climbing a mountain trail that disappears and reappears, making you wonder if you're still headed for the top or if you're stranded on a cliff. But parenting in a divorced or remarried family is harder—it's like climbing that same trail in a blizzard, blinded by emotions and events out of your control. You have no clear path, no idea of where you're going. You may not even realize that you're lost.

Almost every week I get letters from bewildered parents:

"My attorney says that the custody plan she worked out for my kids, who are five and eight, is a good one but they've never been away from me. What should I do?"

"I'm worried that my son will think I don't love him if I agree to joint custody. What should I do?"

"My teenage son wants to live with me but his mother objects. What should I do?"

"My new wife says that my daughter will ruin our relationship just like she ruined her mom's remarriage. What should I do?"

Let me warn you right now. People will offer a lot of advice that won't be all that useful for you or your child. Much of it will revolve around the breakup itself. You'll hear from experts who swear that if you mediate your differences, your children will be home free. Some argue that joint custody will protect your children from feeling that they've lost their family while others insist that if you refrain from fighting, your children will slide easily into a new life chapter. Attorneys, mental health professionals, friends, and other parents are going to tell you that you can do things to ensure that your divorce has no lasting consequences.

But of course it will. You know it and every other parent knows it. How could a child not be affected by the major changes that divorce and remarriage bring? Divorced families are altogether different from intact families. So are remarried families. Your relationship with your children changes the day you divorce. It changes again when you remarry. With luck and good judgment, the divorce will turn out to be a turning point that leads you to greater happiness and to be a better parent. But the change that you or your spouse or both of you seek voluntarily will necessarily involve sorrow and loss for your children. They're going to need your help in coping with the losses, now and later.

What happens to your children in the long run is not governed by events at the breakup but by what occurs through time in the post-divorce and remarried family.

You see, divorce is not a single event. Like marriage, it's a process that has many stages for you and your children. Divorce begins with the escalating distress of the marriage breaking apart—a crisis that often peaks when divorce papers are finally filed—and ushers in several years of disequilibrium for everyone in the family. Many parents say that the low point doesn't occur until two years after the divorce.

So what do you need to know to help your child? Does age matter? Does gender matter? What if your child is shy? Does an outgoing personality help? Where will the effects of your divorce show up in your child's life? In the classroom? On the playground? At home? Now? Later? Maybe never? How do you cope with a crisis within a crisis?

One of the first divorcing parents I ever talked to was a young father who called in a panic. His two-and-a-half-year-old son refused to move from a chosen spot in the living room where he seemed to be standing guard. As far as the father could tell, there was nothing special about this location in the room. It was halfway between the couch and the window, off to the left. His son, holding a ragged toy rabbit, would not budge. Every time the father tried to pick him up to take him to bed, the child screamed in terror.

I asked the father, who was trying his best to calm his son, when his wife had left and where the child was when it happened. He recalled that his son had been playing in the living room when his wife stormed out of the house in a towering rage. The little boy had waved to his mother from the very spot he now refused to abandon.

"Have you talked to your son about this event?" I asked.

"Oh no," the father replied. "He's much too young to understand."

"Talk to your son immediately," I said. "He's not too young at all. You're making a mistake by thinking that. Tell him that his mother is coming back to visit him. Get her on the phone and let him speak with her. Then tell him he doesn't have to stand and wait for her."

My advice worked. The gallant little sentry allowed himself to be carried off to bed with the knowledge that he would see his mother again. The father learned the importance of communicating with the son he thought was "too young" to understand. He also laid important groundwork for talking directly to his son and in later years remained especially sensitive to the boy's feelings.

My goal is to give you advice that you can use during your divorce and through the years ahead. If you're in the thick of the crisis, you can look up specific ideas about your three-year-old who won't go to bed, your eight-year-old who is having trouble at school, or your fifteen-year-old who is angry all the time. You can find out how to explain divorce to children in ways that they will understand at each age and that will help them cope. I've included information to help you decide custody and visitation.

But I hope, too, that you'll use this book in the many years after your divorce for ideas about how to protect your children in the ever-changing post-divorce family. I offer specific advice on what to say to your children when they reach adolescence and young adulthood, explaining how you can help them avoid being afraid of love and commitment in their own lives. I tell you what you need to know before you commit to a second marriage and give advice to stepparents, who need all the help they can get.

I suggest that you read the whole book first and then go back to specific topics. This way you'll gain an overview of what lies ahead and be able to plan.

I'm firmly convinced that one reason divorced families have problems is because most people don't have the help that they need. All of us want to shut our eyes and believe that "everything will take care of itself," as if life after divorce will unfold according to some magical formula. But nothing about divorce and remarriage is simple. And if you are yourself a child of divorce, your own journey down this road will be complicated by your earlier life experiences. I wish I could say you are automatically wiser and better able to help your children than people who have not been touched previously by divorce, but that's not how it works. It may be harder for you when you recall your own childhood pain or you may be able to draw on your experience to help yourself and your children.

Each decision to divorce begins a long journey that holds surprising, unexpected turns. We begin, in the next chapter, with you.

PART ONE

THE BREAKUP

Chapter 1:   Take Care of Yourself

After Hurricane Andrew slammed into the Florida coast in 1992, killing twenty-six people and causing more than $30 billion in property damage, stunned residents were slow to pick up the pieces. Whole neighborhoods had been destroyed. Utility lines were knocked out. Businesses failed. Gradually, though, people put their communities back together. Streets still had the same names. Familiar movie theaters reopened. Stores restocked their shelves and opened for business as usual. Everything was the same but everything was different. Everyone who walked down the street was proud of the rebuilding but knew in his or her hearts that it was not the same city as before.

What happened after Hurricane Andrew is equivalent to what happens after you divorce. Divorce is an end and a beginning. From the moment you walk down the courthouse steps, you're going to need new knowledge and new ideas and most of all a new you. Even after the disequilibrium of the breakup is restored and you've found balance in the various spheres of your life, you're a different person. But most of all, you're a different kind of parent.

One of the many things I've learned is that parents can't help their children until they've thought about themselves, about where they're coming from. So let's begin right there.

First you need to take control of your own life. I wish I could tell you that it's okay to lie down and pull the covers over your head, but that's not possible. You may feel like you're the only person in the world who could ever feel this bad, but let me assure you, you have plenty of company. Once you've decided that "it's really over," you'll have set into motion the task of becoming a different person and, to your surprise, a different kind of parent. While your decision marks the end of a marriage, it's also the formation of a new kind of family. It's a new play with different characters in strange settings, changes in parent and child relationships, and predictable transitions that most parents fail to anticipate.

Most people don't understand that divorce follows a long trajectory. What you feel today is probably not going to be relevant to your life three, five, or ten years from now. The quick fix that you want to put into place tomorrow won't be of much use down the post-divorce road. You can take steps to ease your immediate pain, but the really hard work comes one day and then one year at a time with changes that ricochet into your life and into the lives of your children.

You're about to undergo a metamorphosis. To succeed for yourself and your children, you're going to have to create a self-image as someone who can cope with the demands set before you. You can't become an effective parent until you've regained your footing and begun to repair the damage done by the failed marriage and the inevitable stresses of the divorce.

How fast or how well this happens depends on how you respond to the challenges and frustrations that lie ahead. There's no way not to cry. Whether you left the marriage or you were the one left, crying is good for the soul. It doesn't banish the hurt but at least you can get the pain out of your belly. But if you're caught up in the image of having failed in your marriage—because you were betrayed or you're guilty of breaking your marriage vows or your judgment was just plain lousy—your parenting will be burdened. Nor can you muster the strength you need if you think of yourself as a victim. It may be grossly unfair if the person you trusted most in the world is the cause of all your pain, but that feeling must yield to the tasks before you. As strange as this sounds, if you find yourself raging at your husband or wife, it really doesn't matter if you're right. What matters is that being enraged will eclipse your ability to be a good parent. It will cloud your judgment and make it harder for you to take care of yourself or see your children as being separate from you, with different needs and priorities in their young lives. Worst of all, it will make it much harder for you to be a compassionate, loving mom or dad.

If your divorce is like most, only one of you wants to end the marriage. Never in my thirty years of working with divorcing couples have I seen two people sit down quietly at the kitchen table and say, "You know, we both made a mistake, let's go our separate ways." There's almost always pain and palpable grief. At this point, the hardest thing you face is the need to avoid getting stuck in your pain. Think of Lot's wife. She was offered escape from Sodom and Gomorrah, which were due to be destroyed by God, on condition that she refrain from looking back. But tragically for her and her children, she did look back and forfeited her only chance for rescue. The decision to divorce requires that you focus on what lies ahead, unrelated to how or why the divorce happened.

If you are the one who wanted out and are feeling great relief and pride at having, at last, done what seemed impossible, you are to be congratulated. But you're still going to face problems with your children. I assure you that you cannot expect instant support or even understanding, even if they've seen you suffering.

A NEW KIND OF PARENT

Divorce creates two separate single parents with two homes, two sets of furniture, two refrigerators, and separate insurance policies. Each of you wakes up every morning to discover that when your children are under your roof you have responsibility for their well-being, discipline, and entertainment. As single parents you can surely cooperate, but you are no longer joined at the hip as mother and father over each twenty-four-hour day. Even in bad marriages parents often protect each other against the anxiety and fatigue of parenting. If a child is sick, parents who no longer share a bed still take turns getting up during the night.

But with your divorce, true shared parenting evaporates. You have no one to call on for help. Whatever happens during the days or nights that your children are with you, it's always your turn. Of course you can work out a cooperative arrangement with your ex-partner and I surely hope that you will. You can divide custody. You can decide to split errands and soccer games. You can share the children's favorite recipes. But coparenting after divorce is not the same as coparenting within marriage. If the nursery school calls to say that your previously well-behaved son is biting the other children and breaking toys, you can't set the clock back. You certainly can't say, "I want to talk this problem over with my husband." There's only you talking with the teacher, trying to keep your child in the school he's disrupting. If you let your seventeen-year-old borrow your car and he's several hours late, you walk the floor alone. You can call your ex or the police, and probably you should, but they will not pace the kitchen floor with you. You can turn to your family for help or hire a nanny, but no one will supplant a full-time partner. A successful divorce requires you to be stronger than you've ever been, as if you are one person doing the work of two with the tenacity of ten.

Divorce forces you to become a new person. It really doesn't matter who made the decision or whose "fault" it was. The transformation is similar to what happened to you when you first had a baby. From day one you embarked on a new adult role for which you had no dress rehearsal. The birth certificate didn't make you a mother or father. You remade yourself into a parent. Remember when you suddenly found yourself getting up in the middle of the night to carry out new and unfamiliar duties? You learned to be responsible in ways you never imagined. Your hearing got sharper. You could detect your baby's breathing a room away and you could hear her faintest cry. You carried a constant awareness of your child's needs whether you were one mile or three thousand miles from home. So, too, divorce requires you to rally yourself to carry out new responsibilities that are every bit as difficult and demanding as those you learned after your first child was born.

WHO WERE YOU BEFORE?

Unfortunately, the legal change noted on your divorce papers does not usher in this change in identity. You do. Divorce doesn't happen in the courts, although the public record is what makes it official. It happens in the psychological changes that occur over time in both you and your ex-partner. Most of the changes occur gradually, with the result that you wake up one morning and realize that you're a different person. You no longer cry yourself to sleep, wake up angry, berate yourself for your poor judgment, obsess all night about whether you made the right decision, or feel like screaming much of the time. After weeks or months, indeed sometimes years, of feeling shaky and bewildered, there will come one psychological moment when you become this new person.

How can you tell? You'll know that you've begun to acquire this important new identity when you finally excise your partner's voice some-where inside your head berating you, accusing you, pleading with you, or hounding you. You are a new person when you finally stop feeling like a failure who says, "I tried so hard but my best was not enough," when you feel free, even hopeful, and can make decisions without trembling inside. In taking these new steps toward a new identity, reward yourself with something real that makes you feel good. Try a massage, a night out, a new hairdo, or go for broke and get a whole new outfit or set of golf clubs. As it is after any shock, you may start out walking a bit unsteadily but then you will gather strength as you go forward.

To begin the healing process, you might try this simple exercise. In your mind, go back over the years and try to recapture who you were before you got married. Are there earlier self-images that you can substitute for the sad ones linked to your failed marriage? Were you hopeful as a young man or woman? What happened to that hope? Did you have other choices when you chose your husband or wife?

One woman told me, "I was a very attractive and popular girl. I had several men vying for my attention. I'd already enrolled in law school but gave it all up when Jim came along and swept me off my feet with promises of everlasting love that turned out to be false from the honeymoon on. I look at myself in the mirror and can't believe the worn-out image with dark circles under her eyes that looks back at me. Even my hair has lost its curl. What happened to the real me?"

A man told me, "She was the prettiest girl at school and the mayor's daughter to boot. I was from the wrong side of the tracks. I thought that with her at my side we would reach the moon together, have a wonderful gracious home, and create the family I always longed for. But the marriage drained my self-confidence and my drive. For years I almost suffocated in boredom."

So try to find your earlier self-images and use them to rekindle the hopes and strengths that you need to move ahead with your life.

At some point every man and woman, whether left or leaving, has to face up to the hurt and disappointment that go with a failed marriage and the continuing tensions of the divorce. Resolving grief means letting go. In divorce, it's letting go of the memories collected over many years of being together. It means letting go of the hopes and dreams that led you to marry this person in the first place. You need to pull up the memories of your courtship and all the good times you had together, to mourn each recollection individually and put them to rest. Many people find that therapy helps them in this process. A sensitive therapist can provide support as well as understanding that can break into your loneliness and restore your perspective. One man credited his therapist with restoring his sense of humor. "I was beginning to bore myself with self-pity," he said. "Thank God she helped me snap out of it."

Mourning loss is a process that takes time. But you need to know that after divorce you enter a new kind of attachment with your former partner, one that is not born of love but one that arises from the role of being coparents. As one of my colleagues put it, divorce is the end of love and the persistence of attachment. This enduring tie can be based on anger, tenderness, friendship, or any combination of powerful emotions. It may change over the years. When you meet at your daughter's wedding or as new grandparents at the baptism of your first grandchild, you may feel friendly or you may still be raging. Whatever the mixture, the tie will endure for as long as you both shall live. As human beings, we're blessed and damned with memories.

Be aware, too, that before you can give your children the attention they need, you need to gain control of your own emotions in general. In the early weeks and months after the breakup, you may be more upset than you've ever been in your life. Many people admit that they allow themselves to scream at everything that crosses their path. An hour later they want to crawl into a dark hole and hide. People who have been wonderful parents and rarely raised their voices in anger slam doors on their children, cry in closets, and erupt in anger over nothing in particular. The feelings that now pull you apart from the person you married are as powerful as the feelings that once drew you together. Propelling yourself out of a marriage where there was once love or at least the excitement of coming together invades every domain of adulthood. As much as you want to disappear into the woodwork or stay in bed for a week, because you have children you are not free to do this now.

By their presence, your children remind you that you have big responsibilities, and that is the last thing you want to think about. I have found that many children are terrified by the change in a parent's behavior. They have no way of knowing that the loss of control is temporary. Being children they think the changes are forever. Many children have said to me, "My mom is different. She screams all the time like the witch on TV. My dad yells so much he's lost his voice."

If you're honest, you'll realize that although you're worried about your children, you mainly want to think about yourself and your own problems. Meanwhile the legal system is demanding that you make choices. In your weakened condition you are called on to be wiser than you've ever been before.

In this chaotic mental state, you may push your children to the periphery, emotionally and sometimes physically. The trouble with chaos is that it escalates. The more chaos, the crankier your children become, the more they scream at each other, and the more you're going to lose self-control. As one mother put it, "I felt like a thousand ducks were snapping at me." But children also have a funny way of calling you back to reality. One woman showed me exactly how that works. She said, "Just as I was getting ready to lose it, my eight-year-old said, 'Mom, if you keep getting mad your face will freeze that way.' I was so astonished, I burst out laughing. She said she learned it from her teacher. So I hugged her and she broke the spell." Children can drive you up the wall, but they also have a marvelous recuperative influence.

MEN AND WOMEN FACE DIFFERENT CHALLENGES AT THIS TIME

If you're a woman who has never made financial decisions alone, now is the time to learn Economics 101. You'll probably have to work full-time, run your home, be a mom, and try to carve out some time to live life as an independent adult. You may also have to return to school to improve your market skills or launch a new career. Many divorced women say that work provides welcome structure to their lives. If your job is gratifying, it can greatly help restore your self-esteem. But if your job is demeaning or difficult or occurs on weekends or nights, so that it creates an even greater gap between your wish to be a mom and your need to work, then the job can have the opposite effect.

Ask yourself how your work affects the rest of your life. What pleasure or support does it provide? Are your coworkers a source of friendship? Does your schedule dominate your life and wipe you out? If you possibly can, make plans to get a more civilized schedule. Your children need you more than ever. It may be worthwhile to borrow money from your family, in-laws, or friends to enable you to pursue a career that satisfies you. Or it may be possible to get your ex-partner to help you for a year or more, especially if he can see a financial advantage in having you upgrade your skills or education. Several women I know well from my long-term studies of divorce borrowed money from their former husbands to finish college or graduate study or even pay tuition to law school. One divorcee who had been a full-time mom and housewife got a Ph.D. in musicology with a loan from her ex-husband and went on to a brilliant career at a first-class university. Several women who had no former business experience established successful companies. Work is important. Whether it provides support and pleasure or is only drudgery and a necessity will make all the difference to you and your children. Lots of studies show that when a woman feels enhanced and happy with her work she brings her good feelings home to benefit her children. But when she feels exploited and exhausted her children suffer doubly. They are deprived of their mother's presence and they have to contend with her ongoing depression.

If you're a man who never took care of the kids day-to-day, welcome to Home Economics 101. You have to figure out how to entertain, feed, and care for your children. If you're like most men and you have exited the family home, you'll need to find a new place that has room for your children. Make sure that each child has his own bed and a place for his special possessions. It's not a good idea to vacate your bedroom to sleep on the living room couch when your children are in your custody because it'll make them and you feel very uncomfortable. Get a decent-size refrigerator and kitchen table. Make sure that there's a place to do homework that's not in front of the television set. Start checking the newspapers for details of entertainment aimed at children and families. If your child enjoys baseball, get some season tickets. All this takes planning as well as serious consultations with your children. If they're preschoolers, check out playgrounds and library programs that include reading stories to young children. For older children check out recreational programs. Whatever your children's interests—theater, sports, movies, all sorts of hobbies—they'll be very grateful if you show interest in helping them pursue their goals while they're with you. Furnish their rooms with appropriate toys and games. Get their input before you lay out the money, but also get some help from friends with children the same age.

Most youngsters need help in setting up their activities outside of school. A visit to the local recreation center or Y is a must. Have a talk with your children's teachers. They may be surprised that you took the trouble to consult with them, but I predict they'll be happy to make suggestions and also keep in touch. Ask about community programs and how good they are. Some activities may be new to you. It would probably be better not to include adult friends at the early stage after the breakup. Your hardest task in these early days is to keep your children and yourself from being bored and fatigued with each other's company. You don't have to be a playground director, but you have to create a new, welcoming, and interesting environment when your children are with you.

MORE RESPONSIBILITY, LESS CONTROL

Now comes one of the hardest parts about raising children after divorce. This message is very important because hardly anyone will prepare you for this big change. Both of you need to come to terms with the fact that while you have greater responsibilities for raising your children, you have far less control as a parent than you had when you were married. I will be blunt. Although you're divorced, you'll never be free of your ex-spouse. If you hoped to expunge him or her from your life, you'll find that you're only out of his or her bed and bank account. Because you have children together, you won't escape having a continued relationship. Whatever your custody arrangement, you're yoked. Divorce in a family with children is always partial. The other parent is always there. Each time you exchange your children within your custody agreement, you may run into the other person. Even if you try to avoid personal contact, you'll see your ex-partner in the facial expressions and behavioral quirks of your children. Everything you do as a parent is still constrained by what the other person does. If you have a good relationship with each other this is good news, because it means that you can help each other in the challenges of parenting. But whether you do or don't get along, the ties that bind you together still hold.

So what should you do?

If you're a father, you'll continue to share responsibility for your children financially and emotionally. You're expected to help support them and to provide the values that you believe in, but you've lost the powerful role of being a father who always knows best. You have financial obligations with less power. You can yell about these, beat drums, jump through hoops, or join other fathers to complain how you were screwed. But the fact is you are not a carefree bachelor or the powerful dad that you were when you were head of the household and every child knew your role. Forever more you're a divorced father. Your task is to make the most of a part-time role that you share with a woman who is no longer central in your life. This is true whether you're a father who visits his children or a coparent in a joint custody arrangement. You cannot decide on an impulse to take the kids to Disneyland. You can't even decide to go to Disneyland by yourself if it's your turn to take the children. You have to clear everything with their mom, who is expecting you to return the children on a certain day at a certain time where she has dinner waiting. She has a right to say no, that they can't arrive late because you want to do something else. You can't suddenly decide to change their schedules, diet, or bedtime. You can't call your ex-wife and tell her that she's dating a jerk whom you don't want hanging around your kids and expect that she'll listen. You can't satisfy your curiosity about her love life by pumping the children. They'll be uncomfortable and she'll object. You can't suddenly change any of the rules of your agreement unless you both agree to the change.

If you're a mother, you also continue to be responsible for your children but you'll have less power in deciding how to raise them. If your husband never put a sweater on your son before sending him out into the cold air, there's nothing you can do about it. You can't push a sweater into his unwilling hands as they take off and force him to use it. If you worry that he drives too fast, it won't do any good as they leave for you to say, "Don't drive fast." If you worry because he allows unlimited TV or permits the children to stay up too late by your standards, you can't alter his rules in his house. You can't dictate how he disciplines your children or what he teaches them about right and wrong. As for communication, talking will have precious little effect unless you agree to listen to each other. You have power to persuade but none to command. When your children are with their father, you cannot control what happens to them. Like your ex-husband, you can't take off with a new lover to Las Vegas if it's your time with the children. Nor can you take them to Las Vegas without his consent. You can't even move yourself and your children to a new address without his knowledge, and in many states you can't get remarried, move, and bring along your children without his consent and the consent of the court.

These differences can make for great tensions that are not apparent during and after the breakup. But if you divorced to gain total freedom, think again. I'll discuss these problems and what to do about them later in the book.

ANGER

Everyone is angry after divorce. There's no way not to be angry. There's no way to exit a close relationship of any kind, including business partnerships and love affairs, without feeling disappointment and without feeling furious at your partner, at yourself, and at the world that has thrown you a curve. Dreams are always shattered. If you've been betrayed, you may feel ashamed and wounded. If you walked out on your spouse, you may feel intensely angry about all those wasted years. You're angry at the person who disappointed you. How could you have gotten yourself into such an unhappy mess to begin with? How could you have been so dumb, so misled, such a patsy?

Such feelings are inevitable after you decide to divorce. Actually, there's nothing wrong with feeling angry, as long as it doesn't continue.

The problem is—and this may surprise you—many people find that anger makes them feel good. They go out of their way to hold on to it by associating with friends who fan the flames of their rage or by avoiding people who seem unsympathetic. Let's face it. Anger can make you feel righteous, if not saintly. You're a good person and you were wronged. This is a very powerful feeling. What's more, you may be right. You are a good person, a very good person. But feeling that, you may enjoy blaming the other as arch villain, and this can block you. Your anger may even prevent you from realizing how much you are suffering.

In Cher's immortal words, "Snap out of it."

Anger may make you feel better but it is dangerous. If you let it spin out of control, it can all too easily dominate your life. Anger that endures can turn to bitterness, cynicism, and suspicion of people who deserve better. I'll talk later about anger that lasts and what to do about it in Chapter 19. For now, I want to focus on the first year after divorce. You are angry. What should you expect?

First, you can use your anger to mobilize yourself. Think about it. You don't need that other person anymore. You're free to organize your new life as you see fit. Anger can give you an aggressive push from behind. Nothing will get you up faster in the morning than the feeling that you are hell-bent on setting things right. Anger can persuade you that you'll do things differently this time around. You'll never again make such foolish choices. So be aware that there's "good" in being angry if it drives you to restructure yourself and your life. Forgiveness can wait.

The danger is that anger can spill onto innocent people around you. For example, Jennifer, a thirty-two-year-old computer programmer whose husband recently walked out on her, called me one morning in a panic. She explained that she had lost her temper at her six-year-old son. After being screamed at for ten minutes, the small child turned with a hurt look and said, "Mommy, what did I do?"

Jennifer realized that she was on the verge of losing it, that her anger was spinning out of control. Her son's reaction triggered in her recognition of what was happening. She broke into sobs.

An hour later, Jennifer was in my office discussing the situation. I told her that I was very concerned at how her anger at her husband was spilling onto her little boy. I gave her the names of two good therapists and urged her to seek counseling. A year later, Jennifer called to say that things were going well. She had never worked harder at anything in her life, she reported, but she had regained self-control and understood the roots of the fury that had spilled onto her innocent child.

Another danger is that actions you take on behalf of your children may be guided by pure anger, and nothing else. This is no way to behave. You can't make helpful decisions about your children if you're driven by rage. I remember a woman named Sarah who had been planning to go to court to request that her husband's visiting rights with their daughter be severely limited. I said, "You know, Sarah, he's her father even though he's no longer your husband. She'll want to make her own judgments about him. If you curtail his visits now, she may be very angry at you someday." Sarah called the next day to say that she stayed awake all night stewing but in the morning decided that I was right. She really had no right to interfere, other than being angry. She called her attorney and canceled her request to return to court.

So what can you do to recognize the power of your anger? How can you stop yourself from making mistakes? It's very important during this first year to simply watch yourself. Ask yourself, How am I doing? Observe your own behavior. This is a moment of truth that only you can recognize. No one can overcome your anger for you. You have to do it by yourself.

If you're like many people, you'll find that your anger gradually diminishes as the months and years go by. You'll be able to seal it off into a past part of your life and keep it from spreading. Most people let go of anger—or at least enough of it—to regain control. They don't expect it will go away entirely. But they don't feed it so that it burns ever brighter and stronger. They don't go looking for anecdotes that will help them feel certain of their victimhood. They don't look for opportunities to say,

"See, I told you so." They turn instead to valued friends, relatives, therapists, anyone they can really trust to tell them the truth. They're ready to listen when someone says, "You are not being rational."

A word of warning: anger fueled by jealousy is especially toxic. If you're alone and unhappy while your ex-partner is dating other people, your mind can turn any relationship into a torrid romance. These fantasies are dangerous because they can lead to stalking and to violence. If you find yourself haunted by such ideas I strongly suggest that you get some professional help. Sometimes you can bring yourself back to reality by reminding yourself that you're the one who is conjuring up those images and giving them the power to hurt you. You are your own tormentor. If you are the victim of jealous fantasies and threats have been made against you, I urge you to take them seriously and seek protection from the police.

If you find your anger is increasing—and you're beginning to convince yourself that all men betray women, all women betray men—I advise you to think of your rising anger as a residue of the divorce that is blocking your progress. It's something that needs to be under your control, rather than letting it control you. A lot of anger is based on self-pity. If all your energy goes into remembering how you were hurt, how can you have the strength to move ahead in your life? If you're mired in anger, how can you recognize new opportunities? Anger blocks the kind of self-scrutiny that you need in order to change. It can lead you into repeating the same kinds of mistakes and prevent you from really understanding what happened. There's no substitute for saying to yourself, "I am not going to remain stuck. I'm getting out of these habits of thinking. I'm determined to change."

Many people can help you make the transition to the "new you." Loyal friends and new people you befriend after the breakup can ease the way. Your family, including former in-laws, may want to help, especially with the children. New relationships, especially lovers, will see you in an entirely different light. When someone new finds you desirable, your self-esteem can soar. But beware of these so-called springer relationships. The person who springs you out of your misery may not be as wonderful as you think. Don't make the mistake of thinking that your judgment is restored. This is not a good time to make a major commitment, unless you're courting someone you have known a long time. You need plenty of time to explore your options in the world of romance, and you will need lots of time to learn how to be a single parent.

I can tell you that if you feel more confident as a parent, you'll gain a great deal of strength and comfort in the role. Being a good parent during this transition helps diminish the grief, guilt, and tremendous upheaval that divorce causes. In the storm, your ability to be a good parent will anchor you. You'll be aided by the knowledge that you are helping your children through this difficult transition by not overburdening them with your own pain. You're clear about what's happening and you're able to comfort them. That will go a long way in easing your path.

If all this sounds like mission impossible, it is. It's a real triumph if you do it right. If you divorced to regain the freedom of your dating years, think again. But if you hope to become a different you, to have a happier life, to improve the lives of your children, and to feel more in control, read on.

Chapter 2: Telling the Children

The first question I usually get asked when speaking to parents is heartfelt and direct: "How should I tell my children about the divorce?"

I want to answer this in some detail because what you say and when and how you say it is very important. This conversation raises the curtain on the changed family, so you need to give it careful thought. I suggest you call two family meetings rather than one to make sure that each child has a chance to mull over what's been said. You'll have second thoughts and your children will have a lot to ask that they didn't bring up the first time.

Just as your life will never be the same after the breakup, divorce is a critical turning point for each of your children. Sadly, many parents don't realize this. They hope that their relationships with their children won't change very much after divorce. They've probably been told by attorneys or therapists that if they behave with civility toward their ex, make a fair financial plan, and allow each child to have good access to both parents, the stress of the divorce will be short-lived. There should be no long-term effects on each child's development. Moreover, parents hope their children will feel relieved and will welcome the divorce as a remedy to the parent's unhappiness.

But that's not the children's experience. They're intensely aware that their family has changed forever. Even the littlest ones sense the difference. If you want your children to feel secure and protected after your divorce—and I know that you do—you will need to provide that security and protection.

Children have an entirely different take on divorce compared to their parents. For starters, most children want the marriage to be preserved. They feel better protected in a two-parent family. They like having Mom and Dad live together, even when their home has become a sad place because their parents are unhappy or fighting. No matter the history or family background, every young child who entered my playroom at the Center put the mother doll and the daddy doll in bed together.

Second, although it is hard to believe, many children are content in a marriage that the parents find unhappy or unfulfilling. They don't know or don't care that Mom and Dad aren't sleeping in the same bed or haven't communicated for a long time. If one parent misbehaves, they assume that he or she will straighten up and fly right, just like kids are expected to do when they're naughty.

After divorce, most children look back longingly on the intact family that they fully expected would last until they were ready to leave home. No child expects a parent to leave home before she does. These feelings can last well into adulthood, when some grown children of divorce confess with embarrassment that they still harbor the wish that their parents would get back together. In my experience, parents are surprised when their grown children speak frankly about the divorce and about their fond memories of the family home, the Christmas tree that everyone decorated, and their playmates who lived next door before the breakup. These are often cherished memories that last over many years.

WHEN TO TELL YOUR CHILDREN ABOUT THE DECISION TO DIVORCE

The kindest and most important thing you can do for your children is to tell them what's happening in the family before it comes apart. How can they trust you if you withhold information that changes their lives? It's very serious if they think you knew you were breaking up but didn't tell them. So if at all possible, you need to tell them about your plans before you separate, so they have preparation and support from you when they wake up one morning to discover one parent has left the home. Think about it. A four-year-old who finds his daddy suddenly missing is devastated. A teenager feels betrayed. (I'll get into age-specific reactions in later chapters and what you might say depending on each child's age.)

If your children are five or younger, it's best to tell them a day or two before you separate. For school-age children a few days to a week before will help them assimilate what you say. Adolescents often know their parents' plans weeks or even months ahead because they are often the confidants of one or both parents. But they should be told at least two weeks before so they'll have the opportunity to discuss it with their best friends and think about how it will affect them and what lies ahead for all of you.

It won't be easy to tell your children that your marriage is unraveling, but they'll feel comforted by your honesty. It means a lot that they can count on you to remember them and assures them that you are keeping their concerns in mind. Children get very frightened of being lost in the shuffle at this time. I'll never forget a tearful little girl who brought me a flower. "It's a blue forget-me-not," she said soberly. "They shouldn't forget me."

What if your spouse leaves suddenly or storms out in a rage and files for divorce so you don't know in advance? In this case, you can apologize to your children and admit candidly that you just learned of it, that you want to keep them informed, and that had you known in advance, you would have told them. This is no time to equivocate.

The best thing you can do, however, is to gather the children round and tell them that you've decided to separate, what that means, and when it will happen. Again, your goal is to assure them that you're thinking about their well-being from the start. Talk simply and slowly, and keep in mind that they'll remember forever what you are saying. They'll also remember what you don't say. Choose a quiet time when you and the children have plenty of time that's not in the midst of normal activities, like watching television, talking with a friend on the phone, or doing homework. Parents tend to be so worried about telling their children about the divorce that they rush through the process. You may want to get it over with so you can feel relieved. But if you fail to fully engage each child's attention, you'll miss an important opportunity to lay the foundation for the future of your post-divorce family.

Plan to tell your children about the divorce when both you and your spouse are going to be home for the next few days or through the weekend. Don't do it just before a business trip or when you're less available. If you can manage to talk to them together, by all means do so. It's far better to symbolize some harmony than to show anger at the other or point a finger in blame. If you can't cooperate, each parent should tell the children separately but take turns, one right after the other. If you can lay aside your anger momentarily, decide together beforehand what you're going to say so that your stories jibe. It is not good for them to see the two of you together and hear one of you command, "Okay. You tell them!" Parents owe their children the gift of civility and cooperation at this transformative moment in their lives. Tell them that you will be there the next morning and that you'll spend more time with them at bedtime.

WHAT TO TELL

For most children, the news that their parents are divorcing arrives like a bolt of lightning. You may have been talking about it for weeks, but the decision itself typically comes as a surprise. It's incomprehensible. This is because many parents do their best to carefully hide their fights from their children, which is a good thing. Child after child has told me, "I came home from school one day and there was my mom and my dad waiting for me. They looked real serious. And then they said they were divorcing. I was afraid to ask why and they never told me."

As a result, many adult children of divorce report that they're always afraid of being too happy; if things are sailing along just fine, something is bound to suddenly come along and ruin their happiness. This fear is related to the fact that they were stunned by the divorce and have embedded in their minds a kind of fatalism about the fragility of relationships. You may not be able to eliminate this surprise factor, but there's much you can do to soften the blow. Remember this: your children will always recall how you behave at this juncture in their lives. If you're open, honest, and allow them to see your sorrow, including your tears, you'll be helping them. The stiff upper lip approach blocks their feelings.

"The memory of the day my parents announced their divorce is with me today, fifteen years later," said Monica when she was about to graduate from college. "That moment came to characterize our family dynamics for the next decade and beyond. All my mother said was, 'Your dad and I have decided to separate. We will live in separate houses. You will divide your time between two homes.' I remember she made the announcement to my sister and me on the gray couch in the family room. My dad was weeping and my mom was trying very hard to keep the stoic posture that kept her strong in my eyes. My sister collapsed and wept with my father. I think not because she understood what a separation was—she was only three, I was six—but because she felt a rupture and wanted to cling to Dad. They found a way to connect through tears. I resorted to the mechanism that still serves as my crutch to this day—I remained pragmatic. 'Does that mean that we will have a garage sale?' That line became the family joke for years."

I say all this because I know that many parents gather the family together and all they say, and I mean all, is, "From now on your mom will live here and I will live there." When I talk with parents I refer to this as the real estate approach to divorce. I don't mean that children should not be told where everyone will live. But divorce is much more important than describing it as simply a move to another location. I think people do this because they don't know how to explain the divorce to their children, but they do know how to explain a location change. But you have to explain the divorce first and then talk about who will sleep where. So let me give some detailed suggestions about what you should say to explain this major change in everyone's lives.

When I interview adults raised in happy intact families about their experiences of growing up, they often begin by telling me the story of their parents' courtship and marriage. It serves as a platform for describing their own entry into the world and how they consider themselves part of a continuing story.

I believe that children of divorce should have the same claim on their own history, namely that it began with love and, if true, with their being loved and wanted by both their mother and father. You want to protect their self-image and self-esteem by saying that their life story began with love and not, as many children conclude, with rage and failure.

Start by telling them that when you got married you loved each other and fully expected that you would live together forever. Tell them that when they were born, you were very happy because you wanted a family. Why? Because you want your children to feel that they were born into a loving family and that they were wanted. Then—if this is true—you should tell your children that you have not been getting along and that you're making each other unhappy. You can say, "You've seen us acting strangely. Mommy is crying, Daddy is shouting, we're both on edge." If just one person has decided to leave the marriage and the other is completely opposed, you need to say it clearly. But don't explain the divorce, as many parents do, by saying "Your mother and I (or your father and I) are different people." Every sane child past the age of three months knows that his mother and father are different people. You need to spell out differences that your child can understand. For example. "We are different people in how we want to live. Daddy works seven days a week and travels on business. He loves his work, and although he wants to spend time with you, he feels that if he works less he will be unhappy. Mommy is very lonely and unhappy and wants him to stay at home." Or, "Mommy is very close to Grandma and Grandpa. She spends almost all her time over there and Daddy wants a more independent family." Or, "Mommy drinks a lot of whiskey and then gets very cranky and angry at Daddy. She has tried very hard to stop but can't, and Daddy has decided to divorce and move to another house. Mommy and Daddy both want our home to be more peaceful for us and for you." Be gentle. Telling the truth does not mean that you should deprecate or scapegoat each other. Because you and your spouse cannot make your marriage work, and things between you can only get worse, say you've decided to divorce for everyone's sake. You don't want your children to grow up with the wrong view of what marriage is. You don't want to live a lie or mislead them into thinking that your failing marriage is the best that marriage provides. It isn't.

What if one parent blames the other? What should you do if you are being blamed? This is the worst time to hotly deny the charge and get into an angry argument in front of the children. Stay as cool as you can and say that when people divorce they get very upset and blame each other. But when things cool down they start to see things more clearly. You are sure that will happen.

Then tell your children that you tried to fix the marriage so they don't think that you're acting impulsively, irrationally, and foolishly. "We failed and it is a big disappointment." Why would you throw away what your children hold most dear in their hearts without trying to protect it? If you want your children's respect, they have to think of you as someone who is sensible and who is careful not to break other people's treasures. If you tried counseling or talked to a minister or friend, say so. You tried very hard and you are very, very disappointed that you could not make it work out. Tell your children that you have come to a very sad conclusion. The best course of action for you, the adults, is divorce.

If you're honest and show respect for the gravity of the situation, your children will have permission to show their hurt and anger. This is very important because it allows them to cry. If a parent doesn't say how upsetting the situation is, many children feel that they have to behave in a controlled way. They may feel it's taboo to cry or show feelings. While this might make it easier for you and even for them at the moment, it can make life harder in the long run because children will hide their feelings to protect their parents. They'll think, I can't stand the idea of hurting my mom or dad by showing them how awful I feel. So I won't let myself feel. They'll do anything to not rock the boat because they love you and want to take care of you, and they realize that this is a crisis for at least one of you.

Go on to tell the children, "You're not responsible for this divorce," but don't just leave it at that. Spell it out. Mom got mad about your messy room and Dad got mad about your homework being late, but that has nothing to do with the divorce. It shouldn't be difficult to find examples of such stresses in families where people are on edge. Then spell it out further: "You may think that what you did is related to the divorce. But I'm here to tell you that children never cause divorce. Parents cause divorce. Nor can children fix divorces. Sometimes children think that if they are very, very good or if they get up on time every morning, this will make the divorce go away or will bring Mommy and Daddy back together. It doesn't work that way. What causes divorce has to do with parents."

If you can think of something in the house that broke recently and was repaired, use it as an example of how broken things can be fixed and that the divorce means you are trying to fix things in the family that got broken. Lots of times when you fix something it looks different. You will still have a family, you will always have a family, but it will look different. If you don't have an example, you can still explain that the divorce is an attempt to fix the family. It will be different but it will still be their family and yours, so everyone will be better off later on.

Don't try to recruit your children to a particular position. Give them freedom to make up their own minds. Rest assured that they'll do this anyway and not tell you about it. The notion that children buy into their parents' views uncritically is nonsense and ignores all that we know about the sensibility and moral judgment of children and adolescents. You owe your children the honest expression of your feelings and the freedom not to be a soldier in your battle. Your job as parent is to educate them about right and wrong and to help them express their anger and sorrow along with yours. You'll all feel better.

What should you tell your children if there has been an infidelity? What if only one person wants out of the marriage and there were no concerted efforts to save it? What you say depends on the age of each child. Since a child under the age of five would not understand what you're talking about, it's better not to say anything about infidelity. You should speak about this to an older child separately. If your child is ten or eleven, you can say—if you have the courage to be honest—your mom has decided that she loves another person more than me or, conversely, your dad is in love with another person and we cannot live together any longer. It's likely that your children have overheard accusations between you regarding the infidelity. If these are true, it's better to bring the issue into the open. Most children know about infidelity from television and movies. Divorce is a major motif in prime-time family shows, not just soap operas. But leave out details, like, "Your mom has been sleeping with another man." That part of the story should be placed on a shelf. Children don't want these details. They can't bear to think about your sex life and should be protected.

Next, stop and ask each child: "What do you understand about divorce?" You cannot proceed until you know if your child understands what you're talking about. Ask about their friends' experiences. Let them speak. Let them tell you about their worry of losing you, about their strange ideas of having to be put in a foster home, about adolescents not having funds to go to college. Many young children think that divorce means they'll be sent to live away from both parents, or they think they'll never see one of you ever again. Or they think they'll be abandoned as each of you flies off on a broomstick. They may be full of bad information and you can correct them gently.

Some children will be frozen into silence. Try to help them say what they're scared of or relieved about. After all, you know them best. Remember that whether or not they speak, every child will have a mind that's spinning fast-forward. They'll be worried, some realistically, some exaggeratedly. Again, keep in your mind that there are no empty spaces in their heads. Even when they say, "I don't know," they can have ideas that are too scary to articulate. Keep in mind, too, that even very young children try with all their might to protect you, that they're just as worried about you as you are about them, and that they may happily lie to you about what they feel if they think it will comfort you.

If your child says she has no idea what divorce is, press her. Surely she must have heard about it from other children or from something she saw on television. If your child says, "Can I go now?" don't be misled into thinking that everything is fine and your child doesn't care. My research shows that even many years later these children remember every word their parents say. They react very strongly and keep it well hidden—with delayed reactions showing up when parents thought all was well and good. The denial on the surface can mask deep and painful memories being formed at this time, so you really need to keep the conversation open.

Once you have an answer, tell the children what divorce means in this family. Every family makes its own divorce arrangements. Describe what you've been thinking about in terms of who lives where and the arrangements you're making for custody and visiting. Ask them for their ideas and comments and promise to take those into consideration. The worst is when children feel like inanimate objects that are simply distributed between two homes. This is the time to encourage them to discuss their schedules, friendships, and wishes. Children have important priorities. One little boy told me tearfully that he would rather be able to stay in his neighborhood during the soccer season, otherwise he couldn't play. The parents, who opted for joint custody, were able to arrange that during the soccer season the child would live primarily in the home near where the team played. A seven-year-old girl spoke haltingly about playing in the backyard with her friend, how they sat in the oak tree and pretended they were sailing around the world. She didn't want that journey interrupted or that treasured friendship disturbed. Her parents promised her that they would do their best to keep up the friendship by arranging frequent visits with her friend. Both children were greatly relieved and elated at having their wishes considered. Maintaining whatever stability in their lives that you can preserve helps them adjust to the inevitable changes. Thus it's extremely important to hear what your children have to say. So many children of divorce have the sense that no one has listened to them and conclude mistakenly that their parents don't care.

End the conversation by saying, "We all have to be brave. We will do this together and will all help each other." It's okay to ask them to have courage. They may happily rise to the challenge. It's okay to end the conversation with pizza or anything that cements the idea that you are still a family. Done in accord with these suggestions, this discussion, although sad, can be a growth experience for you and your child.

At this point make a date to have a second conversation in a few days or a week, especially with your older children. You have told them about your decision, asked their opinions, said you're sorry, and laid out what is about to happen. You can afford to stop the conversation here with the promise to continue. If they want to talk more, by all means keep going. But there's some advantage in letting what you have just said sink in. Two sessions acknowledge the importance of the family meeting.

The second meeting should begin with a review of the first meeting.

Your children may have gone out of their way to try to forget what you said, hoping that the divorce will go away like a bad cold. Begin by saying, "Remember we talked about the divorce. What do you remember?" This will give you a chance both to find out how your children are coping with the new circumstances and to repeat what seems to need repeating. Don't be surprised if a child comes up with a lulu of a memory and attributes it to you. Jenny, who was five, turned to her mother and said sweetly, "You were talking about death." Just correct her gently.

Then lay out the arrangements for life in the post-divorce family— where people will live, when they will see each other, the works. Many children worry about their pets. Who will walk the dog? Where will the cat live? Does Dad's apartment have a phone? Does it have a computer? Some of the questions are very strange to adult ears, but let them come out. What will happen to the baby in Mom's tummy? Bring along a big calendar and show the children what you're talking about. Show them where they'll go to school, how they'll get there, who'll pick them up. This is the time for details. If your work arrangements are also changing and you'll be using more sitters, tell them now. By the end of this second meeting, children should have some clear notion that you're in control and that you're considering their needs and wishes. They should also feel confident that you will keep them informed.

Allow plenty of time for comments and questions. Elicit these as best you can. Tell them how proud you are of their understanding and their questions or whatever you can find that makes commenting appropriate. Finally, close the meeting before all of you are exhausted. You'll be living one day at a time in coming months.

Chapter 3:   The Developmental Ladder

When parents consult me about their children during divorce, I always ask two questions: how old is your child and are we talking about a girl or a boy? This is key because your child's reaction to the breakup depends on where she stands on the developmental ladder, which is related to but not completely governed by her age. I'm talking about psychological milestones. Development is a ladder that your child mounts from infancy to adulthood. How your child responds to your divorce now and over the years, as well as what you can say and do to help her, depends very much on where she stands on that ladder. Boys and girls also react differently at certain ages. This chapter tells you why.

To climb the first rung on the ladder, an infant has to learn to sit up, crawl and walk, play peekaboo, begin to talk, and develop relationships with the people around him. Once he has achieved these tasks, he can move on to being a toddler who learns to talk incessantly, play with others, pick himself up when he falls down, and reach for independence with his first emphatic "no!" To achieve these steps he needs a lot of praise and encouragement from you. In elementary school years, the child's job is to get along with other children and adults, master the rules of the classroom, play fair on the playground, and learn to hold his own in a group of peers. In middle school and high school, his relationships with peers, including the opposite sex, and adults become more important, and serious learning takes center stage. For these accomplishments your child needs good teachers and concerned parents who are able to coach from the sidelines every step of the way.

Each age brings with it new tasks, and each task provides the foundation for the ones that follow. Every child has to keep moving along that ladder. And here is the problem in a nutshell. Your divorce may interrupt your child's developmental progress. Many children get stuck temporarily at the time of the breakup because they're exhausted by what's happening at home. Unable to keep up with other children, their play becomes listless and unfocused. They're much too anxious and worried about you, and their own future, to listen to the teacher and do their homework on time, and so they fall behind. Sometimes their anger can stall their developmental progress. They're so angry, they refuse to listen to anything adults have to say and sidetrack themselves from making important social, academic, and psychological achievements.

In many families, the delay following the breakup is thankfully temporary. Children usually regain their foothold in a matter of weeks or a couple of months. But if the delay continues for several months or years, children need help from parents, teachers, and other professionals to get them back on the appropriate rung as quickly as possible. If a child doesn't learn to read in first or second grade, he's in trouble. He can make it up for a while, but at some point he will begin to fall further and further behind. If he antagonizes other children and doesn't learn to make friends on the playground, kids will make fun of him. Children tend to tolerate some measure of angry behavior, but if it continues too long, a child who is acting out will be isolated. Parents need to keep an eye on their child's behavior at home, at school, and with friends to make sure that his development is not off course. If it is, they need to do everything in their power to help their child catch up as the crisis recedes.

Sometimes the breakup results in children shooting ahead developmentally before they've consolidated an earlier phase of development. We see this most often in preadolescents who adopt the swagger of adolescent behavior long before they're able to to control their impulses and exercise any semblance of good judgment. I discuss this at length, including advice for what you can say and do, in Chapter 8.

Now that you have a grasp of what I mean by development, I think you can understand why I want to know your child's age in assessing her reaction to divorce. Her age, and where she stands on that ladder, help me determine what she is capable of comprehending about divorce and what she is likely to worry about most. Children within the same age range tend to see family relations and breakup in similar terms. A four-year-old from Tampa has a lot in common in her response to the divorce with a five-year-old from Kalamazoo, even though they're being raised in different families a thousand miles apart. Six-year-olds from California and New York are more or less at the same level in their thinking, which means they have a beginning grasp of time and distance, barely understand the concept of marriage much less divorce, and will struggle mightily to understand the changes that divorce brings to their homes. Age tells me what a child is likely to understand about schedule, time, how long a week is, and distance, and how to answer questions like, "When will I see Mommy?" or, "Where is Daddy?" Age will clue you in about what to say in comforting your child through the ordeal.

It also matters if your child is a boy or girl. Boys after divorce tend to be at greater risk than their sisters for learning difficulties all through elementary school. Girls are at a higher risk than boys for getting into trouble in early adolescence. They mature earlier. Boys and girls react differently when a father leaves the household. Girls often soften the loss in elaborate, touching fantasies that can last for years. Boys, on the other hand, are preoccupied with "Where's my dad? I need him now."

Boys and girls need different things from you as they grow up. In an intact family, this doesn't present much of a problem. You're all under one roof so your children can gravitate to the parent they need during a particular developmental stage. This is harder to carry off in a divorced family when children are more likely to live on rigid schedules. The fact that a child becomes less interested in one parent as she enters a new developmental phase doesn't create undue anxiety in the intact family. Each parent is secure in his or her role and importance. But in a divorced family, when a child turns away from one parent and gravitates toward another, the parent who gets less attention may feel rejected. He or she may even rush to an attorney to claim there's conspiracy afoot.

I want to emphasize that age and gender don't tell you everything you need to know about how to decide what's best for your son or daughter. Children show great variability in the course of their development depending on their genetic makeup, experiences, and temperament. Temperament, in fact, plays a major influence on a child's response to divorce. As every parent knows, each child is different from birth. Jimmy is flexible, moving easily from one setting and developmental stage to another. He's a friendly, sociable kid who lights up the room when he smiles. Mary has a hard time with change. She was a clingy baby who woke up every night and needed to be held before she could calm down. She's reticent, shy around other children, and gets upset with change. In between Jimmy and Mary are all the children in town—and one of them is yours.

Thinking in terms of your child's temperament at the breakup will provide you with valuable clues about how he is likely to respond to your divorce now and later and how to decide what kind of help you need to give. Emily, age eleven, sits politely as she hears about the divorce and calmly excuses herself to do her homework. Jack, age thirteen, starts yelling at the top of his lungs—"What the hell is the matter with you?"— stomps out of the house, heads directly for the gang on the street corner, and doesn't return until dawn. Obviously Emily is easier to deal with and can probably manage for the time being. But Jack needs your immediate attention. He panics while Emily stays calm and takes life in stride. So even though both children are close in age, their temperamental differences dictate different strategies for you. Of course, you have to be wary of reactions that appear too calm. Children like Emily may be working overtime to deny any feeling, and it might be helpful if you spent extra time with her to make sure that she's not sitting on a cauldron of feelings. But there's no denying that some children are genuinely able to keep their attention on their own agendas and get around to dealing with family issues when they are emotionally ready.

Given these differences in age, development, gender, and temperament, what kind of reactions can you expect when you announce the divorce? I'll go through the age-specific behaviors in the rest of Part 1. For now, I want to describe some general behaviors that can emerge in children at the breakup independent of age and gender. The more you know about what to expect, the more you can help your sons and daughters.

Divorce frightens and upsets children from the time they're toddlers to when they enter adulthood. Children panic at the breakup because they fear that your divorce threatens their lifeline. There is an unspoken contract between you and them. Parents are responsible for every part of their young lives, providing food, nurturance, protection, and everything that creates continuity in an unpredictable, sometimes frightening world. Divorce threatens to undo that contract. Where can they turn and whom can they trust if their closest family relationships come apart before they're ready to leave home? When parents fight bitterly, the children's terror is boundless; they feel in danger of being crushed by two giants who are scarcely aware of their presence. Even if you don't fight, the notion of family breakup is terrifying. More than children in any other species, the human child cannot survive without a committed adult. Every child, even the rebellious teenager, knows how much she needs you in order to stay alive.

There is a wide gap between your understanding and the way children perceive events in the family. I am always startled to discover that children often make no connection between the parental violence that they have witnessed and the decision to divorce. This all has to be carefully and patiently explained, and I will talk about it later. But here I want to emphasize that you can take almost nothing for granted about your child's understanding. You and they think differently. For instance, many parents comfort themselves with the notion that their child will not be upset because a third of the children in his school are children of divorce. But that's not the way life works. Children experience divorce in single file. They are not in the least comforted by the fact that other children at school have divorced parents. Adults may feel better if they find others in their predicament, but each boy and girl feels intensely alone and lonely at the breakup. They're focused on their own families, their own ordeals. At the breakup each child struggles alone in the dark with big questions. Why me? What will happen to me?

You may find it difficult to know how your child feels about the divorce because few children talk about their feelings directly. Children don't sit down, look you in the eye, and tell you that they're worried or unhappy. They show their unhappiness by making sudden changes in their behavior. Your sweet-natured daughter becomes irritable and cranky. Your well-behaved son who was the teacher's pet starts clobbering other children at nursery school. A child who is angry at you will hit a younger sibling or the dog or threaten to run away. Indeed, a frightened child will often hit anything in sight or scream in defiance as a way of coping with his fear of being forgotten. Or he can become temporarily disorganized.

Feelings of sadness are very hard for children to bear. It's sometimes easier for them to clown around and pretend that everything is just fine, like nine-year-old Peter who was beside himself with grief at the thought that his beloved father didn't care about him. After the divorce, Peter would visit his father's office after hours, leaning back in the teak executive chair. While his father was working out in the gym downstairs, the boy called his mother on the telephone every ten minutes to brightly tell her that he was "feeling great."

Many of the youngest children tell me, years later, that the time of the divorce was the loneliest period in their lives. Both parents had their attention glued elsewhere and often no one was home. Yet most parents I talk to at the breakup and years later have no idea that their child is lonely or longing for "someone to speak with or play with." Unfortunately, siblings did not undo their loneliness because older children often handle distress by watching a lot of television or otherwise shutting out the world. They don't as a rule reach out to the baby in the family, tendering the kind of comfort that they themselves crave.

Your children have another reason to try to conceal their true distress. At a very young age they realize that you're horribly upset and they want to comfort you. I've seen two-year-olds sitting on their crying mothers' laps, reaching up to stroke Mommy's hair. It's very moving to see a child's love for and devotion toward a troubled parent. I know it's heartbreaking to think that your six-year-old is trying to hide his feelings and thoughts from you because he's concerned about you. But after divorce many children are vigilant in just that way. They watch you carefully to make sure that you're all right. They love you and they need you to be strong for you and for them. It's very important that you recognize and acknowledge your children's loving efforts to help you. If you can, tell them you're feeling better and you're getting stronger every day.

Soon after the breakup you need to get in touch with your child's school. In my experience, only about half of all divorcing parents talk to their child's teacher at this time or in the early years of creating a post-divorce family. You may be embarrassed to do so. After all, you don't want to burden the teacher with your personal problems. You're also afraid that you might break down and cry. Teachers for their part are afraid of intruding into your private life. They don't want to meddle.

But I assure you that a heart-to-heart talk with the teacher at this juncture will help everyone immensely. Children behave differently at home and at school. For example, eight-year-old Kyle was extremely aggressive at home, stomping around and screeching orders to his little sisters. But according to his teacher, Kyle was the meekest child in the class. He basically had no friends and was entirely withdrawn. This information surprised Kyle's parents and cast his rebellious behavior at home in a different light. They began to regard him as a troubled kid who was blocked in expressing his feelings appropriately. At my suggestion both parents talked with him separately. They told him what the teacher had said and wondered aloud how to explain the contrast between his too quiet behavior at school and his rambunctious behavior at home. Could he just tell them straight what was on his mind, without acting too good or too naughty? Kyle lowered his eyes and explained, "The kids think I have something wrong with me because I don't have a dad." This opening gave both parents the opportunity to explain that divorce didn't mean that Kyle had no dad. In fact, his dad was just as strongly connected to him as before. It was the connection between his parents that was severed. Gradually Kyle's behavior became more normal both at school and at home.

Six-year-old Marisa told her teacher that there was a new baby in the family and that she and her mother got up every night to take care of the infant. It wasn't until the end of the school year when the teacher made a house call to see the baby that the teacher discovered there was no baby. Marisa, who missed her mother who was now working full-time until late every evening, had created a vivid fantasy reflecting her wish to be cared for. Marisa's mother had been tempted to scold her daughter for telling the teacher a lie, but I explained that she should feel pleased. Marisa loved her mom and missed her. She invented the baby to recall the many times she had been cared for lovingly. Marisa's mother was very moved and made arrangements to spend more time with Marisa, setting up a time two days a week for them to be together.

Many first grade teachers tell me how they hold sobbing children on their laps to quiet them. Others describe children who follow them around the room wanting to hold on to their hand or dress. Teachers also tell me that older children arrive early before school starts and hang around when class is over. They're reluctant to go home. Some children are bullies on the playground while others prefer the company of much younger kids. These are all danger signs that the teachers will know about but may not tell you about unless you ask. But they are excellent clues to your child's concerns.

On the other hand the teacher may say that your child has redoubled his efforts to learn and that he is progressing splendidly. This, too, is an important discovery that should help relieve your concerns. You should tell your child how proud you are of his achievements at school and that you recognize this is not an easy time for him. If appropriate, provide a reward. Also have a look at your child's life and try to figure out what's keeping him in balance so that you can continue it. Maybe your child enjoys visits with his grandparents or his after-school activities or his music. Whatever buoys him up, keep it going.

I hope you will make an appointment to sit down with the teacher. For older children, you may want to talk to an assistant principal, guidance counselor, or school nurse. Find out how your child is doing academically, socially, and emotionally. Some teachers like to give younger children simple tasks, like erasing the blackboard, so they can reward them with welcome praise. Some will direct a classroom aide to pay special attention to your child's needs. Others have access to resources for children of divorce. Sometimes all that's needed is your attentiveness and expression of concern. Your child may need extra tutoring because he has fallen too far behind in schoolwork that can no longer be made up easily. In elementary school children learn long division and other skills that are harder to catch up with later on. Teachers can be very inventive in dreaming up simple projects in science or environmental issues or art that the distracted child can work on when he is unable to concentrate on the curriculum. Such projects can be a lifeline to a worried child, especially if they earn the teacher's praise. With the information you get from the teacher, plan a heart-to-heart talk with your child. Tell him what you have learned and discuss it. He has a right to know. This will also give you an opportunity to find out about his friends and what he does after school. Be sure to ask about his new schedule since the divorce, how hard it is, what's good about it, what he would like to change. If he's in trouble, ask what you can do to make him feel more comfortable. Don't hesitate to offer him special help if it is indicated. That's part of your job description as a parent and not something reserved for emergencies or cataclysmic events. National studies report that children of divorce are referred for mental health consultation about three times as often as children from intact families, so don't be surprised if the teacher recommends it. Symptoms are much easier to eradicate if they're treated soon after they emerge.

A SPECIAL WARNING

If you're a child of divorce who is undergoing your own divorce as a parent, many memories will resurface at this time. The feelings that go with these memories are also reawakened. Divorce will be even harder for you because you feel that this is exactly what you did not want to happen. You'll feel angry and discouraged. Can't you ever escape? Are you being pursued by fate?

Let me be frank. I worry that your anger and discouragement may make it harder for you to help your children. I realize this may sound paradoxical. Logically, as a survivor of divorce, you should be better prepared to help your children. It isn't that long ago that you stood in their shoes. But while you may remember your feelings from that time, you may want to suppress these feelings for fear of being overwhelmed by them.

On the other hand, even though the memory is painful, you certainly have a storehouse of information that could be helpful to you and your children if you can reach back. You may remember clearly how much you felt shut out because no one talked to you about the reasons for the divorce. So talk to your children in ways that they can understand. You may remember feeling as if you were the only child in the world whose parents divorced. So tell your children that divorce happens in a lot of families and that most kids feel the way they do; you did and you know. Tell them not to be ashamed of their tears. You can sympathize with their anger. Talk about your loneliness as a child and tell them that you don't want them to be lonely. How can you cheer each other up? I think that once you begin this conversation and overcome your own anxieties about dredging up your past, you can be enormously helpful to your children. The danger is that you won't see your children for who they are, as individuals with different life experiences, but as a continuation of yourself. The choice is yours. Your divorce can become a second chance for you to understand more about yourself and, at the same time, to help your children fight off their unrealistic fears.

Chapter 4:   Zero to Three

Let's start with babies. Many couples are happy with each other during pregnancy. The husband cares for his wife with love and tenderness. She looks forward eagerly to motherhood and creating a family. Many couples report that their sex life during pregnancy was the best ever. But then "Her Majesty the Baby" arrives and all bets are off.

Contrary to what many people think, a new baby does not necessarily cement a marriage. It's not only that the new mother and father don't get much sleep, feel depleted emotionally and physically, and have no idea of what they're supposed to do next. In addition, a new baby is sometimes perceived as a rival who can threaten the marriage at a fundamental level. If a mother, in her effort to care for her baby, ignores her husband, he will feel hurt and angry. She, in turn, will feel unappreciated and unsupported. If he's aroused by the sight of a woman who is nursing, and finds out that his tired wife is not interested in sex, he may feel jealous. If becoming a mother brings up long dormant problems for her, she may blame him irrationally for her discomfort. If he was weaned harshly in early childhood by the arrival of a new sibling, and the memory is preverbal but powerful, he may feel outrage at the infant's presence. In short, the baby's arrival can be a setup for hurt feelings, explosive anger, and, sadly, divorce. It can also be a foundation for an expanded sense of self, pride in the infant, and a stronger, more mature love within the couple.

So let's look at the baby. What does she need? She's at the very first rung of the developmental ladder that I talked about in the last chapter. She needs to establish confidence in the world around her so that she can build a strong foundation for mastering each milestone in her young life. She needs to be encouraged to smile and take delight in the fact that she's moving ahead. She needs to feel from your expression and your admiring, happy gaze that she's important and lovable. As she learns to roll over, sit up, crawl, walk, and, in one of the miracles of human development, talk, she'll become a toddler and full-fledged member of a family that is enchanted with her progress.

But before all this can happen in ways that meet her needs, she must feel safe. She needs to know that someone she trusts is close by her side. Trust begins when she learns that her cries bring you quickly to her side. You respond by picking her up, rocking her, soothing her, and meeting her needs. When she's older and falls down on the playground, you hold her, you kiss the boo-boo on her knee, and she hugs you back. This is what psychologists call secure attachment. It means feeling protected and safe from danger because that special person—Mommy or Daddy or both—is there to take care of you.

But if you're divorcing during these years, you need to know that babies and toddlers are especially sensitive to tensions and conflict around them. They begin imitating adult facial expressions at the age of two months. If you're depressed, a nursing infant will see it and turn her gaze away. If your baby witnesses real anger between you, she will fret, cry, and show all the signs of distress that babies use to communicate their anxiety. She may reject the breast or the bottle, refuse to sleep, and not allow you to comfort her. A toddler may shut down, rock in a chair, bang his head, or cling to his mother's leg. While your days may be burdened by working out details of your divorce, your nights may turn into a living hell of walking or rocking your inconsolable baby or holding your frightened two-year-old.

If you find yourself alone and caring for your baby, feeling blue and overwhelmed, I recommend very strongly that you let your pediatrician know and that you get professional therapy. Postpartum depression is a serious disorder that can be exacerbated by separation and divorce. We know a lot about depression, so avail yourself of what medical science has to offer. Medication and psychotherapy often work well together and can offer quick results. Depression can harm both you and your baby by making you less attentive, less responsive, and, despite your best intentions, less loving and even resentful of your child.

This is when the relevance of your baby's temperament comes into play. If your baby is a serene, stable child, she'll show relatively few signs of being upset. Indeed, she may be able to sleep, eat well, and smile happily when you play the games that parents and babies play the world over. But if your baby is colicky, and restless, and does not respond easily to being comforted, then the impact of your troubled marriage and divorce is likely to be more severe. You may see delays in her development accompanied by chronic cranky demands that disturb your rest and your mood. If your toddler has a calm temperament, he may continue to practice walking and talking without interference; or you may see a delay in his progress or even regression.

You need to think about the fact that all of your child's experiences in infancy and toddlerhood lay the foundation for what she thinks about people and for what she thinks about herself. The ambiance that you create around her deeply affects this process. Distrust begins when she learns that her crying has no effect. She believes that she is powerless. If her calls for help go unanswered long enough, she learns to feel unsafe, unprotected, and helpless. Without going into the neurobiology of the mother-infant bond, research shows that a mother's moods play an important role in shaping her baby's moods. If you're crying, upset, overwhelmed, and angry, you'll transmit some of those feelings to your baby. If you feel happy, loved, and taken care of, you convey those feelings to your fortunate child and she responds in kind.

WHAT YOU SAY AND DO

With a preverbal baby, the most important advice I can offer is that you try your best to maintain an oasis of calm around the infant and yourself. If you can—even for a few months—keep the crazy-making events of the divorce at bay or even delay the divorce; it might be a lot better for you and your baby. You need these early months after her birth to get to know and love your child. She needs the peace and the time to learn that she can absolutely count on you. The parent-child bond that is central to your child's future also needs time and space to grow strong.

How can you achieve this? First, if you and your estranged partner can call on your mutual concern for the baby, you will have taken the first important step. You should both know how important a calm environment is for the infant and that a mother's capacity to nurse and her supply of milk depend to some extent on feeling relaxed. Also keep in mind that father-child relationships need support from the mother in the early months and years of a child's life. So if you're in conflict, try to call a moratorium. People in battle call a truce, why not the two of you? It should be possible for two people who once loved each other to find ways of cooperating temporarily on behalf of their child.

If your toddler is walking and talking—and one of you has moved out—the primary caretaker should explain that the absent parent is coming back and in fact will be there soon. You need to say this before you see signs of your child's grief or acting upset. Babies and toddlers are acutely aware when a person they are used to seeing is suddenly missing from their surroundings. If you're the mom and your husband left, you need to say repeatedly, "Daddy is coming soon." If you see your toddler looking behind curtains or under the furniture for Daddy, repeat the message: Daddy is coming soon.

Fathers often fall madly in love with their toddlers and develop a special relationship that includes gentle roughhousing. They throw their children high into the air and catch them with mock difficulty—a kind of play that is hard for many moms to do. Little children look forward to this kind of play, squealing, "Let's play horsey again." Both parents should realize how important this kind of activity is to young children who are developing their sense of balance, learning to master their fear of falling, and beginning to recognize differences in gender roles. Ideally, despite your differences, you should both try to protect these patterns of early childhood.

Now look around for where you can get help. Is your mother or mother-in-law a soothing person? Is there someone in both your families who would rise to the challenge to pitch in? Could one or more of them help on a regular basis?

If you, as mother or father, must bring a new caregiver into the house because you have to go to work, be sure to ease in the person gradually. Make sure that she knows how to do things your way. Teach her how you want her to talk to your baby. Show her how you give a bath. Have her spend a week, not a day, following you around, getting to know your baby. Most of all, make sure that your baby knows her before you leave. Spend as many hours as you can playing together, just the three of you.

If you decide to place your baby or toddler in day care, try to wait a few months after the breakup. Then give your child time to get used to the new setting. If she's unable to be without you after several efforts, take her message seriously. Delay the change. In all of these moves, your baby's response can guide you. She won't be spoiled if you follow her lead. On the contrary, a healthy, happy baby will reward you long into the future. As she gets older, you'll need her cooperation and she'll be able to give it. Take seriously your observations about her temperament. The fact your sister's child loved day care from the first day is not relevant to your little one. Your child may need more time to adjust to change. It doesn't mean that she's mentally backward. She may bring home a

Nobel Prize someday. Be guided by what you see and what your heart tells you about your child.

You may have to put your other obligations on hold for a while. If your baby is used to seeing his daddy frequently, try to keep that going at the same level. If you're both close to your baby, you should do your best to support each other despite your differences. Keep in mind that pushing each other's buttons will have a severe effect on your baby and on your relationship with your baby.

A final note, if your divorce results in court-ordered physical joint custody for the baby—and one of you objects to this strongly because you don't want to disrupt the baby's environment—you are facing a different set of issues. Unfortunately there are many conflicting views on babies, overnight visiting, and custody arrangements. Some experts base their views on research about parenting in intact families, which says infants need the company of both mother and father. By extension, they say, the more your baby goes back and forth between your two homes for overnights after divorce, the better. This, they argue, is the only way your baby can achieve a good relationship with each of you.

I have serious misgivings about using studies done about parenting in intact families as a guide for parenting in post-divorce families. Like many viewpoints in the divorce marketplace, this argument about overnights seems loaded by a political agenda that says a child's equal time with both parents is central to her well-being. There's no research evidence that this is true. There's certainly no evidence that this is true for infants and toddlers.

The only study done of infants under eighteen months at the breakup shows that court-ordered overnight visits with the father, over the mother's objection, where the parents are in conflict and don't communicate, led to babies being insecure with both parents. Dr. Judith Solomon, who directed the 1998 study, which appeared in the *Journal of Attachment and Human Development*, found that babies suffered the most when the parents fought while exchanging custody. The study also reported that the lack of communication between the parents extended to refusal to follow medical instructions when the child was ill with an ear infection or other complaints that required medication at certain hours.

By age two, if your child is developing well, and is comfortable with both of you, and if the two of you are communicating well, there is no reason he can't spend occasional overnights with Dad. Two nights in a row may be difficult until he's older. You don't want him to worry that Mommy has disappeared. But as long as the same routines are followed, I've seen curious toddlers thrive in such arrangements; it's a big achievement to go to another parent's house at this tender age. If your child can carry it off, you should both praise him for his wonderful behavior.

If you have to go back to work right away, and many mothers do after the breakup, I want to make a special appeal. If there is any way for you to reduce your hours in the first year of your child's life, try to arrange it. It would be a great boon for your child. In some jobs the nursing mother can bring her baby to the worksite. See if your ex is willing to maintain support beyond the usual amounts for that first year. If he can't or won't, maybe someone else in your family could provide the financial assistance you and your baby need at this time. It's worth borrowing money if that's the only way. Consider asking your in-laws as well as your parents. They are all grandparents and they may be willing to do this for you.

And then take care of yourself. Put the future on hold. Just clear your mind the way people do when they meditate. Actually learning to meditate and exercising to get your figure back are both top priorities. Try to be kind and loving to yourself. Elicit all the kindness and cooperation from your family and friends you can, and resolve to protect your child. You may be lucky and find that your ex shares your view of giving the baby's needs priority and that grandparents are eager and able to help. In any case, learn to ask for what you need. Some people find that's the hardest thing to do. But remember, you're asking on behalf of your child. What could be more important?

If you're a new father, I urge you to consider your baby's needs for consistency and trust. There are countless ways for you to stay involved in your infant's life without disrupting that security. You can do this by learning as much as you can about infant and early child development and then making yourself available to help the baby first and foremost. As you will soon learn, babies change rapidly. Your role as your child's biological father can never be usurped, but only you have the power to nurture it in a healthy, loving way.

I should tell you that I have known a number of new mothers who were able to maintain their balance despite going through a difficult divorce. They did it by deciding that they were not going to miss out on this wonderful period of their lives. They weren't going to relinquish this magical time because they made a mistake in who they married. The sooner you can regain your equilibrium and the more you can transmit that sense of calm to your baby, the better both of you will feel.

Chapter 5: Three-, Four-, and Five-Year-Olds

An average child in this age group is under the impression that the grown-ups in her life control everything, including the weather. When she gets hurt, you can kiss away the pain. When she's hungry, food appears miraculously. When she's sleepy and closes her eyes at night, it's safe to go to sleep because her mommy and daddy are there to protect her against all the scary shapes that come around in the dark.

The child's entire sense that the world is a secure place where all her needs will be met is rocked by divorce. And so, not surprisingly, the first response of the little child is acute fear. What's going to happen to me? Who will feed me? Who will take care of me? Since young children can't tell time, don't comprehend how long a day or a week is, or even that day and night follow each other, and have no concept of distance, imagine how they feel when they don't see one of you for a week, let alone a month. They figure that you've simply gone away and left them. It takes children several years of development to understand that when someone disappears from view it doesn't mean he won't be back.

They also don't understand the rapid changes in your mood, your new impatience, your sudden unavailability at bedtime to play and carry out the many activities that are a treasured part of their lives. One curly-headed five-year-old made a deep impression on me when she came into my office a few months after her parents separated and explained soberly, "I need a new mommy." It was my task, she implied, to go out and get her one. From her perspective, the loving, available mommy who took her to playdates, brushed her hair, read to her at bedtime, and snuggled her tightly in the rocking chair had vanished. She'd been left with a harried, worried lady who no longer had time to put her to bed, read, play, or arrange cookies and milk before bedtime. Like all other intelligent pre-schoolers, she had no way of knowing or understanding that her mother's distress was temporary and that her home life would regain order and that within in a year or so her care would improve. Of course, for a four-year-old, one year is a quarter of her lifetime, two years is half. It's a very long time to feel pushed to the margin of your parent's life. Moreover, in many families it's unlikely that the divorced mother who has to work full-time and run her home, and understandably wishes to resume her own social life, will ever again have the schedule that permitted her to devote so much time to her young child. It's no surprise that children remember their loss and their grieving well into adulthood. Fortunately, a young child's sorrow can be alleviated by attentive parenting.

When I assess children this age, I invite them to join me in my Center's playroom, which is stocked like a miniature toy store—two dollhouses (very useful for children of divorce), puppets, blocks, puzzles, playdough, stuffed animals, drawing paper, crayons, Lego, funny hats, dinosaurs, toy telephones, and, of course, toy pistols. Amid this plentitude, where most children have a great time playing, many children at the time of divorce sit wanly or hide their heads in my lap, too worried to play with the pretty toys. Or when they do play they arrange the animals to represent kittens or other baby animals whose food has been snatched by monsters. The logic of their childlike thinking terrifies them even more. If one parent can leave another, why won't both leave me? This is their central worry and burning question. And since most young children are not told ahead of time about the divorce and wake up one morning to discover that one parent has left the home, they fully expect the second one could take off as well and they, like the kittens, will starve. Put yourself in their little shoes. How could they think anything different? This is why telling them ahead is so important and why repeated assurances from you are essential. While grown-ups can sometimes leave each other, they never, never, never leave their children.

Moreover, small children suffer more than older children because they have so few ways to comfort themselves. They're too little to know how. They discover that a warm thumb helps, rocking helps, pretending that you're a small baby helps. Even tantrums can help. A child will do anything that will bring Mommy and Daddy running and focus their attention where the child wants it. Children often abandon their latest civilized achievement, be it toilet training, speaking whole sentences clearly, or going in the carpool to nursery school. Your child may cling to you, not let you out of his sight, and refuse to stay in day care or the nursery school he had been happily attending. He may cry when you leave for work, even though you haven't changed any familiar routines around leaving for work. All the separations of day and night are filled with his anxiety. Will I see you again? How can I be sure? You can also expect to see a general rise in crankiness and aggression at home and sometimes at school. Don't be surprised if you get a call from the nursery school teacher saying, "I don't know what's gotten into Michael. He's such a sweet boy, but now he's biting the other children." And of course, unlike older brothers or sisters, a young child can't turn on the television by himself or call a friend to complain. He's totally dependent on the comforting he gets from you. When you're preoccupied, unavailable, or absent, he suffers loneliness and a continuing fear that you've forgotten him and will never return.

As adults we underestimate how hard it is for a little child who is used to thinking of her parents as a caretaking unit to separate them in her mind and feel safe and protected. Little girls cling for weeks, some-times months or years, to fantasies that Daddy will come back and stay with them. "When he grows up, he'll come back to me," said Diana with stars in her eyes. Little boys are distraught. "I need a daddy," wailed Bobby. "Get me a full-time daddy." When a small child wakes up in the morning and finds Daddy or Mommy has gone, familiar routines—watching Daddy shave or Mommy pour breakfast cereal—are not happening. In a flash, the world becomes a strange, worrisome place where the closest relationships in the known world can no longer be expected to hold firm.

Adding to their unhappiness is the fact that little children are especially likely to believe that they're the cause of the divorce. They're trapped in the belief that they were responsible by the immaturity of their thinking, which is something you won't be able to eradicate until they grow older. You can feel reassured by the fact that as children grow older, they can revise their understanding of the divorce, especially with your help. But for now, cause and effect are personalized—Mom did it, Dad did it, I did it, or, conveniently, my baby brother did it. Since half of all divorces occur in families with children under the age of six, I think it's fair to say that the majority of children whose parents are getting divorced will to some degree blame themselves for the breakup.

Why? Because they still have virtually no capacity to grasp impersonal causes. The intellectually sophisticated notion that two people can have different views and feelings is not within their cognitive domain. A concept like no-fault divorce is light-years away from their thinking. They're used to being reprimanded for some breach in behavior such as spilling the milk or calling endlessly for a last drink of water after bedtime. It's far safer for them to blame themselves than to think of their powerful parents as the culprits of their distress. They say, "I did it." Or, "My puppy messed up and so my dad got mad and he went away." Five-year-old Juliet said, "I forgot to tell Mom that the bread burned in the oven and then she got mad and they had a big fight and then they divorced." You have to appreciate the unfamiliar logic of the child's mind to understand the force of the self-accusation and how much children suffer.

WHAT TO DO

The good news is that children this age are the most responsive to your reaching out to comfort them. Soothing words always help. Hugs are invaluable. But that's still not enough. This is not a time for you to be away from your young child. She'll need more of your time on a regular basis because she's haunted by her fear that you're abandoning her the way you and her dad abandoned each other. Your unexplained absence, even for a day, can seem like an eternity. I realize how hard it is for you as a newly divorced parent to follow this advice. You have so much to do, you're going crazy. With so much to think about, your head is taking off without you. Nevertheless, the most important thing you can do on behalf of your child is to try to keep routines much as they were before the breakup. If your child was in nursery school or day care before the breakup, try your best to help him continue there. Ask the teachers for advice. They, in turn, should be encouraged to greet your child warmly and tell him what fun activities are planned for that day. You may need to spend a little time at the school before leaving for work, just like you did when he started day care. Most important, be on time when you come to get him. If your child has a special stuffed animal or blanket, be sure he has it with him. Some children at the time of the breakup refuse to enter the carpool, even though they had no difficulty beforehand. Speak to whoever is driving and ask him or her to engage your child in some playful conversation. Maybe make a game of looking for dogs or children or traffic lights on the way to school. Another game involves learning landmarks on the route, which can help your child feel the road is familiar and safe. Your goal is to recognize your child's symptoms and do whatever you can to assure him that his world is secure. It's very likely that he will calm down in a few months.

I also think you should try to stay home most weeknights, as much as possible, after the breakup. Encourage your child to play with you and with other children. Play is a great restorative of emotional equilibrium.

Young children are inventive and charming. Despite your adult concerns, you will also feel restored by playtime. Tell your child that you're proud of him and that you love him when he builds with blocks or puts his teddy bear to bed tenderly. Give him a soothing bath and read a favorite bedtime story. When you tuck him in, assure him you'll be there in the morning to greet him. If he seems fretful, and he will be, if he clings and begs for you to give him more time, or to turn on a night-light, or to lie down with him for a while, do it. Explain that this is very special because he has been so good or tried so hard or whatever. Tell him, even if he has been very naughty, that you know how hard he is trying to help and you appreciate it. Perhaps he can try even harder in the morning. If you haven't done so, tell him what the plans are for the next day so he can look forward to something predictable. I'm sure that as a sensitive parent you know your child well and don't need details from me. What your child needs is a parent who can relate to his anxiety and calm his fears that he's likely to be abandoned. You can restore his confidence in you by providing him with a stable, dependable world.

Bedtime routines are more important than ever. All children have trouble in the dark when they can't look around and see familiar objects to keep them anchored to reality. The darkness is more frightening when the family breaks up and everything in life feels dark. I remember Anita, who at age three refused to lie down in her crib at night. When I interviewed the family, Anita's parents told me that they had been fighting every evening and that their daughter couldn't help but overhear the arguments from the next room. The mother and father both said, "Every time we try to put her down to sleep, she screams. What should we do?" I advised them to tell Anita that the divorce meant there would be no more fighting, no more yelling, no more danger. Now she could lie down with her doll and go to sleep. She was safe and her baby doll was safe, too. Once Anita realized that she didn't have to stay up to watch the fighting and was assured that both parents were unhurt, she was able to lie down and go to sleep peacefully.

Parents ask me whether they should sleep with their children after the breakup if a child requests it. There's no harm at all in taking a frightened child into your bed for a few days to calm him. However, it's not a practice that should be continued on a regular basis. An important part of growing up is to learn to separate from your parent at night. If you allow your child to sleep with you for months, he'll soon find it very difficult to sleep alone and you'll be tied to his sleep schedule. That's not good for either of you. I've known several families where a mother sleeps for months with a young child, sometimes going to bed at the same time. But later, when she resumes her social life or becomes interested in a lover, the child is suddenly displaced. Then the child who couldn't fall asleep alone feels thrown out by his only source of comfort. This is a recipe for acute sorrow and weeks of severe fatigue as you both struggle to establish normal sleeping habits. My advice is to avoid this dilemma by making bedtime a healthy transition as soon as possible.

If you have not been working full-time and you can afford to further delay going back to a demanding schedule, do so. Many children suffer a double trauma—the family breaks up and Mom is not home as much. I know many families have two parents working full-time and that most children tolerate this well, especially if they have close contact with loving parents at the end of the day. But it's more difficult for a child to tolerate the absence of both parents during the day right after a divorce. Little children do better if the changes in their lives are introduced gradually. Of course, resilient children are better able to handle multiple changes, and if your child is flexible, count yourself fortunate. You need to take all these considerations seriously because they affect your child's sense of security and overall development.

If you cannot reduce the hours you work and continue in a full-time job, you need to keep a very close eye on your child. You need to find a way to provide affectionate, responsible care in your absence. Your parents or in-laws might be able to help. Or you may be better off with help that you hire and train. In either case, you'll worry unless you know that the person you leave in charge shares your values about how to care for and discipline your child. There are many places to look for that right person. But whoever you select will require your supervision and guidance. When you interview applicants, ask about their own upbringing.

Do they have children? How do they feel about discipline? What is their top priority in bringing up children? Are they willing to accept your ideas and implement them? Keep in mind that you want someone who will stay a while. Your child has just suffered loss in his family and you want to spare him future losses if possible. To the extent that you can treat your helper with kindness and understanding and generosity, your child will benefit.

Many people rely on their older children to provide after-school care, especially when the youngest goes to kindergarten or first grade. Whether this can work depends entirely on the relationship between the two siblings. How do they feel about this arrangement? Some older children are wonderfully loving and responsible caregivers. Others resent the responsibility and threaten or even hit the younger child. After all, they're children, too. Such arrangements require close supervision. Be sure to reward your older child with high praise and material gifts she appreciates. Also be sure to give her some relief. A ten-year-old is too young to give up her own activities and friendships every day after school to take care of younger siblings. Three times a week is better, if you can swing it. You might also come home once in a while unannounced to check on what's really happening.

WHAT TO SAY

Your child needs help in understanding the changes taking place in family life. Your remarks are best aimed at explaining these changes and dealing with their central fear of abandonment.

Remember my message about the importance of telling the children ahead of time about the separation. Then, as weeks go on, you should continue to say something that may be obvious to you but needs lots of repeating: "We both love you and will continue taking care of you."

When you put your son or daughter to bed, you need to say, "I will be in the next room, reading a book" and, "I will be here when you wake up." When you take your son or daughter to nursery school, say, "I will be here to get you this afternoon" or, "Grandma will be here" (or whomever, as long as it's someone they know well and like). And, "I will be so happy to see you and hear about your play with your friend Timmy." Any assurance you can give that you or someone they know and like will be there at the moment of reunion is critical. Any way that you can convey that there's continuity in the child's life, even when you're apart from each other, will be comforting. You can say, "I'll be thinking about you when I go to work and I will be here smiling when I see you tonight."

A five-year-old is likely to worry that her father is not being taken care of. So you both might say, "Daddy is going to have his own house, his own refrigerator, his own bed." Similarly, "Mommy will have her own house, refrigerator, and bed." You might say, "Of course you can take your favorite stuffed animals and toys with you. Daddy and Mommy will have plenty of room so you can take whatever you need and not leave anything behind. You'll get to play with Daddy and sleep in his house. You'll get to play with Mommy at her house. You'll have your bedtime story in two places." All these details reassure the child that he's not facing losses in all parts of his life. Explain slowly and carefully to your three-year-old, who is still learning to count and whose understanding about days of the week is limited, about back-and-forth visits. He will gradually accept the idea that he continues to have both parents. The important thing for a child this age to understand is that he's not losing his parents, that he will be with his siblings, and that his favorite toys will not vaporize.

It's extremely important that you treat your son or daughter with great tenderness and sensitivity when traveling between your two homes. Many parents fail to understand that going back and forth, whether to visit or for joint custody, is a major accomplishment for a small child. What may appear to you like a short trip of a few blocks by car may loom as a long, frightening journey for a small child. Try to remember what it's like to be powerless in a huge, confusing world. Once again I remind you that you should watch how your child adjusts to this task. Is it easy for her? Or does she hang back in fear? Her response should help guide your efforts to help.

When your little one goes back and forth the first few times, treat it as you would the first day of school. Take your child by the hand and point out landmarks that will soon become familiar along the way—a big tree, the white church, the ice cream parlor. Help him fix each landmark in his mind so the journey grows less frightening. If it interests your child, teach him to count blocks, telephone poles, or mailboxes along the route. It becomes a fun game, and because counting is also a method of building confidence, it will help him gain some control over the unfamiliar journey. You might also give him a sheet of paper and ask him to draw a map that you can later pin over his bed.

Like so many protagonists in fairy tales, children are not only worried about leaving home, they worry about returning. The story of Hansel and Gretel is about children's ingenuity in finding their way home with the help of a trail of crumbs. The story captures the fears that all young children have about losing their way. My concern is that we have underestimated the effort required of the young child in making the transitions called for by divorce. Little children in all homes dread getting lost, but you can help your child cope with the dread after divorce.

What else can you do? When your child leaves your home to visit his other parent, he needs your permission to enjoy himself and he needs assurance from you that you'll be there happily awaiting his return. It would help him if you could send him off with cheerful words like "Have a wonderful time!" Mention that you'll be there for his return. Both are important, but few parents do it. A child who has mastered visiting or joint custody has taken a huge developmental step forward, but he cannot do it without your help. Ideally, if your relationship with your ex-partner permits it, you can call ahead to ask what plans have been made for the next few days or weekend. Then you can say, "When you visit Daddy (or Mommy), you're going to the zoo" or to McDonald's or whatever the plan might be. The parent at the other end needs to convey the same message, that it's fine to go and you'll be welcome when you return. To the extent that both you and your ex can summon the kind of encouragement that parents show for excursions to the outside world, you will both ease the journey.

Most five-year-olds have some mastery of numbers and a rudimentary grasp of time. Take a big calendar and mark in bright crayon when your child will be at each home. Show him the intervals of going back and forth. A four-year-old will barely understand details but will be reassured by the regularity of what you describe and by the rhythmic motion of back and forth. And he will have gotten the important notion that he will continue to have both parents, and that unlike in the story about the Little Red Hen, the sky is not falling down.

Remember, your child thinks that since one parent can disappear, so can the other. His trust in you has been shaken by the breakup and his fears run deep. This is the one time in your life when it's a good idea to sound like a broken record. Keep repeating this simple message: I'm not going anywhere. I'll be here for you as long as you need me. If you do that, your child's anxiety will subside and he'll conclude that he can trust you.

Chapter 6:   Six-, Seven-, and Eight-Year-Olds

If your child is six, seven, or eight years old, he's straddling two worlds—one with you at home and one with playmates at school. He's in the process of shifting his main attention to the playground, where he expects to learn how to get along with the other kids. If you think back to your own childhood, you'll recall that this is a daunting task that will take all of his determination and courage. Games have rules that can't be changed by tears or running home to Mama if he messes up a turn. Catching a ball without missing earns him a lot more status than picking up his toys. He's also had his first encounters with the disciplined demands of classroom learning, the challenge of sitting still, watching the teacher at the blackboard, and remembering what she said. His intellectual capacity has expanded. He has a better understanding of cause and effect and knows that Mom and Dad don't control the world. He understands about numbers and time and has even acquired a sense of the ridiculous, delighting in riddles and funny stories. He's terrified of being laughed at. He's able to amuse himself within reason, can feed himself if you put out the food, and can even put himself to sleep.

I remember one six-year-old who put at a sign at the end of his bed, "Don't be afraid, Jimmy, go to sleep," and it worked for him.

Because a child this age has one foot in the family and the other foot in the outside world, his greatest fear at divorce is that his recent gallant advances into the social world of his peers may fail. With his family life crumbling, the foot he has planted outside begins to wobble. If he's really worried about losing his balance, he may retreat from the outside world and regress to a younger developmental stage. Bed-wetting and thumb-sucking can reappear.

To move along the developmental ladder, a six-, seven-, or eight-year-old needs to feel secure in having a family he can count on. How can he concentrate at school when he's thinking about you and the divorce, which at the outset may be all the time. I mean that literally—all the time. He just can't keep his mind on his schoolwork. He also feels angry and cranky, which may cause him to jump on his best friend and hit him. Such behavior soon isolates him on the playground. Now he has more worries to keep him from enjoying the games he loved before. He worries that when he comes home from school you won't be there. If his daddy is late to pick him up at an agreed-upon time, he worries that Daddy may never arrive. If Mommy doesn't come home exactly when she said she would, then Mommy may have disappeared. The fear "Who will feed me?" of the younger children gets replaced by worries such as, "Where are my parents?" "Will they hold things steady so I can count on them when I need them?" Or when he really lets himself worry, "Will I have the same home?" And believe it or not, he worries, "Is my home still there?"

Children this age tend to show their main reactions to divorce in the classroom or on the playground. Many of them lose a year of school-work in the elementary grades during and after the divorce. It's simply too much to do it all. One youngster sat in class a whole year refusing to remove his jacket. He explained to the teacher that he had to be ready to go at any time. "Go where?" she asked. "I don't know," he wailed.

Fortunately for these children there's a lot of repetition in the early grades that enables them to catch up for lost time in that first year after divorce. Some, however, continue to lag behind and need extra help later on when they're better able to concentrate. Learning to read is the primary task for children this age. It can be harder to do when your mother and father divorce and you can't pay attention to the teacher.

You need to understand that your child's inner life is likely to be dominated by sorrowful thoughts about you and your ex. Is Mommy going to let her beautiful garden die? Will she ever smile again? Will she have more time someday? Where in the wide world is my daddy? Does Daddy have a place? Where will he stay? Does he have good stuff to eat? Who washes his socks? Since your child assumes that parents come with families, he may worry about being replaced—will my daddy get another mommy, another dog, another little boy? His longing for the absent parent is heartbreaking to witness. "My daddy went to Oakland," wailed six-year-old Roger. "Where is Oakland?" he asked me, not knowing it was close by. "Is Oakland in Mexico?" Since at age six or seven children have no concept of geography, space, and distance, their thinking is bounded by the neighborhood they know. But their sorrow has no bounds.

Like the younger girls, girls this age often weave powerful fantasies to comfort themselves when their yearning for the departed parent is overwhelming. I call these Madam Butterfly fantasies because they remind me of the tragic opera heroine who waited for many years for her husband to return, refusing to believe he could have abandoned her. Carla, who had not seen her father in four months, told me matter-of-factly, "My daddy sleeps in my bed every night." She confused her dreams with reality as her longing for her father amplified. On reaching her eighteenth birthday, still needing to keep the fantasy in place, Carla drove seven hundred miles to see her father, who had only visited her once since the breakup. Her courage failed her as she reached his street in a distant, unfamiliar city. She turned her car around and came home without seeing him. "I was afraid to find out that he didn't care about me," she told me.

While children this age don't suffer as much loneliness as younger ones—unless they give up on friends and school to linger listlessly at home—they do blame themselves for the divorce. But they do it in ways that are typical of six-, seven-, and eight-year-olds. Their explanations never cease to amaze me. Heather, age seven, said it was because she failed to deliver a telephone message from her mom to her dad. Marion, who was eight, explained that she was a witch, like the pretty witch in her favorite TV show, and that she could make things happen just by thinking about them. She then confessed that she had thought that her parents might divorce and then they did. Eight-year-old Philip, who was dyslexic, confessed to his dad many years after the divorce that he long believed the split happened because he couldn't read.

Despite their greater ability to understand cause and effect, their maturity doesn't yet include psychological understanding. Children this age won't make a connection between conflict and divorce. Even if you've been fighting like banshees, your child will probably not associate the arguments with the divorce. Indeed, the capacity for children this age to deny what they've witnessed—shouting, yelling, slamming doors, crying—is astonishing to most parents. Parents reason that an intelligent seven-year-old who has seen open arguments will recognize that there's trouble afoot. Don't count on it. Children at every age, but particularly this age, have the capacity to deny what their eyes and ears tell them. They especially don't want to see their parents fighting. If they continue to see Mom and Dad as being together, they're secure in pursuing their own developmental agendas.

WHAT TO DO

The fear that Daddy has gone to join another family and your child's painful longing for his presence should encourage you to arrange very quickly for continued father-child contact. It should encourage you, the father, to quickly set up a home where your child can visit or reside part of the week. You can allay your child's anxiety about your welfare by showing her that you're reasonably comfortable in your new home. I recommend that the visit to Dad's new place occur within a week or so of telling your child about the breakup and that the visit be set up at that time.

If your housing is only temporary, as it often is at that time, tell your child about your plans. He should also be told as soon as possible what schedule of custody or visiting will be arranged. He should also be consulted about how this would work with his own new schedule of activities like Little League and other activities that he values. These measures will go far to reassure your child that you, Dad, have not been thrown out of the home or run away. Your child doesn't need to mourn your absence because you're a continuing part of his life. This should be at the top of your agenda in helping children this age cope with divorce.

It's very likely that you'll receive complaints from teachers because your child is acting angry and not paying attention to his lessons. This is especially true among boys. When you talk with the teacher, tell her that you're divorcing and what your plans are for the immediate future. If the teacher says that your child's behavior is very difficult if not totally obnoxious, take a deep breath and get ready to intervene. It's relatively easy to calm a three-year-old who needs you by sitting at her bedside when she goes to sleep as opposed to a six-year-old who's kicking up a fuss on the playground. It's going to take all your patience and then some. You and the teacher can work out a plan for your child.

At home, tell your child that you met with his teacher and that you're both concerned. Ask if there's anything you can do together to reduce his worry. Your son may have specific complaints that you can remedy. In these talks, be sure to swallow your own anger. Your child is not acting out because he wants to make life miserable for you, even though it may feel that way. When he fails to respond to the teacher's questions, he may be near tears. When he squirms out of his chair during quiet time, he may be worrying about where his dad is. You need to be patient. Don't rage at him for not keeping up at school or for disrupting the class. A child who is depressed often acts out with angry behavior. It's not fair for you to blow up when your child is hurting and needs your support. He needs a firm hand but a loving one.

When the teacher calls to tell you that your son's behavior has improved, celebrate. Treat him to something he really likes. Lavish well-deserved praise for his cooperation.

The most important thing for you to keep in mind is that your child needs to get back to his normal activities and to find them challenging and absorbing. That's his current developmental step on the growing-up ladder. His job is to attend to learning in the classroom and to develop friends and playmates. His job is every bit as important as yours and needs your full support. It's true. Both tasks take all his energies. So while your child may worry about losing one or both of you after divorce, his central need is not necessarily more time spent with each of you. Take seriously your child's burgeoning friendships and activities. He needs to carry on with sleepovers, birthday parties, and other group occasions where your job is to fetch and carry. How to arrange this when you're both working full-time is a perennial problem. How to cultivate friendships with other parents when you're running faster to stay in one place is crazy-making. But if possible, you should not allow your child to lose out on extracurricular social activities because of the divorce. Music lessons, baseball teams, and the like are critically important. Hire a college student to be your chauffeur if you can't do it. Adult children of divorce report that they felt deprived of many activities and much fun. They envied their peers from intact families who had parents willing to be soccer moms and dads. How can you make the playoffs if there's no one to take you to the game?

If your child is hanging back, if she comes home to spend her time alone after school, if she seems listless and withdrawn, take it seriously. Have a talk with the teacher to find out if he or she has some thoughts about how to help. And, of course, talk with your child. Ask her how you can help because she seems not to be having fun and seems lonely. Find out whether there is a specific worry that you can remedy and what she would like you to do. The most important thing at this early stage of the divorce is to show your awareness and concern. I will talk in Chapter 21 about what to do if your child continues to be troubled. But don't say to yourself or listen to others who advise you that she'll outgrow it. It's important to help her by showing your genuine interest and concern for her pain.

Be sure that your child has both your phone numbers and has memorized them. And be sure the school knows where to reach you and whom to call under what circumstances. Accidents do occur on the playground and the school is often confused about who to call when parents have divorced. I recall one episode where a child was taken to the emergency room for what looked like a broken arm. The staff was unable to take any action until a parent had been notified. The father directed the call to the mother. The mother directed the call to the father. The child was in limbo and sat in pain in the waiting room for many hours until one parent arrived to sign the needed permissions for the medical staff to treat him.

Finally, keep in mind that your school-age child is still very young and needs a lot of care. A six-year-old can make herself an occasional lunch, but she should not have this as her full responsibility. She will forget. Many first grade teachers have told me how they regularly have to pool their own lunches to take care of children from newly divorced homes who forgot and were ashamed to admit that they were hungry. Teachers also complain that children from newly divorced families come to school sleepy and often fall asleep in class by midmorning. Bedtime is hard to enforce when you have so much to do and you're on the phone or working on needed papers. But sleep is very important for your child. With everything going on, you need to maintain your child's regular schedule. She needs your continued reassurance that you love her, that you're concerned with how she's managing, and that you're available when she needs help with school. She needs to count on you to provide comfort and encouragement.

WHAT TO SAY

Children this age need to hear all the things I mentioned in Chapter 2—they're not responsible, your marriage started with love, they are wanted, you promise to protect them. Then you need to say some extra things appropriate to their age and their reactions to the news of the divorce. Your goal is to encourage them to stay tuned to life at school and to keep moving up the developmental ladder. Children at this age may need your help in learning how to read and to master numbers. You need to allow for this in your harried schedule. They may also need advice in handling problems that arise with friends and playmates on the playground. This is a new and challenging world in which many youngsters can get their feelings badly hurt. You can also offer specific instructions about what they can do to keep school the main center of their lives. "I expect you to pay attention to what your teacher says. I want you to make friends, stay on the soccer team, keep up with your piano lessons." Say it clearly: "I know it's not easy, but we are all trying to do our best."

If your child is disruptive in school, tell her that you cannot permit her to make trouble in the classroom because she's worried, unhappy, or angry about the divorce. Rather, you want her to come tell you how she feels. If she starts screaming at you, say firmly, "Stop. You may not talk to me this way." If necessary put her on your lap and hold her like a younger child. Don't let her boss you around.

Some children start acting out at home. Boys in particular may try to move into their father's former position by putting on articles of his clothing and strutting around like lords of the manor. My advice is for you to kindly discourage this behavior while keeping in mind that your son is trying to symbolically reconstitute the family. If the behavior does not get out of control, you can let it alone. But if your son starts to talk like his father at the height of an argument, yelling at you, then stop him firmly. "You may not talk to me like that. I know you're angry about the divorce and I know you want us to be together again, but we've made this decision. It's not going to change."

If you can't be home after school, make it your business to know where your children are. And be sure that you or someone they know and like is there after school. The transitions from home to school and school back to home are not easy for children this age. Because children are anxious, you should try your best not to change things without notice, and above all, don't break appointments at this time. Think about what they don't understand. You shouldn't call and say, "Sorry, I'll be late picking you up. I was held up at the office." Your child doesn't have the remotest idea what being held up at the office means or why your work is so important to you. If you're newly back at full-time work, explain why this is something that you need to do and how your child will benefit. Walter explained to me soberly, "My mom is a cash register. All she cares about is money." Although Walter's mother was working very hard to support the family, he did not make the connection between her long absences at work during the day and her efforts to take care of him and his sister.

Since this is the age when children need to be making friends, getting involved in sports, and joining other after-school activities, let's talk about how you can help. First, you need to understand how important these relationships are for your child's development. While you may be strapped for time and extra income to support this extracurricular world, you need to make it a priority. In this, you may have a certain disadvantage. Parents in intact families have an easier time paying for baseball uniforms, music lessons, ballet shoes, and the like—but you need to find a way to make the same opportunities available to your child. Many children of divorce complain that they don't have the same freedom to play as do their classmates from intact families. For starters, they don't have a built-in mom-chauffeur with a built-in backup dad-the-driver. They often have conflicts caused by visiting or custody arrangements. If no one can pick them up when the rehearsal ends or the game is over, and the school bus is not running, they can't join. If you can't be available, perhaps your ex or someone in your family or a hired student can provide the needed transportation. If these arrangements are impossible, explain the difficulties to your child, tell him how sorry you are, and promise that as things settle down you will do your best to make sure that someone will be available. But don't just let it slide and hope that your child will adjust. He has a right to hear your apology and your concern. You will both feel better.

If you move after your divorce, I strongly recommend that you do whatever you can to help your children build new friendships. Tired as you are, go to the PTA meetings and join family groups at your church or synagogue. Parents are often eager to welcome new members and to support families that have come through a divorce or other crisis. Try to make friends with adults who have children the same age as yours. Talk to the new coach or new ballet teacher in your new community and tell them about your child. When birthdays roll around, invite your child's new and old friends to the party. Share picnics and holidays with other families, single and intact, where there are children. Many children of divorce say sadly that their friends are not allowed to come over to their house after school because no adult is present. Perhaps you can figure out how to have someone there, at least one day a week, to welcome your children's friends with cookies or brownies and milk. I remember when my children were in elementary school my son had two friends who used to march into my home demanding, "Where are the brownies?" We all laughed and we loved it. Children this age need your help in moving into the neighborhood, in establishing new friends, in thinking of activities they can share, and in holding on to the children they left behind.

Keep in mind, your child is moving into the world of peers and academic learning. He may be thrown off course by your divorce. Most of all, he needs to feel that things are settling down at home and that you're in control. You've helped him maintain his relationship with both you and your ex. He needs encouragement from both of you to enjoy learning and to enter into new activities. By encouraging his efforts to succeed at school and on the playground, you're both building a strong foundation for his future success.

Chapter 7: Nine- and Ten-Year-Olds

I n the pecking order of elementary school, boys and girls in the upper grades enjoy a special status. Seen through the eyes of younger kids, most fourth, fifth, and sixth graders look pretty cool. They can go to the movies on their own. They can get dropped off at a friend's house. Depending on where they grow up, many are free to ride their bikes all over town, anytime they want. They've got wheels. They've got attitude. Some even have cell phones.

Parents of most nine- or ten-year-olds can't help noticing that their children have entered a new developmental spurt, one that draws them further away from home and out into the world of peers. If you have children this age, you may be pleased to see that they're increasingly able to spend time alone, take more responsibility for themselves, and define the interests that they want to pursue, like sports, music, dance, and other group activities. Enterprising youngsters are able to establish and conduct rock band trios, write and stage skits, and organize other complex projects—although their capacity to sustain these over time is very limited. They can think for themselves and distinguish their thinking from what other people believe. They can say, "My mom says this, my dad says that, and I say something different." Or, "I don't agree with my mom or dad." Whereas children in the early school grades are often in love with their teachers, children this age are not only impatient but quick to criticize or even make fun of teachers whom they find tedious. They have reached a skeptical stage when adults are expected to earn their respect and their affection.

Nine- and ten-year-olds are better able to plan for the future and think about moral issues. They're able to distinguish good and bad behavior according to their own lights and to criticize one or both of you for deception, unjust treatment, or just plain repeating yourselves. Alan was ten when he told me, "My mom and dad lied and cheated on each other. I've decided to be different. I'm never going to lie."

You may find that your child sometimes gets bored by your company, preferring to spend time with peers or adults with specialized skills like coaches and selected teachers. By the same token your child may disapprove or flatly reject other adults. One mother was a great success with her children at this age because she was an exciting storyteller of adventure tales. One father was an amateur magician whose backyard performances drew children from all over the neighborhood.

You may notice that children this age are newly responsive to how you feel. They can read your moods accurately, even when you try not to reveal clues. They can handle abstractions and are beginning to understand behavior, their own and yours. Indeed, they're growing up fast. They like it. They also find it scary.

So when you tell children this age about your decision to divorce, what can you expect their reactions to be? Obviously, they don't worry about who will take care of their physical needs on a daily basis. In a reasonably functioning home that's taken for granted. But I can tell you that they'll be terribly upset by the disruption in their home life. Consider their predicament. Life is just opening up in exciting ways. They're fast acquiring new skills and new opportunities. They're gifted performers who scamper all over the stage, interacting with friends, acquiring new knowledge, showing off their prowess, taking chances.

From their perspective, your job as parents is to hold up the stage.

Your child expects you to provide the foundation that won't let the stage tip over or the lights go out. In the child's mind, he belongs on center stage and you should stay in the wings concentrating on keeping everything stable. You're supposed to remain invisible, in the audience, coming into the limelight only to applaud or to come running when he calls for help, which he hopes he never has to do. But during divorce, it seems as if you pull the stage and audience out from under him and focus the attention on yourselves.

I'm not saying that children are right to be this self-centered. But it goes with their age and development. Actually, if you weren't over your head dealing with your own crisis, you'd likely be relishing this developmental stage in your child. These are blue-ribbon years, when proud moms and dads admire their children's science fair experiments and whistle and stomp with approval at all the kids playing in the school musical concert. I think it will help you to understand your child's reactions if you understand how concentrated he is on his own growing up and why your divorce seems like an interference that he hopes will just disappear.

Moreover, as children this age gain competence, they sense that adolescence lies over the next hill—a notion that is thrilling and terrifying. What will happen to them if the family is disrupted? Who will keep things on an even keel? Beneath their cool façade, I assure you that their anxiety level is sky-high.

ANGER

A key reaction to your divorce, befitting your child's somewhat grandiose conception of himself as being the center of your family, is anger. Whether the anger is directed at one of you or both of you, your child will be fuming: How could you give priority to yourself and not to me? How could you be so selfish? Underneath the bluster is a worried child who fears that he may lose you as well as the scaffolding he needs to support his growing up.

This anger causes children to enlist younger siblings in the criticism brigade. They'll start to reproach you for your behavior, turning the tables on who gives the orders around the house. Parents are startled to hear things like:

"Stop smoking!"

"Come home on time."

"You're thirty-one years old and you want to go out dancing? How could you? That skirt is too short."

"Dad, you look ridiculous in that shirt."

"I remember there was no conflict when they were married and how awful it was to leave my home, my school, my friends," said Sara, who at age twenty recalled her parents' divorce ten years earlier. "We had a great garden and big trees and then we went to live in an apartment. I still remember the climbing wisteria and how much I cried and how angry I was at both of them for disrupting my life and being so selfish."

This rising anger may soon manifest itself at school or on the playground, sometimes as mischievous behavior like petty theft, truancy, or alignments with one parent against the other. But the anger is directed toward you, not their playmates. Their real goal is to force you to reverse your divorce decision. Basically they want you to stand still and watch them as they continue to move forward in growing up.

Some children get most angry at whichever parent they hold responsible for the divorce (usually the person who wanted out) and form a close alliance with the parent left behind. These alliances, which I'll talk more about in Chapter 23, can be hurtful and enduring. The parent who gets attacked may not be responsible for the divorce but that's not the issue. A lifetime of loving care and devotion can be wiped out overnight by the children's anger. They don't understand complex feelings and may fail to comprehend your unhappiness despite having witnessed your humiliations and pain. And, of course, they have no way of understanding issues like your loneliness or sexual deprivation.

Nine- and ten-year-olds are adept at playing one parent off the other, going from one to the other until they get what they want. The strategy can work well in intact families, but it works even better in divorced homes because there is usually no reality check. Obviously, if you can maintain a united front and know what the other person has said, you can limit this kind of manipulative behavior. But this is much harder to do when you live apart.

If you can't communicate well and are tempted to believe whatever your child says about your ex, try not to get caught in the web. One father in our study always said to his son, "Tell me what you want, not what your mom said. I'll make up my own mind." Just make it clear that you make the rules for your turf. You're not responsible for what happens in the other household. Moreover, you don't want to get drawn into issues that are not worth fighting over. One nine-year-old girl in our study liked to tell her mom about her dad's girlfriend and all the tattoos on her body. Although these stories drove the mother wild, she wisely decided not to say anything. "I was furious," she said, "but I clamped my mouth shut and acted bored. I decided that unless I went to court, I had no recourse. What would the judge say? Is there a law against showing a child a tattoo on a woman's thigh?" The mother's strategy worked and the exciting stories soon stopped. The moral is that you should do your best not to be drawn into the good guy–bad guy kind of games that children play. They act this way to promote their own agenda, which is to keep the two of you involved with each other, no matter the consequences.

It's very difficult to deal with anger coming from a child you love. It hurts to be told that you're being selfish. You may be haunted by feelings of guilt for even going through with this divorce. Is it the best decision? Are you taking the right step? You've tried so long to be a loving, nurturing parent, and now your child turns on you at a time when you feel alone and overwhelmed. Shouldn't you have the right to expect their support? In the face of such assault, it can be hard to maintain your balance. When your child contributes to the misunderstandings between you and your ex, things can get pretty rocky. But read on. The situation is not hopeless.

COMPASSION

Having just told you how mischievous your children can be and how much they can contribute to your distress, let me say clearly that there is another side. Along with anger you'll also experience extraordinary love and compassion. Although girls are more able to express these feelings, I have seen boys open their hearts the same way. Children at this age worry about you. They examine your face to assess your mood and they learn to read your body language. They can be surprisingly accurate in these judgments. There's no mistaking their genuine sweetness and eagerness to comfort you, to put an arm around you, to hold your hand and sit by your side when they feel that you're discouraged or overwhelmed. "My daughter understands me," one mother said, "even when I say nothing. If I look sad she will come silently to hold my hand." One ten-year-old called her depressed father nightly to ask how he was feeling, to tell him to eat a decent dinner, and to get some needed rest. Sometimes children can express their feelings with a burst of passion. One boy turned to his father when they were passing some power lines and said, "Daddy, how much electricity is in those power lines?" On hearing an estimate of the voltage, the boy said, "Dad, I would hold on to those wires for you. Daddy, I would die for you."

Morality is an important issue at this age. Nine- and ten-year-old children are very concerned about right and wrong. Their conscience is growing and their minds are racing. They look to you for guidance, which is as it should be. But they can also become disenchanted with you. If your child sees you doing things he cannot condone, the consequences can be very serious. To develop a conscience that knows right from wrong, a growing child needs to respect his parents and think of them as virtuous. When he finds you at fault, this can cause him a great deal of suffering. I recall a heartbroken nine-year-old, Sam, who told me tearfully, "Dad and Mom were always telling me to do right and look at them now." His father, whom Sam idealized, was deserting his wife for a woman who lived next door.

So if you or your ex are involved in an infidelity, you can expect that children this age will take you to task. It's important for you to have an explanation that they'll find credible and that can enable them to respect you. (More on what to say in the next section.) I remember a ten-year-old telling me how silly his father was. "Every week he introduces me to another lady," he moaned. "Dad calls each of them his significant other. What's the matter with grown-ups? Or is it just my dad?"

Finally, children this age feel safe and comfortable when they're part of an ongoing family. They enjoy doing things as a family, especially if their wishes are respected and their friends are sometimes included. Their anxiety about your divorce is tied to the fear that they're losing the family structure that sheltered them. They're still children. They need you and the circle of activities that families engage in. There's a lot you can do to continue this protection, especially if you realize its importance.

WHAT TO DO

Your child's anger and righteous indignation can challenge you to the limits of your patience. Of course, you can decide to ride out the storm, knowing that it will end faster if you maintain a safe distance. But there are better ways to contend with children who are scolding you for your decision to divorce. First, you need to provide clear rules against rude language and against hitting or yelling at school and at home. More than ever before, this is the time when limits are important. It will be better for him and for you if he feels that you are in control. Try not to become defensive and don't get caught in self-accusation. While it's tempting to think that your child is being coached by your ex, this may not be the case. Children this age are perfectly capable of mounting their own campaigns. In fact, the typical nine- or ten-year-old will try to deal with his own anxiety by attacking you, your ex, or his siblings. If you're tempted to yell at him, it's not so terrible if you do. But try to keep in mind that he's frightened that he'll be left to raise himself while you go gallivanting off into the sunset. If you lose your temper, as you undoubtedly will when your child taunts you, it's not the end of the world. Calm down, say you're sorry, and explain that this behavior is unacceptable. Tell him why it upset you. In other words, be kind but don't let him run wild. Keep reminding yourself that his independence is only skin deep and that he's fighting to maintain the home that he believes was caring and protective of him.

If your child breaks into a rage and accuses you of being the cause of his misery, you need to hold your own against the assault. Try to keep in mind that the hype that he uses does not reflect his feelings. Many a child this age has said to a beloved parent, "You're ruining my life," when all the parent did was ration television time. Don't be frightened and try not to feel guilty. Unfortunately when your child yells, "How could you do this to me?" and accuses you of selfish behavior, it may make you tremble. But it's important to take the accusations seriously without collapsing in a heap. If violence is threatened, and it sometimes happens, don't hesitate to call for help.

A number of parents I know successfully dealt with rambunctious children by introducing a time-out or injecting some humor into the situation. One woman who could hardly stand her daughter's yelling decided to communicate by e-mail. She wrote, "Dear Melanie, I got your message and I am proposing a truce. For a week, no talk about the divorce. How about a quiet dinner and a movie? Your choice. Your hopeful mom." At the end of the week, she wrote again, "Dear Melanie, this week has been divine. Can we renew the truce? Your hopeful mom." After two weeks, the household was no longer in turmoil. It was possible to discuss rationally the issues that were on Melanie's mind and to explain calmly why her mom and dad had opted for the divorce. Melanie and her mom both cried. What happened? Once the yelling subsided, Melanie's mother could assure her daughter that she was aware of her daughter's fear that her life would be disrupted. She would do everything in her power to protect it. Melanie in turn was given the opportunity to get past her anger and express her worries about her future. She had been worried that her mom wouldn't be able to manage alone and that she, Melanie, would be forgotten.

Not all children act out in anger. Your child may get discouraged and withdraw from the rough pressure of school, including academic and athletic competition. She may begin to come home right after school in the hope of finding you there, or she may simply sit and watch television alone. Or she may be more comfortable engaged in fantasy play, spending her time with younger children. Ten-year-old Patricia, whose father had moved away immediately after the breakup, developed a fantasy game that she played every day after school. She came home, dressed her dolls in all their finery, and sat them at the table in the dollhouse. Then she and her dolls quietly waited for the father to join them at the dinner table. He never appeared. The story repeated endlessly, frozen in time.

Ten-year-old Jamie raided his mother's purse to buy gifts for schoolmates, saying that no one liked him now that his parents were divorcing. Children who respond to the breakup by taking a step backward or standing still on the developmental ladder seriously need your attention. Their reaction may be temporary but you cannot ignore it. Your child may be ashamed of what happened to her family or she may be worried about herself or you. Children like Patricia seem stuck in a fantasy world from which they cannot extricate themselves. They need professional help so they can resume their developmental progress. Unfortunately, many children this age tend to be isolated when they're in trouble. They're too young to get relief by sharing their concerns with other children; they don't confide in friends the way teenagers do. Moreover, talking about family is too painful because they feel like they're betraying you.

If you sense that your child is withdrawing and moving backward in her development, you need to ask if she's sad or worried and whether you can help her feel better. Tell her that you hate to have her miss out on the fun of being ten years old. Ask for details. Did anyone hurt her feelings? Is she distressed about the divorce? What is on her mind? A little time well spent at this stage of the divorce can break into her loneliness and belief that you don't understand her distress. Also, contact her teacher to find out how she's doing at school. It's sometimes helpful to have a three-way conference with her, you, and the teacher on hand to ask what the grown-ups can do.

But if your child, like Patricia, seems withdrawn from friends and social activities and is preoccupied with unhappy fantasies, it's a good idea to get professional help from a well-trained mental health expert. Often someone at school has a list of experts who work with children, or your pediatrician may be able to suggest someone she has used before. Investigate carefully before you arrange to take your child to a therapist. Ask your friends, but be sure to ask only people whose judgment you trust. Find out what you can about the training and experience of the person you're considering. Then arrange to talk with that person and decide for yourself. Ask whether she can see your child for an evaluation and proceed from there. I'll discuss this in greater detail, but for now I want to impress on you the fact that if your child needs help, you should get that help before the onset of adolescence. Children need to be strong to take on the challenges of being teenagers. This is an important time to provide any needed academic or emotional help.

How you and your ex treat each other is a subject of special interest to children this age. They're watching your every move in making their own moral judgments about you. A parent who continues to fight or who complains bitterly about the other parent may soon be an object of disdain. Keep in mind that children this age are especially likely to see their parents as being in two warring camps, even if you're getting along reasonably well. If you want your children to respect you and to learn from you about proper behavior, you need to treat each other with civility. This means that you try your best not to criticize the other parent. But beyond that it means that if one parent is physically or emotionally ill, you treat that person with consideration, not only because it's right but because your children are watching and judging. You want your children to grow up to be moral and considerate in their relationships. Sometimes after divorce parents forget how important they are as role models for their children. Being a role model is even more important because your children are watching you very closely.

This is a time for you to behave morally and sensibly—not to let loose because you think the children are older and won't be shocked. The opposite is true. You'll need all your moral authority to help your children move into adolescence and to help them deal with their own rising sexual and aggressive impulses, which are part of normal maturation.

Because they're older, they're drawing conclusions for themselves about what is right and wrong in relationships. They're making very clear judgments about you. Hardly anything escapes them. If you or your ex are in the midst of a rising love affair, it's very important to be discreet, especially if the relationship started before the marriage ended. Whether your behavior was right or wrong, a better time will come to discuss these issues when they're older. Nine- or ten-year-old children don't have the frame of reference or the understanding to sympathize with you. They'll be very excited, very angry, and very distressed. So it is better to say, as I said earlier, that you both tried to get the marriage to work and you're sorry that your efforts failed. You're trying your best to get things in order and you would appreciate their help.

If your ex has left and made no attempt to contact the children, this is something that obviously will be part of their lives for many years. This is a time to comfort your children by being honest. Tell them the truth about your spouse's whereabouts. One woman sat her three children down and said, "I don't know where Daddy is. To the best of my knowledge, nothing bad has happened to him so he's probably okay. I don't know why he hasn't been in touch with us. But as soon as things settle down, I'll try to find out and will tell you what I learn. I know you miss him and I'm very sorry that you're hurting. He loves you but he's unable to show it right now." As she reported to me, the children sat silently. One was crying. When she got up to comfort the crying child, the other two crowded around her. She said, "You are all such wonderful children and I am so proud of you. If Daddy were here, he would be proud of you, too." This mother intuitively touched all the bases that I am recommending. She told the truth, she assured her children that their father was not sick or dead, she acknowledged their suffering, and she made clear that they did not need to hide their anguish from her or themselves. She did her best to address their self-esteem by saying how wonderful they were. She also left the door open for the father's reappearance.

WHAT TO SAY

I assume that you will have explained the divorce as suggested in Chapter 2. Such an explanation is important at every age, but now more than ever you need to stress that you will need and appreciate your child's help and cooperation. You're still a family and you expect to do things together just like a family should. Talk with your children about current and future plans that might include one or more of their friends, or make plans with other families to go out and have fun.

If your child engages in petty theft and truancy, march him right back to the store. Say firmly, "You need to return all those things immediately. If you want, I'll go with you. But I don't want it to happen again." Or tell him that you expect him to attend school and that is a nonnegotiable expectation. At the same time, you can help your child by acknowledging that you understand he's feeling confused and unhappy. But he can get your attention a lot better by simply asking for it. He doesn't have to get into trouble. In fact, you think about him all the time, even if you can't always be present. Be direct. Be sure to say clearly what you expect in behavior. These are the rules. When things calm down, there'll be plenty of time to talk. Right now, you can say, "Stop it. We're all doing our best. You have to do your best, too."

If your child continues to blame one of you for the divorce, don't try to explain why she's wrong or sit down and offer details of the breakup. Better to say, "I know you're really mad about the divorce. But you don't have the story right. When things calm down, I'll be happy to explain it to you."

It's important to acknowledge your child's concern and kind efforts to help. You can say, "Honey, it's lovely of you. It means a lot to me that you're concerned. You're a wonderful kid and I love you. It makes me feel good to have a daughter [or son] who is so considerate and sweet." All their efforts to help should be rewarded generously. At the same time keep your eye on your child's total schedule to make sure that she has allowed time for play and friendships, which are very important at this age. One father earned a hundred points from his anxious son who came for a visit and offered to weed, vacuum, walk the dog, and wash the dishes. The father said, "Look, I really appreciate your generous offer. But I want you to have a good time when you're here. Choose one chore you love and one you hate. I'll do the same and that way it will be fair. Then we'll do what's on your schedule." The boy was delighted and relieved to have such an understanding parent.

If your child waits up for you at night or lectures you about smoking, it may be helpful to discuss why he's worried about you. Is he saying that he's afraid he'll lose you? Thank him for his advice and say that you're trying to take care of yourself. You appreciate his concern. (As for smoking, you're on your own.) Tell him, if it's true, that you're in good health. Like any tired adult in good health, you can feel fatigue. But take his concerns seriously. He loves you.

I urge you to cultivate a sense of an ongoing family as soon as you can. Set up a recreational plan that you can all do together. Play together, dine, camp, go bowling—do things that build a sense of family structure so your children don't feel that they've lost their family. Make jokes. Plan activities for the family as it is, not as it was. Include your children's friends whenever possible. Some families have a custom at dinner where each person reports on their activities for that day. You can use this to strengthen the sense of your post-divorce family. If possible, you and your ex can divide your expertise in helping with homework assignments. Intact families do this routinely and there's no reason not to continue it. Overall, you want to set an example of courage, honesty, and respect. You do not tolerate rudeness or breaking of reasonable rules. Once you get past his anger, a child this age can keep you on your toes in being strong and maintaining high ethical standards for the whole family.

Finally, since children this age can tolerate your absence for a day or two, this is a good time, by the end of the first year, to give yourself an occasional weekend off. Go have some fun, or better still, find some quiet place where you can feel restored. You'll find it much easier to deal with your children and with all the other issues that you face after a quiet weekend away. Do it.

Remember, don't overreact to your child's anger. This is not a time for you to fall apart. Your child is simply telling you how much he needs a family and how much he's worried about his entry into adolescence, which is just a few years off. Your job is to protect him and keep him on course. He needs structure, kindness, and rules. He needs to understand from you that his post-divorce family is stable and that it will protect him morally and physically.

Chapter 8: Eleven-, Twelve-, and Thirteen-Year-Olds

I f you have a young adolescent, be prepared for anything when you announce your impending divorce. Reactions range from panic to doe-eyed nonchalance and everything in between. But no matter what expression your children show, they'll most likely be taken aback by the news. They're also capable of shielding their feelings from themselves as well as from you.

John, who was twelve, ran into the street after his parents told him about their plans, screaming, "You're going to kill us all!" He panted as if he were running from a fire.

Karen, age eleven, ran to her neighbor's house after dark and shrieked, "My parents are getting a divorce!"

Lily was totally calm. She listened politely, hands folded in her lap, coughed a few times, and then went off to do her math homework.

David rejoiced. He turned to his mother and said, "Great! Now we can do anything we please!"

Let me assure you, many of the more dramatic reactions reflect temporary panic. The panic almost always subsides after twelve to twenty-four hours. Although some children have a strong impulse to run away, they're simply too young and inexperienced to carry it off; some do, however, disappear overnight or trounce out for a few days, announcing that you can find them at their best friend's house. You may get a call from the friend's parents saying it's okay with them if it's okay with you. By all means, say yes. Thank them for their support; you may need to call on them again. But ask to speak to your child first. Tell him it's a good idea to spend the night with his friend, but you are looking forward to seeing him in the morning.

The lack of age-related symptoms in this group—such as the typical fretfulness of a three-year-old, the sleep problems of a five-year-old, or the learning difficulties of a seven-year-old—is not grounds for celebration. While you can do something fairly quickly about the symptoms seen in younger children, the risky behaviors you observe in these older children are a more serious challenge.

If your child is on the threshold of adolescence when you divorce, you're facing issues that will tax your parenting skills. Along with very early childhood, this is arguably the most hazardous time for a child to experience divorce. The little ones, as we saw earlier, are afraid of abandonment and can feel profoundly lonely at the breakup. Moreover, there's not much they can do to relieve their feelings. Not so with eleven-, twelve-, and thirteen-year-olds. These youngsters can take vigorous action to relieve their fear of loneliness and abandonment. If there's a single "reaction" to divorce among children this age, it can be a headlong, headstrong rush toward risky teenage behavior.

The problem for so many eleven-, twelve-, and thirteen-year-olds is that your divorce can propel them into the exciting world of full-blown adolescence long before they're ready for it. If your child believes, as some this age do, that the divorce has lifted constraints and loosened the rules, then she may get involved in hazardous behavior that can have serious consequences. I've seen too many thirteen-year-olds engage in unprotected sex after the breakup not to warn you that this can happen.

Another reaction that I've seen in this age group is almost total denial of any change in their lives. This is more common among children who are doing very well at school, where they get a lot of recognition.

The denial may last for years. Of course, at times denial can be a wonderful thing. As long as your child is doing well, you have no reason to insist that she start feeling troubled or worried. There's much wisdom in respecting your child's need to gradually resolve the issues in her life and to rely on her intuition. By all means watch your child to be sure she's managing, and if she is, let her be. I've met many young people who seem entirely unmoved by the events swirling around them and who continue to move ahead until they're ready to talk about the events at a later time.

For example, Sally was a bright, studious twelve-year-old who showed hardly any reaction to her parents' divorce. She simply continued to devote herself to schoolwork, winning awards at science fairs and the like and graduated from high school with honors. But when Sally was seventeen, she fell in love for the first time and was suddenly very frightened that her boyfriend would leave her. During her freshman year she called her mother from college to talk about the breakup. She was finally ready. Sally confessed how difficult it had been for her to acknowledge the events but that she needed several years to figure out her feelings. The lesson for you is that if your child shows no reaction to your divorce and if she's doing well in her school and social activities, be patient. Wait for her. Once she's open, you can move quickly to address both your concerns.

To understand what your preadolescent is going through, try to recall how you felt at this age. One day you were playing on the jungle gym at school, hanging upside down and yelling friendly insults at the opposite sex. This was the way you consulted one another. "Hey, toad breath, bet you can't do five chin-ups!" Total disdain was the only way to go.

But then, gradually, something changed. You felt nameless stirrings in your body. More and more, you glanced at yourself in the mirror. Maybe you should cut your hair. Maybe you shouldn't hang upside down anymore, now that you're into short skirts. Maybe you could get that cute boy Johnny to look at you. You look in the mirror again and again. Am I too fat? Too thin? Too short? Too tall? Am I attractive? Am I cool?

And all the while, in a sub-rosa compartment of your mind, are all the images of people "doing it" in the movies or on TV or from jokes you've sniggered at. What's it like to do "it"? What is "doing it" all about anyway? How does it feel? Will I like it? Do my parents do it? How disgusting!

If you can recapture these feelings, you'll have a better understanding of what your child is experiencing. It happens sooner to girls than to boys, but both are struggling with powerful hormonal shifts, a rise in sexual drives, the urge to separate from you, and the determination to hang out with kids their own age. Moreover, you'll see this transformation occur differently in boys and girls. Both experience a greater interest in the opposite sex and begin pulling away from the family. But girls show more changes in their external appearance—their clothes, makeup, hairdos, and general demeanor are noticeable. They laugh more, begin to flirt, and are intensely aware if a boy is nearby. Boys, on the other hand, don't show as many changes in clothing, hairstyle, or outward manners. But they are intensely aware when girls are present. They engage in a profusion of daydreams and fantasies that can lead to sudden, embarrassing erections. One important difference between boys and girls this age is that girls are observed by older males, including men. This greatly intensifies their self-consciousness, anxiety, and pleasure. Older teenage girls and young women do not as a rule ogle pubescent boys.

In either case, you may find yourself living with children who can drive you crazy. Risks seem to excite them. Their judgment is terrible. Why not try out new things? Jennifer did it. Morgan tried it. What am I waiting for?

The problem, of course, is that your child's ego is not strong enough to control these urges without your help. Her judgment and ability to stop herself from acting impulsively are no match for what's stirring inside her. She needs parenting badly. She needs a stable family at this unstable time in her life, and deep down she knows it.

And then you announce your divorce. No matter how you try to soften the blow, divorce weakens the family when your preadolescent needs you most. Your child will feel anxious about having less to hold on to as she realizes she has fewer bonds to hold on to her. After all, a father in one place and a mother in another place, whether they are civil or fighting, do not comprise a secure family. Moreover, you are both very busy attending to the divorce and reestablishing your own lives. She feels unmoored, less protected, and alone.

The problem is that your child is not physically or emotionally ready to leave her childhood behind in a scrapbook. She's still collecting important pieces to paste into the pages of her young life. She needs time to develop a sense of who she is, what she likes and doesn't like, and who she wants to spend time with. She needs time to control her biological drives. Her psychology and her conscience have to catch up with her body.

But divorce is likely to change the tempo of your child's development. Without active guidance and strict limits from adults, boys and girls alike will be tempted by what I call "the voices of the street" and by peers who are out to make trouble.

Modern American culture holds startling temptations. Exciting voices beckon like sirens of old, and you can't expect your child to plug her ears. The voices are flattering. They whisper to your daughter or son about how they can become grown-ups on a fast track. These are the subliminal and open messages of television, movies, and advertisers seeking to exploit the rich teenage market.

As your children look around the school cafeteria, they'll see all the cliques clumped at little tables, whispering their secrets, glancing at the new kids, sizing everyone up. So many groups: the cool kids, the dopers, the jocks, the nerds, the Dungeons and Dragons set, the loners, the gangsters. Which group should she join? Who will accept him? Who has the most fun? Who is safe? Who is dangerous? That ninth grader is making sexual advances. That tenth grader is selling pot and Ecstasy for Joe's party Friday night. And there is the older guy who hangs around the school entrance.

With these choices, your child can slip into early delinquency, be mocked as a goody-goody or uncool, or hold back in confusion. But know this: your child will find it very difficult to talk to you about her anxiety because you are dealing with your own issues, just as she is dealing with hers. She's probably upset with you for making her life even more difficult right now. If you're rarely home and she feels like the world is collapsing on her head, she's more likely to be drawn to other children who are troubled and upset. Young adolescents from divorced families are more easily influenced by their peers than those in intact homes. Laurie put it this way: "I hang out with all the other fat kids from broken homes."

Don't panic. Troubled kids after divorce are certainly not inevitable. What happens depends on both you and your child, and my plan is to help you. You can make it clear to your daughter in a friendly, nonthreatening way that if she plans to change any part of her life, she needs to talk to you about it first. You have an interest and a right to know what is going on. She has a responsibility to keep you informed. If you weren't close before the divorce, these conversations will be harder, but you can do it. I'll get to how very soon.

First, I want to go back to girls. A girl entering adolescence concentrates on the most interesting object in life—herself. Her moods fluctuate from total despair (I'm so homely and unlovable) to elation (make way for me, I'm a star!). There's no balance wheel to even out her self-esteem and hardly any stability to her self-image. Much of her attention is taken up comparing what she sees happening to herself and to her friends. Who has breasts or pubic hair? What will we do about those short boys? All their giggling covers anxiety.

As her hormones surge, your daughter is preoccupied by sexual fantasies, romances, rock stars, sports heroes. And this is a good thing. Fantasy helps children prepare for the future. As she paints her toenails and thinks about the cutest boy in the rock band, she's taking the time she needs to grow up. This is why your role as a parent is so crucial. She needs your guidance and support. She needs to hear from you about what growing up is about, about what it was like for you, and about the importance of self-esteem and how much self-esteem has to do with being a moral, decent person. She needs to hear that how people will treat her depends to a large extent on how she treats herself and others. She needs you to be proud of the changes in her body. She needs you to set boundaries that will keep her safe.

The same biological surges hit boys a few years later. Their voices change, they sprout little mustaches, they get pubic hair and have wet dreams. Your son is preoccupied with questions about his body. How strong am I? Will I be a shrimp? He needs to hear from his dad something about his dad's struggles at this age. He'll spend hours in front of his bedroom mirror flexing muscles, wondering if he's attractive. His idols and heroes are drawn largely from entertainment and sports, glamorous figures that rarely embody values beyond competition and sex appeal. He needs to hear about giving himself time to grow and that becoming a man involves more than muscles. He needs to learn from you about decency, morality, courtesy, and how both boys and girls have feelings that make them vulnerable to being hurt.

In their busy lives, none of these children have time for your divorce because they need to feel calm and protected within their families before the storm of adolescence hits full force. Early adolescence is the necessary preparation that divorce has the power to cut short.

WHAT TO DO

Many people don't have the luxury, if that's what you can call it, to choose when they get a divorce. It may not be possible to hold off for, say, a few more years until the children are older and more mature. It would be nice to have that kind of control over our lives, but that's not the way it usually works.

So if you find yourself divorcing with a preteen child, my advice is simply to hold your breath and try to keep your home as safe as possible and household routines as consistent as you can. Even though your world is collapsing, you need to maintain a steadfast, stable, available presence.

Realize that your importance is greater than ever. As a parent you need to know that children can get swept away but that you can take steps to keep them on course. You can help them gain control over their impulses by enforcing rules and teaching them to look and listen instead of making rash judgments. Keep in mind that coming home nightly to an empty house terrifies them. Obviously they can handle this occasionally, but it arouses too much anxiety if they confront emptiness all the time. Several youngsters have told me, "There was never anyone at home. That's how I got into drugs and sex." Make arrangements at least once a week and preferably more to meet your child at your office or for an ice cream at the local café after school. Make plans for the weekend and ask whether your son or daughter would like to bring a friend along. A popular sporting event would be a good choice. In brief, try to provide some structure for after school that would include you and your child or that would involve your child in an activity that she finds rewarding. Keep in mind that despite her independence, being alone can make for anxiety when your child is besieged by angry thoughts and bewildering feelings over your divorce.

Too much freedom is not helpful to your child at this critical time. He's too young for a real job, but you can surely provide some work for which he will be paid. Boys and girls at this age can make excellent babysitters for you and others. It will give you a chance to emphasize how important the job is, to suggest some simple first aid instructions, and to call attention to how much you value taking good care of children. If your child works for you, you should pay the going rate. It would also be helpful to encourage volunteer work in the community. Children this age are often proud to help others and gain an important sense of responsibility and compassion. Any job that makes use of your child's skills is welcome. It also guarantees some order in your child's week.

In your own home, boys and girls can help repair things. Many children this age are very good at computers. They can do simple cooking. They can help with cleaning up and gardening. And they can help with younger siblings. If they do help care for little brothers and sisters, make sure that you're not taking advantage of their availability. It's important to ask what's fair, but be sure that they don't feel that all of their playtime and friendship time is being sacrificed on your behalf. Keep an eye on what you are asking. It's very important that they respect your sense of fairness.

Make it clear that although you don't mean to follow them around, you absolutely need to know they're okay. A cell phone is a great invention for children who are not heading home directly from school. When they call to check in with you, thank them and say something pleasant. Don't ask for a rundown on their immediate plans because that will make them feel that you don't trust them. They don't want to be treated like babies. But do say that you will see them later and designate where and when. If you are held up, extend the same courtesy you expect from them. Call and apologize and explain when you'll be home. All of these rituals are important because they teach responsibility by example. Most of all, they help your child feel that what he does matters. It matters a lot to you and to him.

It's always very important for you and your ex to treat each other with civility, but this behavior takes on a special quality in this age group. Your preteens are watching you very carefully. Parents are always important models for children's behavior, but after divorce this is magnified. I'm not telling you how to live your life, but I can say that this is not a good time for you to date a lot of different people within a brief time period. You don't want your child to think of you as undiscriminating. If you have a thirteen-year-old at home, your behavior can be profoundly upsetting, no matter how casually you treat it. Your child will be stimulated by all your sexual liaisons. And you in turn will weaken your power to reestablish your authority and to parent.

WHAT TO SAY

Don't be fooled by your child's pseudo-sophistication. He's pretending to understand adult issues that I guarantee are beyond his ability to comprehend. For example, I don't think a child this age can handle the notion of sexual behavior by one or both of his parents. The very idea of your having sex makes him extremely anxious. If he asks you directly, "Are you having an affair?" I suggest you do your best to answer without going into detail. I never recommend lying to children, so you might say something like, "I like so and so a lot and we are getting very close. But we haven't decided on future plans. When we do, I will surely tell you immediately." You can even expand on your relationship by saying that you and your new friend like being free to explore a new and happier relationship. You share interests in theater, politics, gardening, or whatever. You make each other laugh and you respect each other. You are giving your child clues to use in evaluating your relationship with this new person without referring to sex. And you are educating your child about good aspects of male and female relationships.

This is the time to initiate the first of a long series of conversations with your child. You may feel like you're talking to yourself, but don't be discouraged. Your child is listening to your message, which is that he's dead wrong about your lack of interest in him. This is the time you reap the harvest of your earlier relationship with your child. If you're close and have developed mutual respect, it is easier to talk frankly about your concerns. You expect your son or daughter to follow the standards of behavior that you think are correct. This is a difficult time, but it doesn't mean that kids have freedom to do whatever they please. There are rules. Don't hesitate to say so. Talk about your standards, about decency and kindness in relationships, about courage to think about what is important to you, about valuing yourself and others. Use humor if you can. Talk about yourself and your history, ask questions about school and friends. "What's happening at school? What happened to your interest in history? Math? Basketball? I notice you're hanging out with a different group of friends. Do you think this change has anything to do with our getting a divorce?" Don't withdraw even if they appear not to listen. The important thing is to hang in there. If your child slams the door in your face, you open it and start again. If he says, "Who are you to tell me what to do? Look at you getting a divorce," it's a question that deserves an answer. "What am I doing that you think is so bad?" This is the time to talk about moral issues with your child, especially if he's veering off course. This is also the time to talk about your mistakes honestly if he points those out. There is no harm in saying, "Dad and I made a serious mistake in getting married when we did. You are right and I hope that you learn from us what not to do."

Parents who are the same sex as their child can do a lot to protect kids this age. Moms can help their daughters not by being a buddy but by being a loving, sympathetic parent. You can listen patiently as your daughter describes how her best friend is choosing another best friend and how hurt she is. Don't hesitate to give advice based on your own experience as a young girl.

Dads can have especially close relationships with their sons. It's a time when boys move away from their moms, so knowing that Dad is available helps them feel secure. Keep in mind that a boy this age does not need a pal. He needs a parent to respect. Both boys and girls need parents who are not afraid to talk about moral values, about love and friendship and loyalty, about how they can acquire respect for themselves and for the opposite sex.

Your sexual behavior is an issue at this time. Since you're divorcing, an affair is no longer an infidelity. But if you're involved in a relationship that started before the breakup, your children will know it. And they may try to punish you for it. Children this age have poor judgment and need adult discipline. One girl told me, "I decided to lose my virginity the day I discovered that my mom was having an affair." But what do you do when you cannot honestly say that you want them to follow your example? The answer is straightforward. About yourself, you tell the truth. "Yes, I did fall in love with John during the last year of my marriage to your dad. I was so unhappy and he helped me a lot. I'm very grateful to him. Whether we get married is still not decided, but when we decide I will tell you. But this doesn't mean that you're ready to have a similar relationship now that you're thirteen. You need to give yourself the gift of growing up slowly and allowing yourself to find out about love so when it happens you can fully enjoy what you have. As for sex, I'm sure that you are not ready. Sex separate from love rarely makes people happy. In fact, it often can make you unhappy because it feels empty." As this conversation continues, you need to take your cues from what your child says about her life. You probably didn't expect to have to talk about these matters until your child was older, but you can't put it off.

Another issue arises when your ex is playing the field and your children know it. If this is happening, you can suggest that they talk to the other parent directly. And you can add, if it's true, that you think your ex is unhappy and desperately looking for someone who will meet his needs. You hope that he succeeds because he's really troubled. Your goal is to help your child feel that he can ask questions and get a straight answer. You're teaching respect for other people by modeling it and by respecting your child's right to know what is going on.

Both parents should probably discuss birth control and safe sex at this time. Many people may not agree with me, but I think the world has become much too dangerous to ignore in this regard. Given current epidemics of sexually transmitted diseases, teens need sex education that includes knowledge about birth control and safe sex and not an admonition to just say no. Studies that tracked high school kids who pledged to say "no" found that they do delay having sex by a few years, but when they start they are more likely to have unprotected sex than their peers who started earlier. Children this age also need knowledge about drugs, smoking, and alcohol. It's a good idea to find out what they're being taught in school. Perhaps you can use the school's presentation as a jumping-off point. Your immediate goal is to rely on your relationship with your children, including your expectations of them and yourself, to hold them back from reckless behavior. Your long-range goal is, of course, to keep their development on track and to help them grow up to be moral and loving adults you can be proud of.

Remember, early adolescence is a perilous time for every child and is especially difficult when the family is weakened. Children this age need you to help them with their rising sexual and aggressive impulses. Try to maintain open channels of communication with your preteen. Set clear standards of behavior. No matter what your child says or does, he needs you to be the kind of parent who is ready to listen, to learn, and to grow with him.

Chapter 9: Fourteen-, Fifteen-, Sixteen-, and Seventeen-Year-Olds

When you come along in the midst of your teenager's very full life, which has an agenda well into the night that includes boy-and-girl relationships, and announce that you are getting a divorce, what can you expect? What's the initial impact?

Probably nothing you'll be able to notice. Unlike younger children, teenagers do not exhibit typical age-related reactions to divorce.

First, the fact that your marriage is in trouble probably won't come as a surprise. Most adolescents, yours included, have some inkling or direct information from you about what's going to happen. They may have even shared in your thinking and decision making. So while they may be shocked to hear that you're getting the divorce, which makes it real, they're not surprised. Nor is divorce itself surprising. They all have friends whose parents have split up and they've heard lots of stories about what happens at this time. But you can be sure they won't feel it's okay just because so many families have gone through it before them.

Most teenagers do have some awareness and dread that belts will have to be tightened after divorce. No more vacations or summer camp or even new clothes. The family home may have to be sold. You may all have to move to a less expensive community. Most worrisome of all, they may have to change high schools and, if there's no promise for financial support, revise their plans about college.

But even these realistic fears are hazy at this early stage. Your teenagers will have theories about what's causing your divorce. Thanks to television and movies, they're well educated in matters of infidelity and marital problems, even violence. Sometimes they'll be astute observers and at other times they'll be incredibly naïve.

When I asked Mimi, a sophisticated fifteen-year-old, why she thought her parents were divorcing, she replied solemnly, "That's easy. They each gave too little and asked too much."

I remember Jerry, a handsome sixteen-year-old who, in response to the same question, explained that his parents were building a new house and couldn't agree on the number of bathrooms. So they divorced.

"You're joking, of course," I said.

"No," he said. "That's the truth."

"That sounds to me like a foolish reason."

"They are foolish people," he replied with a shrug.

However your children explain the divorce to themselves or to their friends, you can be sure they'll try to play it cool and maintain their distance and keep their feelings from you.

Don't be fooled. While you should be prepared for an initial cool, almost detached response to your announcement about the divorce, be aware that still waters run deep. Very soon you may be on the receiving end of a blast of anger from your teenager followed by a crying spell or a dramatic door-slamming exit depending on whether it's a girl or a boy and your child's personal style. Your announcement evokes powerful fears and passions that lie very close to the surface. How could you do this? How could you do this to me? How could you do this to each other?

What teenagers do not say, but is uppermost in their minds, is their immediate conclusion that you failed to hold the marriage together—

and this sends shivers down their spines. They don't see your divorce as a solution, though they may view it as being more honest than a pretense of a marriage. Rather, they see divorce as a failure. The two adults most important to their lives have failed at one of the most important tasks of adulthood—creating and nurturing an intimate relationship. And being teenagers, they think of themselves first. Their first fear is the gnawing question, Does this mean that my relationships are also going to fail? Does this predict my fate? Will I fail to hold a man like my mom? Will my girlfriend leave me? Your example strikes terror in their hearts. As one young woman wailed, "My folks met in college. They fell in love. They have similar tastes and values. What's to keep the same fate from happening to me? Nothing."

To understand their response, I want you to step back for a minute and consider further what's going on at this developmental stage. Mid-adolescence is a complicated time for your children because they're dealing with so many big changes all at once—changes in their bodies, changes in their concepts of themselves and their future, and of course, changes in their relationships with you. Adolescents are poised between two worlds. They have a double self-image of themselves as children and as grown-ups. They need you at this time, although they would hotly deny their need. Much as they rail against your curfews and discipline, deep down they know they're not ready to set their own limits or rules. They need you to be there for them. And they need you to rebel against. They need to sashay back and forth between hard-won independence—Who are you to tell me what to do?—and a retreat to childhood where they remain the favorite son or Daddy's darling little girl protected from bad people out there in the real world. They need to mature gradually at a comfortable tempo so they can leave when they're ready.

Your divorce declares that you are leaving them and not vice versa. Yes, I know this is not your intent. But this is what they feel. Their home is disappearing. Suddenly the house looks priceless. I've known many teenagers who never paid much attention to their home prior to the

breakup but who, with the divorce, look upon it with new eyes, antici-
pating its loss with great sorrow. Along with the loss of the family home,
they lose their childhood as well, feeling prematurely pushed out by your
divorce. In their eyes, you've broken the rules. They're angry at your
audacity. "How could you? You were supposed to stay put and hold things
together until I was ready to leave."

If you must sell the house in which your children grew up, you need
to acknowledge what a dramatic event it is and tell them why the decision is necessary. Try to recognize the magnitude of loss. You're abandoning the symbol of the family and also the place where their childhood
friends reside. Even if you don't share their feelings, you need to talk
about the loss and perhaps have a good-bye ceremony when you leave.
Treat this issue with respect, as if the house were a beloved person. A
solemn getting together or even a bash would be better than letting it
go unmentioned.

This is also a time when all adolescents struggle with moral questions
that are magnified by your divorce. As they tap into the causes and results
of the breakup and observe your behavior, they ask themselves searching
and distressing questions:

Is my mother a good woman? Is my dad a good man? Who's to blame
for the divorce?

They'll carry this question in their heads for years, less related to
what you say but very related to what you do. And, of course, they ask,
what about me? How should I conduct myself? Why not have sex with
my boyfriend? I know that he'll drop me if I say no. But then how long
will he stick around if I say yes?

As you know all too well, teenagers are able to take matters into their
own hands. Their social lives are largely of their own making. They're
not likely to be known to their teachers unless they shine academically,
win at sports, or make trouble. Since you've been so preoccupied with
getting the divorce and getting your own life together, and since they're
angry at you for giving priority to your own agenda, the period easily

becomes a green light for lots of acting out. If my parents can have sex, why can't I? If my parents are free, why can't I be? When discipline is lax and your attention is elsewhere, your teenagers are more likely to rely on their peers to set standards for behavior. Compared to classmates from intact homes, boys and girls from divorced families get more involved in truancy, alcohol, and drug abuse. Girls get more involved in sexual acting out and more often suffer the consequences of unwanted pregnancy. That's why it's so important for you to pay close attention to what they're doing and saying. You should expect to remain an active parent at the time of the breakup and during the years that follow, whether your children remain home or go off to college. I'll spell out what you can do to head off worrisome consequences later in this chapter.

You should also know that your teenagers can be enormously helpful to you during and after your divorce. They want to help, are competent, and can provide a shoulder for you to lean on. With all their self-centeredness, teenagers can also be generous, loving, and capable of sacrificing their own interests to help you. They're proud to be given responsibilities if their contribution is recognized. Many parents have told me that they never would have managed without their teenager nearby. One mother said, "My sixteen-year-old son taught me what I needed to do. He would sit with me and say, 'Let's go over finances. What do we need? How much do we have?' Then he would say, 'What will I need if I go to a private university away from home? How much if I go to a local community college?' He was amazing. Together we drew up a plan that I took to my attorney. My son also told me to get some rest and insisted that I consult my physician about my trouble sleeping. He grew ten years in that first year after his dad and I separated."

Thus your divorce has the power to push your teenager ahead into a greater sense of responsibility for himself, a greater awareness of moral issues, and an enhanced sense of obligation to his family. It also has the power to send him into a tailspin. A lot hangs in the balance at this critical time of your divorce. There are many ways that you can help your child. Keep in mind that his emotional maturity is still new and unstable, his conscience is still dependent on outside reinforcement, and his judgment can fluctuate wildly. Despite his age, and because of his age, your role is critical.

WHAT TO DO

Realize that you're a role model. Teenagers need to think of you as a good person, as someone they wish to emulate. With all their sophistication, they still need you to serve as their conscience and to help them control their impulses. So despite your own upset at the divorce, try to keep in mind that you're setting an important example for moral adult behavior. They're watching you intensely, every minute. They look to see how you treat each other. They listen to you talk on the telephone. They register every bit of corruption and ugliness as well as every kind word and considerate action. Why is Dad dating my ex-babysitter? What is my mom doing with our neighbor? The FBI could take lessons from these kids.

They think a lot about what they observe and draw many conclusions about you and themselves. Probably they talk about it. They talk with siblings and they talk with friends and they make judgments about you. In one family the four sisters discussed their father's behavior for decades, even after he married the lady they discussed. They disagreed for all those years about whether their father had been involved with her during the marriage, with some of the sisters saying that was impossible and others maintaining it was a certainty. They were trying to arrive at moral standards by which they could judge him, as well as define a moral standard for themselves. And they were supporting each other in their quest. The talking that adolescents engage in with their friends serves many purposes. This is the age when it's very helpful to get support from peers. They all face common problems in trying to understand the baffling behavior of grown-ups and the ambiguous world that they're inheriting from you.

Realize that your teenager is not your pal. The tendency for divorce to blur generational differences is reinforced by the many parents who talk to their children as if they were friends, and very wise friends at that. I'll talk about changes in parent-and-child relationships in Part 3, but for now I want to alert you to how the process begins. When you divorce, you may want to solicit the advice of your children about where to live, what house to rent or purchase, and perhaps what job you should take. There's nothing wrong with this. Teenagers are proud to be asked for their wisdom in these matters. They can easily venture into dark basements and explore the foundations of the house you're considering to rent or purchase, but they can also be overwhelmed by your need for help.

Do not burden them with the responsibility of being your best friend, closest confidante, and mentor at the time of the breakup or in the years ahead. By all means ask your daughter for advice on what to wear if she's good at that sort of thing. But don't ask her what she thinks of your latest beau. Get her opinion on the choices you make about jobs and school. But don't ask her whether you should marry Harry or John. Fathers can find it especially comforting to have the ear of their teenage daughters about how difficult their mother was to live with. Don't impose this on your daughter, no matter how good this feels. It really can cause her great suffering. Your confidences can only oppress her and make her feel like a traitor whichever way she turns. She's ashamed to share your confessions with her friends. She cannot talk with her mother, and she does not feel strong enough to tell you to stop.

At the height of the divorce, you can rely on your teenager to help you run the household, take care of younger siblings, and be compassionate when you feel overwhelmed. In my experience, many teenagers take this task seriously and are pleased to be called on to help out in meaningful ways. They say proudly, "I have to be a role model for my younger sister so I can't do any more hitchhiking." They know real responsibility from the fake stuff. In giving them these opportunities, though, be careful not to overdo it. Boys can be overwhelmed by your need for emotional help.

Better to give them concrete chores. Girls can help their mothers in many ways but can be overburdened by the emotional needs of a father. I say this so you can tread carefully and not overstep important boundaries.

When you do ask for and receive help, be sure to reward your teenagers with praise and show how proud you are. Ask for their advice in matters where they can make a real contribution. In appealing to their loyalty and concern for the family, make it clear that you expect them to stick to work at school. Stress the fact that this divorce doesn't change your expectations about academic achievement or the moral standards of the family. Despite your busy schedule, if they are part of a production at school or an athletic event, try your best to get there. Show a lot of interest in what is happening at school and at after-school events. You will find that your children are enormously appreciative of your efforts to attend. They're well aware of the demands on your schedule and they take your being there as a gift of love.

You also need to lay out how the divorce will affect their future, by which I mean the next several years. Obviously, there is a great deal you cannot predict, and you can say this honestly while assuring them that you will consider their needs and wishes and keep them fully informed. Adolescents worry about how the divorce is going to affect their lives. Most high school students have invested years of energy into making friends and cultivating interests. They have absolutely no desire to move to a new school, town, or state and start over. If they have a girlfriend or boyfriend, forget it. Moving away can be a disaster. You can expect major resistance. Whatever plans you work out for the post-divorce family, you need to listen to your teenagers and seriously consider their wishes. Without their cooperation, you're headed for trouble or misery. Far better to compromise than to lose the affection and respect of a son or daughter. One mother whose daughter was a star in the drama productions at her high school was offered the choice of living with a friend to complete her senior year instead of moving away with the rest of the family. This worked out well for her, although it was a hard choice for the mother at the time. Other parents make complicated arrangements for their children to maintain their friendships by arranging visits on holidays and over summer vacations. All of these special plans are much appreciated by young people. In fact, what matters more than the final outcome of where to live is the willingness of parents to take their child's relationships seriously.

If you're going to set up a visiting or custody arrangement that will affect your teenagers' freedom, you need to discuss this in detail and ask their opinions. As much as you can, involve them in looking at the obstacles and decisions that lie ahead. At the same time—and I admit this is very tricky—your teenager needs assurance that you'll still be there when needed and you'll do your best to continue a stable family life. Teens are not adults; they need to focus their attention on school, friends, and activities that remain important to their development. It's a good idea to specifically state your job (keeping life stable) as different from their job (growing up and getting ready to take on the world).

It's also important to discuss future plans for college education with your ex and then let your teenagers know this is being discussed in ways that will protect them. If money is a problem, don't tell them that there won't be any way for them to go to college. These kinds of statements exert a chilling effect on children's ambitions and academic performance in high school. Do tell them that you will try to work things out together. You will find some way to help them get an education. Few children can handle the simultaneous breakup of their family and the loss of their own opportunities.

In an intact family, parents and children tend to sit down together to plan for college. This happens less often in divorced families, but there's no reason it cannot. If you can swing it, by all means sit down together as a family and set down what financial help your child can reasonably expect. This will go a long way toward encouraging your adolescent to trust in your continued help. It will encourage him to do his best and begin to make serious plans. If you cannot sit together with your ex, then have the family conference with just you and your teenager, preferably early in the junior year of high school. Lay out what you know and talk seriously about how you can make workable plans.

Finally, keep a very close eye on your teenager. Your adolescent will probably not seek you out, so you will have to take the initiative to keep the contact going. This involves your giving priority to your child, making yourself available, and instituting meetings that appeal to her. You might say that you're both so busy, you seem to be losing touch and so you'd like to set up a custom of having dinner out together one night a week, just the two of you, "to catch up." On the other evenings, of course, you share dinner with the other children as a family. The goal here is to lay the basis for a more mature relationship between you, to keep in close contact with her and her life. It should not be a reporting session. She shouldn't feel that you're prying. But she should feel that you're very interested in her and that her happiness and plans are of central importance to you.

Boys and girls have special need of their parents at this developmental stage. Boys need a vote of confidence from their dads. In moving into adulthood, it helps them to be told by their father that he's proud of them and that he has no doubt that they'll succeed at whatever they decide to do. If you know something about a field they're interested in, this is the time to share your knowledge and contacts. Fathers in intact families do this routinely. It should be the same for divorced fathers. If your ex does not think of this on his own, there's no reason why a mom cannot gently speak up about the boy's need for encouragement.

Girls also need a vote of confidence from fathers who can talk about their ambitions and goals, giving their daughters the same kind of help that they give their sons. Teenagers appreciate being given contacts and leads about their future prospects. It makes them feel very grown up. And it pays off. Young women who are at the top of their class at leading universities often attribute their success to their fathers' encouragement. The same encouragement should be made available to youngsters in divorced families.

Of course, boys and girls need their mothers' encouragement as well, but this is usually taken for granted. A father's approval plays a special role in enhancing a teenager's self-esteem and hope for the future.

If you find that your child is behaving badly and acting out, don't look the other way. Talk with her. If you feel that you're getting nowhere, call a family conference that includes your ex. In my experience this is a useful technique for families in trouble. The sight of you and your ex sitting at the table together, cooperating, expressing your joint concern about what you know is happening, sends a powerful message to your teenager. Explain why you think her behavior is unacceptable and then ask her, "What are we going to do for you that will keep you on a better path? How can we protect you?"

There are other remedies that you may need to turn to if the delinquent behavior persists, but I will get to these in later chapters. For now, do what you can to turn her behavior around—the sooner the better.

WHAT TO SAY

Teenagers don't need a long explanation of your decision to divorce. It's better to keep your story short and encourage them to ask questions. Your meeting should be as interactive as possible, but be aware of their feelings. What you're saying makes them very anxious, even as they try hard to hang on to their cool. You may want to leave them alone or with each other after you break the news so they can absorb the shock.

Explain briefly and clearly why you've taken this huge step that profoundly affects their lives. Provide a dignified, serious reason and stress the fact that you've given the decision serious thought. Keep in mind that many children complain that they were never told why the divorce occurred. Make sure that they have honest answers to all their questions. You're taking this step reluctantly but feel it's necessary.

You need to understand that your teenagers will judge you at this time. They'll assess your moral stance and they'll be especially concerned with your plans to take care of them and each other. Unlike the younger children, teenagers are aware who wants the divorce. They'll immediately look at each of your faces for signs of satisfaction or unhappiness. Unless there are clear and compelling reasons for the breakup, they're likely to side with the parent who looks most troubled. This is an excellent reason for you and your spouse to treat each other with respect and decency. I advise you to take your courage in your hands and tell them the truth. I don't recommend that you provide details of infidelity. But you are obliged to ask if they have questions, and if infidelity comes up, you have to be truthful. Again no sexual details. Your adolescents, with all their sophistication, cannot bear to think of their parents as sexual.

You need to explicitly separate what is happening today, in your life, from what they think will happen to them when they grow up. To begin, you might say, "This is an important conversation. I want you to listen very closely to what I have to say. Your dad and I have come to a sad decision. You've probably been aware that we've been unhappy for some time. We have tried unsuccessfully to solve our problems so we could stay together. And we've decided to divorce. It has been a very difficult decision. We will try our best to provide what you need and to see you into adulthood."

I suggest that with adolescents you add a new and very important thought. If you can, try to summon up the courage to say, "As we go along, we would like it very much if you could learn from our experience so you can avoid some of the mistakes we've made." This statement may shock your children, and that is all to the good. If they ask what mistakes you made, tell them that you would rather talk about that when everyone is less upset and set a date when you can begin to do so. But don't postpone this extension of the divorce conversation indefinitely. The best guidance that any parent can give is to help children from repeating their mistakes.

As you give the reasons for the divorce, you have to answer honestly in a way that doesn't defame your partner. You may be tempted to say, "Your dad is rotten" or, "Your mom is an iceberg." Don't say it. On the other hand, you'd sound foolish to idealize the person you're divorcing. How to strike a balance?

Let me offer some scenarios. If your husband is having an affair, you can say to your teenager, "Your dad doesn't love me anymore. He's decided that he prefers somebody else. This is not what I hoped for, but it takes two to make a marriage and he doesn't want it. He loves you but he doesn't love me."

"Your mom has been drinking as you know. She's been in and out of treatment programs but nothing seems to stick. And I can't deal with it anymore."

"Your dad and I hardly see each other. He's mostly in Washington and I'm mostly here. We're both very lonely in this marriage. He can't give up his job and I can't travel. We've tried to pull things together and get back to the closeness that we once had, but we can't do it."

"Your mom's been seriously depressed for years. I've tried to get her into treatment but she refuses. Without a change, I can't live with her anymore."

"Your dad says that our marriage is pulling him down. We've had a lot of counseling but it hasn't changed how he feels. There's nothing I can do to change this."

Obviously, your child may turn to the other parent and ask for a different point of view. This is reasonable and fair. You should encourage it. Undoubtedly, she'll form her own judgments.

If, as happens in our open American society, one parent declares that he or she is homosexual, your teenager needs to be told. The parent who is coming out of the closet should say honestly, "It's only very recently that I learned a lot about myself that I know I should have known before. But I have discovered that I am really attracted to men and that my relationship with your mom is not working for either of us. I'm sure that this has hurt your mom and I'm genuinely sorry. I'm sure this may hurt and surprise you as well. And I'm very sorry about that. It's very sad that I didn't know this before, but it is the truth."

If you are the heterosexual parent, you should say, "You probably realize that we are in a terrible crisis. Your dad has just told me that he cannot love me because he really feels drawn to men. It's awful news for me and I feel mixed up and very sad. I honestly did not know this. But he was my husband and he is your father and that will not change. Although he does not love me as his wife, he loves you as your father. And although you may feel sorrow and anger, if you loved him before, you must surely love him now. He needs your love and your friendship and your understanding more than ever."

Is this kind of honesty hard to do? You bet. Is it doable? Yes, it is. But you have to believe me when I say that it will be far worse for your teenager if you let him conclude that he can't trust you to tell him the truth.

I have more to say later about how grandparents can help, but let me say here that extended family members have a special role with adolescents. One young woman who did well later in her life told me that she always sought her grandmother when she felt overwhelmed by her responsibilities. She described her grandmother's garden, how peaceful it was, and how much it refreshed her to sit there quietly for hours, talking or just closing her eyes and meditating.

A temporary retreat is invaluable for you, too, at this hectic time. The strain of raising a teenager and of being a teenager is enormous in every family. But in a divorced family, when you have no help at your side and so much on your mind, it can be too much. Think seriously about giving yourself some "time-outs" to get away and restore your perspective.

Remember, your teenager can be very helpful to you, but don't ask too much. Keep in mind the impact of divorce. She's frightened about her own relationships and she's scared of all the changes in her life. If you respect her need to be with her friends, you can ease the burden of your divorce and help her grow into healthy young adulthood.

Chapter 10:   **College-Age Children**

W hen teenagers pack their belongings for that big move into the freshman dorm, they think long and carefully about what to bring. Nowadays, a computer, a CD player and perhaps a CD burner are near the top of the list. Clothes, books, sporting equipment, and notebooks are essential. But if you look in the moving boxes of the typical college freshman, I wager you'll find plenty of teddy bears and frayed baby blankets among their treasured items. Your child is growing up but still holds on to comforting symbols from the past.

In terms of development, this is the time when your child's central agenda is to explore the world of love and sex. Sure, they're in school to get a good education, prepare for a career, and become economically independent. But once classes are over and papers are written, young people spend a lot of their time looking at the opposite sex, thinking about the possibilities for lasting relationships. The days of high school puppy love are over. Relationships are getting more serious. While marriage is still many years off, it's a time to seek love and commitment on adult terms.

And then you come along and announce that you're getting divorced.

An increasing number of parents these days wait until their youngest child is in college to end their marriage. Their thinking is pretty straightforward: I did my duty. Now that the last child has left home, we're free—or I'm free—to get on with my life. I want my turn at happiness. The kids will be fine.

But don't assume you're home free. How young adults react to their parents' divorce is very individual, but react they will and powerfully so.

College counselors tell me that a large part of their caseload is composed of freshmen and sophomores whose parents have recently divorced or are divorcing. The students show up with myriad symptoms of depression and anxiety—trouble sleeping, difficulty finishing assignments, overeating, undereating, generally feeling miserable. Their suffering can be explained. The message that Mom and Dad are divorcing shakes them to the core. Inevitably they worry that if family relationships don't hold, then love itself is unreliable. They immediately think about their own relationships. Some break up with a steadfast partner, others cling, but many feel a sense of doom. They can't help but wonder, "Will I experience the same fate?" They know it isn't rational to feel this way but that's how they feel. Their worries are reinforced when they look around and see how many of their friends and classmates were raised in second and third marriages. After all, the world is a less reliable, less secure place, even though your parents are no longer responsible for creating stability in your life.

A common reaction for many is to rush home to the rescue. With rising panic, they say, "I must be responsible. Obviously, I was the glue that held the marriage together and after I left, it fell apart." Sometimes this is true. Parents do indeed stay together when there's a child at home who needs care. It's also true that after the child leaves, they face an intolerable emptiness as they look at each other across the dining room table and contemplate the boredom or unhappiness that lies ahead. With this crisis at home, many college students feel compelled to rush home to shore up the marriage or to hold up a collapsing parent. This is a strange role for young people. They're uncomfortable if they rush in or if they stay away. It's a classic no-win situation.

Many young people lose one or more years of college while they're engaged in rescuing one or both parents. Some drop out altogether. While some succeed in restoring the marriage, most fail. Undoubtedly many are very helpful to one parent. But the price may be high and the student may find it emotionally overwhelming. Also they may lose important ground in furthering their own plans. Alice, who was taking pre-med courses, was very worried about her father after her mother dumped him precipitously. Alice's father pleaded with her to come home and take care of him. She yielded, traveling back and forth to help him out of his depression. When she later applied to medical school, her transcripts showed a series of low grades alongside her A's in courses before and after the breakup. She was refused admission because of these poor grades during the time she took care of her father. The admissions committee told her that had her mother died, they would have taken her poor grades for that year into consideration. But they would not make such an allowance for her parents' divorce. Although their decision was terribly hurtful and unjust, it's fairly typical of how reluctant educational institutions are to recognize that divorce can exact a terrible toll on students. Their attitude may reflect the concern that because so many students come from divorced families, they couldn't possibly accommodate all the demands for special treatment. The death of a parent in middle age is rare. Marital dissolution is common.

Given such serious risks to a student's academic future, students who want to help one or both parents might consider taking a leave of absence rather than try combining rescue trips home with a demanding class schedule. The bottom line is for you, the parent, to recognize how hard it is for your college-age child to deal with your crisis at home and keep up with schoolwork. In breaking your news, you should try to pay attention to the timing of exams and class projects. If you can find support elsewhere, you may save your child from sacrificing too much on your behalf.

Like high schoolers, your college-age child is likely to react by blaming one parent for the family upheaval. In most divorces that occur later in life, one person is likely to be very distressed. If you're a mom who has yearned to be free from a disappointing marriage, be prepared for your children's disapproval. If you're a dad who sought freedom, be prepared for their censure.

Another reaction is to mourn the loss of home and hearth. Although your child is living away at school, the house she grew up in is a symbol of her past. She counts on being able to come home for vacations, to see her friends, to hang out like she did in high school. Ask any parent who redecorates a college student's room in her absence or, God forbid, rents the room out. Howls of protest echo through the house.

When children go off to college, your home is a platform for them to spring from. When you pull it out from under their feet, they collapse. Lexi sat for hours on the hill behind her house, looking longingly at her old backyard. She told me, "The house is a part of me and now it's gone. I'm not ready for it to be gone."

What this kind of reaction means for you is pretty simple. Don't sell the house right away if you can afford to wait. Give your children time to absorb the changes. Most important, don't treat this loss as if it weren't important. And if you do move, give everyone a chance to say good-bye with dignity and affection.

Whatever caused your breakup, adult children tend to rally around the parent whom they perceive as being wronged or abandoned. It can be very difficult for many older men or women to bounce back from an unwanted divorce. Depression is common, along with a litany of physical complaints. On the other hand, some older men and women are able to make use of a second chance and turn their lives around. Women and men these days go back to school and finish college or graduate degrees or just take courses without credit for pleasure. They're often very good students. Once they get past their embarrassment at being surrounded by young people, they do very well. There are positions in the workplace. Travel opportunities abound. Gyms are interested in middle-age members. Museums offer interesting volunteer positions. There are, in fact, endless opportunities for people in midlife who have the interest and energy to try new things or return to past interests that they allowed to lapse.

Actually, the extent to which you can rely on your adult child to fill the gaps in your life is limited. Older adolescents and young adults face the challenges and difficulties of building new careers and establishing new relationships. You, in turn, have to rebuild your own life. You can help each other, but this is the time in both your lives to separate. Your goal is to live independent lives that interlock in good ways.

WHAT TO DO

You owe your older adult children an explanation. Don't be so sure they know that you've been unhappy for years. They may have no idea that things have gotten so bad between you. They may never have considered that you were planning to divorce after the youngest sibling left home. In fact, they probably assumed that since you've lived together all these years, obviously you decided to stay married.

If your child is away at college, please do not send an e-mail to announce your divorce. You should go see your child and explain what's happening face-to-face. If you can't travel that far or can't afford the trip, wait until Thanksgiving. If you can't wait that long, each of you should send a carefully written letter or make a long telephone call that explains the reasons for your action. You may not want to face your child, but you owe her this. Be as honest as you can.

Say you're confident that both of you are going to be all right in the long run. Encourage your child to stay in school and carry on with his studies, even if in your heart of hearts you want him beside you. I urge you to put his needs ahead of yours. You can say something like, "I'm falling apart, you're falling apart, we're all falling apart, but let's take a deep breath and not panic. We have plenty of time to talk about this at length. I know you're worried about us but we'll be okay."

Since you and your ex will very likely have very different views of what's happened, there's no reason to tell your child together. But be sure that both of you talk to her. She has a right to hear both sides of the story.

If you're the one who decided to leave, tell her why you're taking this step and why you couldn't work any longer to make the marriage work. Tell her that you're sorry to burden her with this bad news. If you feel free for the first time in many years, tell her.

If you're the one who's been left and if you're going to need your child's help in any way, tell her frankly what you think you'll need. Give her hope that you won't become dependent on her when she's struggling to establish her own life. If you're frightened and upset, tell her.

Don't ask your child to take sides. Children usually love both their parents and don't want to be forced into choosing one of you over the other. If they feel pulled by you, it torments them.

Above all, don't walk away from your marriage as if it never happened. It's an important part of who you are and who she is. If you leave without a backward glance, your child, at any age, will be profoundly shocked and discouraged about her past and future relationships.

To acknowledge this shared history, you should do your best to maintain a respectful consideration of your former partner. Make sure that the financial settlement is fair. Be prepared for questions about how you both arrived at the financial decision. If your partner is ill, you need to express concern, whether you feel it or not. If you want your child to respect you and respect your decision, you have to behave in ways that are in keeping with the image of her having two decent, virtuous parents. The woman you left is her mother or the man you left is her father. She will not and should not be expected to welcome a replacement that seems to you well chosen.

Financial and inheritance issues are important to discuss. Far too many students are asked to switch from private to public universities or told to pay for their own education. While many young people work their way through school, the sudden lack of support from a previously stable family comes as a terrible blow. If a student is preparing for a career in medicine, law, science, or any other profession that involves a demanding curriculum, the need to work and go to school at the same time can throw even the most gifted student off course.

This may be a good time for you to call your ex and discuss how to protect your child's education. If possible, meet at lunch or in either of your offices. Education is a very serious issue. Without a college education your child will enter adulthood at an economic disadvantage. If it's difficult for you to talk alone, invite a trusted friend or a mediator to help you. I know several stories about parents who came through for their children once they were aware of what was at stake. You may have room to negotiate. It's worth a try.

Children also rise to the occasion. For example, Laura was a junior when her parents divorced. Since she was over eighteen, the divorce settlement made no provisions for her college tuition. Laura approached the academic dean for help. He suggested a family conference. As the meeting started, Laura's mother asked Laura to describe her ambitions, which included plans to attend graduate school at a leading university. The dean said this was possible because Laura was a talented and devoted student who showed much promise. Laura's father, who was a busy executive and hadn't spent much time with her, had no idea that his daughter was so ambitious. He was excited and happy to help, given the high caliber of her plans and the dean's plea for her support.

While your child doesn't have a right to see your will, he does have a right to feel that he has not lost an important part of the inheritance he would have received if you had stayed married. When men marry younger women with children or go on to have second families of their own, the first children often lose out. This is a tricky business that arouses intense jealousy. Often this feeling is justified. Sometimes there's plenty of money for the children of the first marriage, but they still feel deprived and angry at you. If you can discuss this frankly and fairly at the beginning, everyone will benefit. You can use prenups, life insurance, or other strategies. The one thing you can't do is ignore it. Even if there's not much money to talk about, the issue needs to be discussed. There's usually a symbolic legacy, a favorite picture, an antique brooch, or a set of china that would have gone to your children without question if there had been no divorce. Often the family home is at stake. This is often of great symbolic significance in addition to its monetary value.

Remember, even though your child has left for college, attachments to her family are deep and lasting. She's extremely vulnerable and you need to protect her as you would if she still lived at home. She may be tempted to leave school to rescue you or the marriage, but you should discourage her in this. Reassure her that you're okay and tell her how important it is for her to continue her studies. You'll have time in coming years to have heart-to-heart conversations about why the divorce happened at this stage of her life. For now, she needs to know that you stand behind her 100 percent, you're proud of her achievements, and she has not lost your love and faith in her.

Chapter 11: Vulnerable Children

Not long ago I had lunch with a friend whose son is a "vulnerable child." By vulnerable I mean a child who suffers from any physical or mental disability or illness. The list is long and tragic: cerebral palsy, epilepsy, asthma, cystic fibrosis, muscular dystrophy, autism, cancer, diabetes, and so on. Children who suffer such conditions require frequent visits to doctors, clinics, and therapeutic programs. They're often in pain. Some require special diets, exercise routines, and restricted activities. Although the care of these children has advanced dramatically, and many can go on to lead reasonably normal lives, their childhood is under the shadow of their care requirements. All need an enormously devoted loving parent to make it all happen.

My friend was explaining what she thought had happened to her son, Jonah, in the years after her divorce. I didn't have a tape recorder, but she was kind enough to send me some long e-mails recapping our conversation. This is what she said.

My son Jonah had a complicated history. After a stressful pregnancy, he was born prematurely and contracted spinal meningitis when he was seven weeks old. He was hospitalized several times as an infant and toddler and once spent a whole month in the ICU where we were not allowed to stay overnight. Visits were limited.

We divorced when he was four and I now believe this was the last straw. It was more than he could cope with after his very stressed history. Both he and I have paid dearly. Although he is physically well today and was finally able to complete college and to get a job, the psychological residues are serious. Separations terrify Jonah to this day. I am sure that his fear is related to all the separations he experienced from being in the hospital, especially that month in the ICU, and then from the divorce. He clings to people, to his friends, to his girlfriends. He seems unable to let go of anyone. He has a hard time leaving to go anywhere—to college, on a trip, to work in the morning. He missed his first semester in college. He usually misses one plane no matter where he is going. His lateness is legendary and affects his social life and his work. His friends are amused and forgive him, but his boss regards his lateness as irresponsible, so Jonah's work history has been a disaster. Although I knew that he was fragile, I really did not understand how to handle him at the breakup. I think I know better now, but it is too late, much too late.

I asked, "What would you have done differently?"
She was very specific.

In retrospect I wish that I had worked fewer hours. It was important for me and for all of us after the divorce to have some semblance of the lifestyle we were used to. But looking back, it would have been better to make more financial sacrifices and be at home with him and his brother after school and in the evenings. Perhaps I should have postponed the divorce until he was a little older and better able to understand that our separation did not mean rejection of him. But the truth is, our marriage had become intolerable. Just too humiliating. My drive to fill the hole and to reconstitute the family had a desperation that was not consistent with good judgment. I always felt that, in my despair, I let my son down. I knew he was a vulnerable child. Look at his history. And I paid no attention.

Parents of vulnerable children face a common dilemma—should I focus on my own needs or give priority to my child?—but for them the question is a hundred times sharper. While all children are vulnerable during the breakup and its immediate aftermath, children who suffer from an illness or disability are in a special category. They seem to need you all the time. Unlike their healthier brothers and sisters, they have special needs that can't wait until you're ready to help. Overall, they have a harder time with delay.

Vulnerable children exert enormous effort in moving from one developmental stage to the next. A healthy baby pulls herself into a standing position, sits back down, wobbles back to her feet and, after a few tumbles, continues to stand without falling. A healthy baby goes from crawling to walking and walking to running with lots of practice in between. If you watch a normal child develop, you'll be amused to see that she practices falling down so she can master that fear and set it to rest. She's determined to walk. She enjoys your praise. She likes an appreciative audience. But she initiates the walking on her own.

For a child with disabilities, learning to sit up, walk, run, and talk are even greater achievements. Depending on his particular vulnerability, he may become as proficient as any healthy child, but it will take him longer to master a skill. He needs your help and special understanding every step along the way. Moreover, he knows that he needs you by his side to survive.

Change is particularly difficult for all vulnerable children. But for a child like Jonah, change is the bogeyman. Separations terrify him. In confronting any change, he becomes frightened and disorganized. He has fewer inner resources to draw on when adjusting to change. The loss of a familiar person, routine, pet, or environment can create panic. Each separation brings up the sadness and pain of all the past ones.

Divorce ushers in everything the child finds most frightening. Changes happen hard and fast. Parents may be less available. The child may need to transfer to a new school, have new teachers, meet new classmates. In struggling to keep up, he may lose some of the hard-won progress he's made. One step forward and one or two back. But there are steps you can take to make the transition easier.

If your child is under medical care or in a special education program, your first step is to consult the people who work with your child. Tell them what you think will change, so they'll understand what your child is struggling with. Discuss your plans and ask their advice about what all of you can do to make the divorce easier on your child.

Whatever you do, move slowly. Try to protect your child by asking her to deal with only one change at a time. If she faces new surgery or has just recovered from a stressful episode, this is not the time to divorce. Wait until her life is without major incident. If the divorce requires you to change caregivers, give your child plenty of time to adjust to the new person. Don't change anything else until she's comfortable with and has accepted the caregiver. If you go back to work full-time, try to do so gradually so you don't suddenly disappear from your child's daytime world. If she'll be dividing her time between your two homes, give her plenty of warning before each move. Easy does it.

Slowly tell your child the reasons for the breakup in an intimate setting. It's better if you can tell her together, but if that doesn't work for you, tell her separately. Most important, double and redouble your assurances that she did not cause the divorce. Tell her that you love her and will continue to care for her. Vulnerable children often feel that they're a burden and disappointment to their parents. And to some degree this may be true. More than healthy children, they blame themselves for the divorce. They think, "If I'd been like other kids, they wouldn't be splitting up."

When you tell her about the divorce, be sure to interweave many expressions of love for her and assurances that her care will continue. Don't expect her to reply. Your message may be too painful for her. She may blot it out. If she doesn't respond, don't repeat what you said in toto but do repeat loving words and assurances that you'll always be there for her no matter what. Let her deal with the news slowly and absorb it at a pace she can manage. A few weeks later, ask gently whether she understood what you said and be prepared to explain the divorce again.

Ask whether she has some special worry or question. Give your conversations time to evolve.

Divorce can precipitate depression and discouragement in your vulnerable child. She may feel that no matter how hard she tries, she won't succeed. And so she puts less effort into learning her next developmental task. These dark feelings can last far beyond the breakup, which means she will need your help more than ever. You'll need to double your efforts to encourage each step forward and to praise whatever progress she makes. Most of all, you need to keep yourself from becoming discouraged and to keep reminding yourself that new adjustments take time.

Think about getting good support to ease your own life and try to arrange for your material needs before you separate. Also, bear in mind that you're not alone. It is tragic but true that many couples divorce due to the stresses of raising a vulnerable child. Now is a good time to seek a help group composed of other parents who can offer support and friendship. Ask your child's teachers or pediatrician for recommendations. One father told me, "I knew that I needed to socialize with adults. Everyone in the group gave me real help when I needed it. I couldn't have done it alone."

You and your ex will need to continue sharing responsibilities for many years after the breakup. If you can sit down and plan together, it will help everyone in the family. This planning may involve financial obligations, such as using both your insurance plans to meet medical bills, and sometimes self-sacrifices. One father I know moved a thousand miles to a city where his son could attend a school for the deaf. The mother called her ex-husband every day and visited her son six times a year. Both parents remarried but continued their joint responsibility for raising their son. When the boy graduated from a major university with a degree in biology, they celebrated as a team.

Remember, if you're the parent of a vulnerable child and you've decided to end your marriage, you'll need to make some tough decisions. When the family splits apart, who will be primarily responsible for your child's care? Who will be responsible a year from now, ten years from now, even thirty years from now? What kind of arrangements can you make to continue his care if you die before he does? Once you answer these questions, you can make plans that will nurture and protect your child for many years to come.

Chapter 12:   What Is the "Best" Time to Divorce?

I hear this question every time I lecture to parents or participate on talk shows. People love their children and they want to diminish any hurt from the divorce. They want to know whether there's an age when divorce is easier on children. What's the "best" time to divorce? The trouble is, there's no simple answer. It all depends on what's going on in your family, what kind of parents you are, how much you can cooperate, and also the age and temperament of your child.

First take a close look at what's happening in your family. If there's chronic violence at home, the answer is "the sooner the better," unrelated to the age of your child. By violence I mean physical attack—hitting, kicking, throwing objects—or chronic threats of physical violence. Exposure to violence has serious consequences for a child's development that may last well into adulthood. They fear for your safety. They fear for themselves and their siblings.

If there's repeated high conflict in your marriage accompanied by yelling, screaming, and pounding the table, then I'd also say the sooner the better. Since there are no meaningful measures of high conflict, this judgment is highly subjective. Some families are reserved, others are operatic. But if you're in a marriage where almost every subject is material for another fierce argument, you know what I mean. In some high-conflict homes, serious differences between the partners are a recurrent theme in everyday life. In other marriages, fights erupt over insignificant issues—a grocery bill, local politics, a bad report card—leading to hurt and a sense of endless frustration. Like violence, high conflict is terrifying for children to witness because it creates a climate that leads to fear and trembling. In such an environment, a child can lose the capacity to trust, even to feel. The longer it goes on, the worse it will be.

Divorce in violent marriages provides important relief for one or both parents and can definitely help the children—but not automatically. When children have witnessed violent behavior, they need therapy in addition to divorce. This is an extremely important recommendation. Children who have witnessed physical abuse in their families absolutely need help in assimilating new and healthier models for male-female relationships. Nor is divorce by itself enough for children who have grown up under conditions of high conflict. They, too, need therapy to help them resume their development without a distorted view of how people treat each other.

The parents who terminate such marriages also need help, not only to protect their children but to learn how to let go of their fear and anger. Divorce does not end fear in a person who has been victimized. Nor does rage go away. After a divorce, angry people often tend to continue fighting. But if you are in a violent or high-conflict marriage, you should keep in mind that anger has the potential to escalate when divorce is threatened or actually filed. While you may not be able to prevent anger from dominating your divorce proceedings, you can be aware of how hazardous the victim-perpetrator interaction is to your children.

If the conflict is low between you—and this encompasses more than half of all divorces—it's a different story. Despite your disappointment in the marriage, you share some mutual respect and common interests. Perhaps you're divorcing because of long-standing loneliness or sexual deprivation, because you have lost respect for your partner, or because of alcoholism, drug abuse, or mental illness. There's a wide range of irreconcilable differences. If this describes your marriage, then you should consider the fact that preschoolers tend to have the hardest time at the breakup and sometimes many years afterward. Much depends on the quality of your child's life after the breakup. A good second marriage may or may not enable you to provide the care that your child needs.

With the risk of repeating myself, I want to emphasize that young children need a great deal of care from their parents. After divorce, many women who were able to stay home part-time with their babies are now required to re-enter the workforce full-time. Mothers who love taking care of their little ones with long bedtime rituals, reading together and playing favorite games, find that they have to cut back these pleasurable activities not because they want to but because they no longer have the time or energy after a long day at work.

So if you can delay your divorce until your youngest child enters school and seems to be adjusting well, your decision will be easier on him. He'll have an interesting world outside your home and a school structure that supports activities and friendships that will keep him developmentally on target. As he begins to find his own interests and friends, you may be better able to protect him from feeling that he has lost more than he has gained with your divorce.

The second most vulnerable age for divorce is early adolescence, when children are developing rapidly and need a strong family to guide and protect them. If you have a preteen child in trouble—failing at school or not keeping up with peers in some important regard—I advise you to hesitate before getting a divorce. Your child may be too troubled to adjust to the demands of a post-divorce family. So before you make any moves, consider whether your child is developmentally on target. If not, try to get her some help before you embark on the divorce.

The bottom line is that if you can figure out how to protect your little one from feeling bereft after the breakup and your young adolescent from feeling unsupported, you will be starting the journey better prepared. But let's be realistic. People can't always prepare for divorce. Traumatic events can engulf families and spit them out in lawyers' offices with shocking speed.

If your partner has done something outrageous and intolerable and you're seething with anger, you're probably going to file for divorce no matter how old your children are or what I say about differences in ages. You won't be able to wait. If this happens to you, keep in mind the importance of maintaining the stability of care with young children and the special vulnerability of children entering adolescence. This is the time to call on your family and friends for help and to set up plans for the young children and young teenagers before you separate.

People also ask me, is it bad for my children if I stay in an unhappy marriage? Or would they be better off if we divorce? I'm afraid the answer to this is yes and no. The notion that your child is unhappy because you're unhappy is simply not true. If your external behavior looks normal and you really enjoy being a parent—while your internal state is lonely or dying from boredom—your child may not notice your unhappiness. Children can't read your internal state unless it shows up directly in your relationship with them. They have no key to your sex life. They're not mind readers. Moreover, they have no way to understand the complexity of your marital relationship. I'm afraid that children who have not yet reached adolescence cannot comprehend why a violent person just doesn't stop if they are asked to show some restraint. They have no clue as to why a person behaves badly when drunk.

The choice to divorce is always a subjective, personal decision. No one can tell you exactly what the future holds. It may bring the man or woman of your dreams. I've seen that happen to young and old adults alike, although your chances diminish with age because the market is smaller. I'm reminded of one woman in her fifties who divorced her husband because she had grown to hate him. Within six months she met a kind, loving man at her church who was exactly what she wanted in a partner. My point is that no one can measure how unhappy you are or predict what new opportunities divorce will bring. Only you can weigh the balance of inner misery and satisfaction in your life. In fact, all of us probably know couples who don't love each other but find contentment in work, friends, and parenthood. Some may have given up the dream of romantic love or perhaps they never wanted a passionate relationship from the start. Clearly, disappointment in a marriage depends almost entirely on where you set your sights to begin with, and these are subject to change. One recent study of unhappy marriages found that many embattled but intact couples, five years later, were much happier and reported that their marriages were good. So it is important not to make critical decisions in the heat of your latest disappointments. Things may look very different if you wait a few months. You may change your mind altogether.

From your children's perspective, the decision to divorce relates to how your unhappiness is affecting your ability to be a good parent. If you and your spouse enjoy being parents and together maintain a moral and protected life for your children, then I think you should consider staying together. I know many couples who have taken this path. They take great pride in their children and decided, on balance, that it was a good way for them to go. Some have discreet extramarital affairs when they are away from home. Others settle for the limited love and sexuality in the marriage that they have. But if your unhappiness dominates your life, then you have to ask yourself probingly if one or both of you will be better parents after divorcing. Will your children be better off? These are hard questions, but again, only you can know your pain and satisfactions and how these play out now in the lives of your children and how they are likely to play out in the future. The familiar question—Is it better to stay married or not?—does not capture the many gradations or nuances of marriage. Nor does it touch on the source of marital problems and the extent to which they can be tolerated within an intact marriage.

On the other hand, if you feel humiliated, emotionally abused, mocked, and derided in your marriage or just wake up miserable each day, you can use the divorce to take new pride in yourself. As an emancipated parent, you can become a far better role model and share with your children your new sense of freedom. You can take the opportunity to improve your life with knowledge that you didn't have when you were younger. You can become a new kind of adult who has had the courage to bring about change in your life and the lives of your children. A new world is ahead of you and it's yours to define.

Chapter 13:   Setting Routines and Structure

After you've explained your decision to your children and helped them understand what's ahead, your first priority is to help them settle into their new routines. They need to feel safe going back and forth between your two homes and to know that they won't lose one of you while they're at the other's house. This may seem easy to you as an adult, but it's hard for young children. You need to help them master the calendar so they can begin to see a pattern in their comings and goings. They'll need to learn to plan their activities with friends according to the new schedule. Their ability to do all this depends on how well and how quickly you restore order to your household. In most homes, including those that have been very well run, routines inevitably get disrupted after divorce. Bedtime often becomes hit and miss. Families that always had dinner together find it hard to continue. Many school-age children get themselves up sleepily in the morning, make or forget lunch, and take themselves off to class, often arriving late. Clothes don't get washed regularly. Children snap at each other and dare you to knock a chip off their shoulders.

To improve the situation, call a family meeting and tell the children that the household has a firm set of rules. Do not ask their permission but by all means indicate your openness to their suggestions. They might enjoy having a suggestion box that you open ceremonially once a week, but it's up to you to decide the routines. To help everyone keep track, write out the rules and chores on a large sheet of paper and put it where all can see. You can promote the feeling of camaraderie—we're going to do this together. But more important is the sense of orderliness that you preserve, the ongoing flow of life and the fact that children know what to expect tomorrow, the day after tomorrow, and beyond.

If your work hours have expanded or if your work demands that you be at the office on evenings and weekends, the children will need an explanation. When very young children see you going back to work and they miss you, they don't understand why your absence is necessary. They certainly don't connect your working with their welfare. You need to explain gently why you need money and why it's important that you work now. Try to put it in concrete terms. One mother explained to her children that the things they needed—a bicycle, a new bed, a warm coat—all cost money that she could only earn by working. Danny, an intelligent twelve-year-old of my acquaintance, told me that his hard-working father only loved his office and didn't care about his son. Danny said, "All my dad cares about is going to work. He shouldn't have had a son." At this time Danny's father's business was in bankruptcy. He was very worried about how he would keep his household going. So if you're working more hours than you did when you were married—and chances are that you're doing just that—explain to your children why you're not as available as before and how your working is related to providing for their needs and wishes. Keep your explanations simple and pleasant. And be sure not to frighten your children. The idea of having to pay the mortgage or rent is far beyond them. I have known children who gave up small things like an occasional ice cream or candy bar because they were worried about their parent working too hard.

A regular bedtime is critically important. Keep in mind that children who are worried or who have experienced radical changes in their lives need help in making the difficult transition from daytime to evening.

You may not have time to read as many bedtime stories, but don't give them up completely. All the bedtime rituals that parents provide are not luxuries; they're not expendable just because you feel pressed for time. These habits have the serious purpose of helping your child close her eyes and go to sleep with the confidence that you and the rest of her world will be there in the morning.

For the same reason, rituals like kissing your child good-bye when she leaves for school are important. Tell your child who will be home when she gets back from school, that she'll find milk and cookies or whatever you instruct your sitter to provide, and the time when you'll return from work. Children need to know who will be home in the afternoon and what's expected of them in the hours before dinner. Tell them before they leave for school. A child who worries about who will be at home to meet her after school can't sit comfortably in the classroom and pay attention to the teacher. Her anxiety about who and what awaits her homecoming can pose a serious interference to her learning. She may also be worried about you at this time, having observed the frantic pace of your life. This makes it doubly important to assure her when you return.

It's a good idea to assign chores, however small, to each child, and if they are done well to reward the children with high praise and a hug for their help in keeping the household order. If possible reward them with a movie or some other surprise at the end of the week. Providing pleasure to offset the pain of the breakup is very important as the new family begins to take shape.

There's no way to avoid asking your older children to help with the younger ones, but keep in mind that your older child is still a child. She does not have the wisdom, patience, or tolerance to raise small children on her own. She needs some time off each week plus a genuine reward for a job well done. Tell her that taking care of a younger child is not a piece of cake. Find out if she's missing out on things she'd rather be doing and try to tune in with what's really happening. Ask what kind of discipline she's using. If you find out she's threatening the younger children, tell her that this is not acceptable, but be sure to explain why.

Don't get angry at her. She's just learning to be an adult and she doesn't understand why bullying her younger sibling is not good. Be sure to suggest better methods for handling conflict. The help she gives you is an opportunity for her to learn about empathy. You can reduce conflict by arranging after-school activities for each child. That way they won't get into each other's hair quite as much.

You also need to keep an eye on your younger children and make sure that they're comfortable with the discipline being handed out when you're not home. Eight-year-old Walter told me about his travails with his fifteen-year-old sister, who had been appointed by his mom to serve dinner, make sure that Walter did his homework, and see that the house was picked up. The sister disciplined him by demanding total obedience, and if he did not do her chores as well as his, she threatened to lock up Walter's dog. Terrified, he did whatever she said. Of course, siblings in intact families can play horrible tricks on each other; such behavior is not limited to post-divorce families. But there's a key difference. After divorce, an older child is often given permission to exert power over a younger one. Without your guidance, this authority can be misused. My advice: you should come home now and then unannounced. You'll quickly see if your instructions are being followed or distorted.

As a general custom when you get home from work, try your best to eat meals together. At the time of the breakup and later, this is often the first routine that gets lost in the confusion. It's a loss that children notice right away and that soon symbolizes the loss of the family. Dinner represents a coming together of the family and you want to preserve that feeling. If you can, take your children out once a week to a restaurant they enjoy. Make it an outing. You don't want eating at home to become dreary. Nor should it be a time for watching television. Better to use the time to turn to each child and ask about their day. Listen carefully to what they say. And then tell them about your day. If you can't eat together every day, do it at least three times a week. This will be hard at times but the payoff is huge. Try for a pleasant and relaxed sharing of the day's adventures.

Other important tasks include feeding your children before they leave for school. I know it's a terrible struggle, but no matter how bad you feel or how fast you have to get yourself out of the house to get to work, try to get up early enough to help your children get ready or at least to see them before they take off. Don't rely on your oldest child to take over this responsibility, although she surely can on occasion. Make sure that they have lunch or lunch money. I've heard from dozens of teachers that after divorce young children arrive without lunch and often without proper clothing for cold or warm weather.

Your rules should be clear: be home at a certain time, call if you're late, ask permission to go anywhere not agreed to in advance, and so on. Strict control is more important after divorce than before it—and harder to enforce. If you were permissive before the divorce, now is the time to rein in your child. You cannot afford to do otherwise.

On the other hand, try not to let your worry spill into over-supervision. Cell phones permit endless contact that can be used too much by worried moms. Your children will think you're spying on them. Each child should know your cell phone number and know how to reach you in an emergency. But be sure that you keep that line free for emergency calls. That will go far to relieve your anxiety. You can ask them to call you when they get home from school, but after that you should be able to trust them to follow the routines you have all worked out. If plans change, they can call. Help them understand that if anything goes awry, you expect a call. And spell it out. If one child fails to arrive home on time, if they're worried about something or somebody, if one of the children is hurt, you want to know about it as soon as it happens. Also try to have somebody nearby, like a trusted neighbor, whom they can call in an emergency.

In talking about this need for structure, I'm addressing both parents. Both of you should provide this kind of help. In real life, however, only one may be able to provide it. Regardless, stick to your guns. You have to maintain your own household, mow your own lawn, make your own house payments. Don't get sucked into "Daddy lets me watch TV until eleven" or "I can eat all the chocolate kisses I want at Mommy's house." You may be called a tyrant for sticking to your rules, but so be it. The worst case is when both parents collapse in the first few years and there are no rules to contain your child's anxiety. Whatever your ex does, the only person you can control is you. If the kids hear you say, "In this home, with me, these are the rules," you will be giving them their due.

Another elusive but important goal is for you to set aside a regular intimate time that you spend alone with each of your children. I'm not talking about big chunks of time—an hour a week just for the two of you, out of reach of the telephone, television, and computer. You can do whatever you enjoy doing together, but I don't recommend grocery shopping or watching TV. It needs to be a protected time that allows you an opportunity to play or talk or even walk. This effort will go a long way in helping each child cope with his fears of losing your attention. It lays the basis for a good relationship between the two of you for years to come. You now have a new opportunity to take a close look at how each of your children is doing. You can be a better parent.

It's very important to bring some pleasure and fun and laughter back into your family life with the children. Long periods of somber looks will take their toll. Think of activities or treats that you can arrange to lighten up this difficult time. You all need some relief. Don't act in ways that make your children think that they have to tiptoe around as if someone were ill. Divorce is designed to usher in a better time for all of you.

During these early years, especially year one after divorce, make it a habit to regularly step back and ask yourself how your children are doing in this new life you all share. Divorce gives you a second chance to pay closer attention to your children—not to berate yourself with "What did I do wrong?" but to honestly ask, "How is each child doing right now?" If you're honest with yourself, you may realize that in the chaos of a failing marriage and divorce, you overlooked your children without meaning to. I've known many families where distraught children were living in a world of their own, yet their parents were too wrapped up in their own problems to notice. Even if you've continued being an attentive, wonderful parent, it's a good time to check in. With any luck, the stresses you've been dealing with in your failing marriage are no longer in your face. If you're open, you can assess what your children have not been getting and what they need most. Have you been leaving them on their own more than you think is good for them? Have you forgotten what it's like to pay close attention to a child's questions? Can you find ways to let them know how much you care about them? If your marriage has been a great disappointment, have you unconsciously let the feeling of regret extend to your children? Can you make new contact with their feelings, thoughts, and interests? Can you improve your self-rating as a parent now that you have made the decision to revamp your own life?

Ask yourself, are my children having any fun? Is there real pleasure in their lives? Do what you can to add to their pleasure so this period in their lives is not all gloom and doom. Rent a movie, make popcorn. Find out what music you can agree on and stock favorite CDs. Buy some board games or play charades, or make up stories or try guessing games. Museums have scientific and art programs for children of all ages. The library has lots of funny rhyme books and limerick collections that the children and you will enjoy. Ask your librarian for some suggestions.

Finally, you need to know that children of all ages have reconciliation fantasies that at the beginning take many forms. Some think, if I'm very good, Mom and Dad will get back together.

If I get straight A's, they'll want to be together.

Mom smiled at Dad when he dropped me off last night. I bet that means they like each other.

Some people who work with children try to eradicate these wishes, declaring them to be a form of denial that prevents the child from accepting your divorce. I disagree. I see no evidence that children who hold on to reconciliation fantasies do any less well over the longer term. In fact, I see their wishes as being positive—a capacity for hope of a better outcome, something that enriches their emotional well-being. Fantasy plays an important role in our lives. Young children feel cut in half by divorce and fantasy helps make them feel whole. It's a protective device that serves an important psychological function. So if your child is wishing on the stars for your marriage to be restored and is acting on his or her best behavior to help make this come to pass, count your blessings and keep your mouth shut. If your child works harder than ever to keep her room clean to please you, let it be. If she asks you point-blank, Are you getting back together? gently say you know how much she misses the family but no, you are not planning to restore the family as it was before.

Remember, all your efforts to restore routines in the weeks, months, and early years after divorce will bring needed stability to your children's lives. It's important for them and for you to feel a sense of order and regularity. That will go a long way in helping your children feel that the turmoil of divorce is over, allowing all of you to look ahead and rebuild your lives.

Chapter 14: Supporting the New Family

As I said earlier, the first thing you need to do after the breakup is to regain control of your life—to define who you are and who you want to become now that you're single again. Part of the new you is to become the architect who rebuilds your family from the ground up. Like architects everywhere, you'll need to come up with sketches. How do you imagine your post-divorce family will look five years from now? How are you going to get there? You'll need blueprints, subcontractors, a foundation, walls, and plenty of supplies. Your vision and creativity will build the new family in ways to protect everyone within it.

Where to begin? At your first opportunity, which can happen before the breakup, sit down and write the name of every person who might be able to help you in the months and even years ahead. List all members of your family, even those who live at a distance, with whom you are on good terms. Then list all of the members of your spouse's family, including those you've been close to in the past. Don't assume your in-laws are not interested in your children. Quite the contrary, they may turn out to be close allies. Then look at the resources in your community—organizations, groups for divorcing parents, activities for children. Finally, make a list of what you want to do as a single person. Which friends are you going to stay close to? Do you want to go back to school? Find a new job? Begin dating again? Make the list as specific as you can.

The items on these lists are your supports—the struts and beams you'll use in rebuilding family life. But I must warn you. Supports don't work unless they're anchored on both sides. You're going to call on the good will and affection of your family and friends. You may be hiring people to help with your children. In every instance, as you accept their help, be sure to reciprocate. Tell each person how appreciative you are. Teach your children to write thank-you letters to grandparents and to send drawings so that others can share in each child's life. If you don't tell the people who support you how grateful you are, you run the risk of exhausting them and wearing out your welcome. If a neighbor stands ready to watch your children when you can't get home on time, take her to dinner or to a movie every now and then. Wisdom consists of knowing how to use what you have in ways that maximally help you and your children.

GRANDPARENTS

Let's start inside the family with grandparents. Depending on their ages, you may have four healthy adults to choose from and, given how many divorces have occurred in recent decades, a few stepparents who might fill the grandparent role as well.

Grandparents can be worth their weight in gold in all families but especially so to their grandchildren in divorced families. Their special emotional connectedness with their biological grandchildren symbolically represents the continuity and the future of the family. The stability that this represents has special importance to children of divorce. Grandparents, in turn, know there is no relationship more rewarding than the love and appreciation bestowed by a child. Holding their grandchildren in their laps, your parents or your spouse's parents feel a special tenderness, joy, and pride. Grandchildren take them back to when they were young parents and remind them of the pleasures and challenges that young children provide. They're keenly aware that time is fleeting and that as grandparents they have another chance to enjoy parenthood without the many pressures they experienced way back when.

At the same time, even your parents may be loath to intrude into your lives, especially when feelings are running so high. They don't want to be rejected. Your parents and parents-in-law may be reluctant to get involved because they're afraid they'll be accused of taking sides, or they worry that their good will and love will be exploited. By all means call them and ask for their help. Strict mothers and rigid fathers can mellow into loving, gentle grandparents. You may be surprised at how pleased they are to be asked, especially when they realize how much your children need them.

Your in-laws may be especially reticent. In your anger, you might be tempted to accuse them for the flaws you found in your spouse. Even if you have been very careful, they may fear that you'll blame them for your failed marriage. But my advice is don't turn your back on in-laws. Given a second chance to hold a baby and play with wide-eyed children, they may blossom into excellent caregivers.

I stress these relationships because all my research shows that children of divorce who had close relationships with their grandparents had an easier time growing up. As adults, they were very grateful for the love and care that they experienced. One woman said, "My grandparents were a model of a loving couple. They really loved each other and seeing that helped me a lot." Another said, "My grandmother saved my life. I spent every afternoon at her house after school when I was in grade school."

Some children were fortunate to have grandparents who lived close by who were readily accessible without complicated prior arrangements. But grandparents who lived far away also played a key protective role in their grandchildren's lives. They regularly called the children on the telephone or wrote letters. They remembered birthdays and Christmas, invited the children for holidays, picked up the tab for some special pleasure like a camping trip or ski equipment that the parents could not afford. A goodly number invited the children to spend their summers. By staying involved, they played a very important role in the emotional lives of their grandchildren.

These relationships helped grandchildren only if the grandparents were truly committed to the children. When grandparents entered into the ongoing quarrel between the parents, their helpful role was greatly diminished. Grandparents who took sides and entered the fray added to the child's suffering.

Once you go through your list and decide which grandparents to contact, you need to pick up the phone and call. Don't wait for them to call you. If they live nearby, invite them over to see how things are going. Tell them directly that you have so much to do right now, you and your children would be grateful if they could spend time with the kids. They may need some suggestions for how they spend this time together. For example, they may not be up to date on your child's school life or latest interests. Tell them about how your children are reacting to the divorce and ask if they have suggestions to ease each child's pain.

Get in touch with grandparents who live farther away and explain to them how they can help. Tell them how important they are. Encourage them to stay in touch frequently. When your children are in a recital or other special event, they should call their grandparents to describe what they're doing. The grandparents should be kept informed so they can send a congratulatory note or a little gift. The continuity in these relationships is very reassuring to your children.

If grandparents have the economic means, don't be afraid to ask for financial help. If you have to move to a less expensive part of town where the schools are not so good, would they consider helping pay for private school? Can they help pay for therapy if a child needs it? I've known many grandparents who paid school tuition for their grandchildren and, just as often, to enable a parent to return to school.

OTHER FAMILY MEMBERS

The next people on your list are your extended family, including siblings, cousins, aunts, uncles, and so on. Your siblings, while likely to be busy with their own lives, will be very concerned about you. If you are close, you can ask for their help, including temporary loans, advice on attorneys, and the like. But even more important, you can ask for a loving shoulder to lean on, a sense of someone who loves you and cares.

But as you ask for their help, be careful that you don't draw them into the fights you may be having with your spouse. As your marriage unraveled, you may have poured your heart out to a sister or other close relative. You wanted commiseration, understanding, sympathy, and comforting. But now that the divorce is under way, your needs have changed. You want help that doesn't further polarize you and your ex. Conversations that were reassuring about how you've been mistreated are not what you need right now. Rather, you need advice about how to pick up the pieces, what plans to make for the future, how to strengthen your family and support your children. So when you call for help, try to move the talk away from what happened and focus on what's ahead. Are they having family dinners that you and your children can join? You may be tempted to keep the complaints flowing, but you shouldn't use your close relationships to consolidate your anger. The people who love you and want to help will follow your lead in setting the tone. If they keep bringing up past hurts, you can steer them to a discussion of future plans and where they could fit in. This may be difficult at the beginning, but they will soon respond to your lead in ways that can benefit you and your children.

SIBLINGS

If you have two or more children, they can help each other during and after divorce by counteracting the loneliness that so many children feel when their parents are so preoccupied and distressed. Siblings often share the sense of bafflement about their parents' behavior. They worry together and reassure one another. They laugh over the madness of grown-ups and then share anger at one or both of you for good or not so good reasons. They whisper confidences and dark secrets when the lights are out. In brief, they form a protective subgroup that is especially important when the family is stressed and parents are less available.

As grown-ups, siblings in divorced families often maintain close ties, and this, I believe, is one of the happier outcomes of divorce. They can express enormous love and gratitude for one another. I have heard eloquent expressions such as, "My older sister was my savior when my parents were going crazy" or, "My brother was a lifeline for years." As adults, siblings also support each other at family events such as marriages and graduations when both parents are expected to be present and the young adults are apprehensive about the enduring tension between them that they fear will mar the festivity.

I suggest that you encourage friendships among your children by planning activities that involve everyone in the family. You can nurture closer ties by telling your older children how much you value their judgment and sense of responsibility. You can tell the younger ones how fortunate they are to have such a wise and kind older sister or brother. You can express your appreciation of their getting along well. But to be perfectly honest, the most important thing you can do is to discourage your children from taking sides in your disputes with your ex. Creating a "his son" and a "her daughter" can block the natural camaraderie that your children have for one another.

If your children are fighting, you need to take immediate steps to restore calm. Don't ignore it and just hope it'll go away on its own. It's more likely to escalate. Your kids may be blaming each other for the divorce or for your perceived absences after the divorce. If you're fighting with your ex, they will be stimulated by the aggression—and take it out on each other. As said earlier, an older child may feel overwhelmed by too much responsibility, or one child may feel neglected. You need to make sure that you treat all the children fairly. If your conscience is clear on this and you've gone out of your way to be fair, call the children together and have a family powwow. Sibling rivalry exists in every family, but parents can be very influential in encouraging it or nipping it in the bud. Tell them how distressed you are and how much it hurts you to see them fighting. You want them to learn to get along. Explain that you need them. You can't micromanage quarrels and judge who hit who first. You don't want any hitting in this family. You can't be available every time one child takes another's toy. Toys are there for everyone. They have to take turns and respect each other's private posessions. These are the rules. Draw up a chart on who walks the dog when. Assign chores clearly and fairly—and make sure everyone sticks to the plan.

With all the demands on your schedule, friction among siblings can only grow if you don't take charge firmly and early. Sitters cannot enforce these rules. Only you can.

If you have an only child, you should know that he may feel he has no one to talk to when you're divorcing. I've heard from many only children that they often feel isolated at home and burdened with the whole weight of their parents' complaints resting on their shoulders. As I said earlier, young children don't confide in their friends. Even young adolescents are reluctant to discuss their parents with other children. Sharing problems with peers comes later in mid-adolescence. Only children, in general, keep their apprehensions private. You can try to help. Cousins can stand in for sibs. If you have nieces and nephews who live nearby, help them to forge close connections, especially if the children are close in age and they get along. They share the same pool of grown-ups and adult rules to unite them. If you don't have family nearby, encourage your child's friendships. Children need other children to play with and to share fantasies and perspectives on the difficulties and advantages of growing up. Only children from divorced families are especially in need of the unique benefits that the company of other children can provide.

FRIENDS

Your friends fall into various camps—couples who were close to both of you during the marriage, those who were friends with one of you, older friends who go way back, and recent friends. Some you will keep after the breakup. Others will drift away.

Friendships offer an enormous source of support during and after the breakup. As your friends, they are likely to share your values. Their life circumstances may resemble yours during the marriage. And undoubtedly several will have experienced marital crises or divorces in their own lives or with someone close to them. They may have a lot of practical wisdom to offer. They may know a lot about community resources and how to get help, which will be very useful to you. They certainly are likely to understand and be sympathetic to your concerns. And they provide a continuing source for the many pleasures of friendship itself and doing interesting things together.

But to be candid, some of your friends may distance themselves from you. They feel they can't choose between you and are too uncomfortable with the schism to take sides. Or they may worry that your breakup will highlight strains in their own marriage. Some couples will be upset by your divorce, fearing that their own marriage will fail. As a result, they may avoid spending time with you. So you may discover that some of the people you counted on are not available. Of course you'll feel disappointed, but don't be surprised. There's a great deal of anxiety about divorce in our society, and many people have problems in their marriage.

You may be surprised to find that as a single man or woman (especially woman), you're considered to be a loose cannon in the eyes of many people. You're unattached and this also means to some couples that you may be a threat to their own relationship. This suspicion is not related to your own behavior, which may be entirely innocent, but it does reflect some people's response to your changed role and their concerns about or mistrust of their spouse. For example, there are men who presume that a newly divorced woman is sexually deprived, and they are more than willing to help her out of her distress. This kind of acting out, even if you ignore it or reject the advances out of hand, can affect the course of your earlier friendships with the couple.

Don't be discouraged by my warnings. Your real friends will rally to you. Some will have children who play well with your children. You can all do things together. You may have to indicate that you would welcome the opportunity to be included. You are in need of adult companionship with men and women alike, from divorced and intact families.

Rita, who is a friend of mine, described how friends helped her after her divorce: "I knew a number of single parents," she said. "I made it my business to seek out other single-parent families, mothers and fathers, often parents of my children's friends, to share a dinner, an evening, a vacation. I needed to socialize with adults and this was a good way to do it. Many of these relationships did not outlast the children's friendships, but they served a good purpose for all of us while they lasted. I was also lucky to have a different experience than many single mothers in that my friendships with married couples, especially with the parents of my children's friends, survived the divorce. These friendships were a source of comfort and pleasure for us all. The girls and I were part of a group of five families that socialized and vacationed together. I was the only single parent. It was great in that I wanted the girls to have time with other kids' fathers. The only drawback was that my youngest girl sometimes really missed her dad in these outings where other children had both parents, but overall these were great memories."

Of course, spending time with intact families will inevitably bring up the pain of the breakup for your children. They may envy their friends whose parents live together. Nevertheless, it's important for them to spend time with all kinds of families. It would not be good for them to experience a world in which all or most of the other children come from divorced families. This is a skewed view of life and poor preparation for adulthood.

GOING OUT ALONE

We'll talk about dating later. For now, let's get back to the new you and how you find supports. Many women lose weight after the breakup and they do look better, prettier, and even younger. They buy new clothes and get a new haircut. One woman threw out her entire wardrobe and instantly regretted it. How could she afford to replace the clothes? She solved the problem by going to several fancy resale shops—the kind that sell scarcely worn designer clothes for a fraction of the original price—and buying five outfits.

If you're a woman, the first time you go to a party alone, no matter how well dressed or attractive you are, you may feel like you don't belong. You may try to convince yourself that you are tired and would rather stay home. Don't fall for your own propaganda. Undoubtedly one of the advantages of being married is that you always had someone to arrive and leave with. In some marriages, the man is always delegated to fetch the drinks for both of you. But now you have to master single entrances and single exits. You have to walk in the door without someone on your arm and walk up to strangers and start talking. You may have to introduce yourself. This may be very difficult at first but you'll get better at it, I assure you. Don't give in to the impulse to flee.

One word of warning, though. Beware that you're an easy mark in the sexual marketplace. Some rogues have an ego that says, "This woman isn't getting any sex, so I'll make her feel better." Sexual loneliness is a problem, but think carefully before you leap into someone's arms. A one-night stand with Casanova is not going to alleviate your loneliness.

A man's experience in entering the social scene may be different. If you're a newly single fellow and you're reasonably put together, you'll be anxious the first time you go to a party alone but your anxiety shouldn't last long. You're likely to learn that you look good to women—and nothing is more reassuring. But be careful. If you liked being married (and most men do), you may find yourself bouncing into another serious relationship much too fast. You may like the comforts of home so much that you let the first attractive woman at the party take you home. You may think that she'll make a great stepmother for your kids. All I can say is please take your time, go slowly, and look around. I know a scientist from a leading university who spent four years looking for a second wife. He was shy by nature and hated going out. He said, "I forced myself to go to every event on campus, to accept every party invitation, to put myself in places where I could meet new people. Finally I met the right woman for me."

Class reunions are another good place to renew connections. You'd be amazed at how often people rekindle old crushes from high school or college days. Couples who meet on old home turf begin their friendship with a storehouse of shared memories—laughing at how young and silly they once were but excited at their freedom to reshape their relationship. Several men have told me, "I found the girl that got away. She's recently divorced."

Wherever you go to meet new people, you'll have to overcome your anxiety and reach out with courage. And humor. Ask a man you like for dinner. Say that you have two tickets to the theater, then ask him if he wants to join you. Chances are that after you overcome your own hesitancy, you'll have a splendid time. If you don't, wait a while and ask someone else. The second time will be a lot easier. Just hang in there.

COMMUNITY SUPPORTS

Now look at your list of community resources, for you and your children together and separately.

Where to begin this process? One possibility is to check out organized groups for newly divorced parents. You may find good advice on how to be an effective single parent. Fathers' groups often organize outings for dads and their kids. Many courts and family agencies offer educational programs for children and parents at the time of the breakup. You may find these helpful, especially those run by well-trained professionals. Children can benefit a great deal from the opportunity to be with other kids whose parents are splitting up. They often make new friends and feel reassured in the various group activities and discussions. Some group programs for children and for parents have been highly praised by the participants. You may welcome the chance to meet other parents in the same boat as you. In most programs, couples are divided, so you have an opportunity to independently meet men and women who share your concerns. I've found that men especially like these groups and are willing to listen to what women have to say to them. You may find others, men and women alike, who want to get together after the program for picnics, carpools, and other shared activities. Your children also may want to continue a friendship begun in the group. By all means encourage this.

Find out what programs are available for children in your community. Many school districts offer after-school programs. Community Centers and Y's have many resources. If your child is talented in music, look around for choirs or orchestras that she could join. If sports is their thing, you should investigate athletic programs. There are many art and dance programs that might be especially helpful and interesting to your children at this stressful time. Anything that helps draw their attention away from the family and into organized activities with other children can be very helpful.

This is a good time to turn to your church, synagogue, or any spiritual group that appeals to you. It doesn't matter if you're a regular or a new convert. You can meet people who share your values and who may invite you to their gatherings. Don't make the mistake of leaving your place of worship after your divorce because you feel or think that people are gossiping about you. That may have happened in the not-so-good old days, but in our modern era many people who belong to organized churches divorce. Ministers and rabbis tell me that they're eager to help parents and children during and after divorce, so if your congregation has a program for divorcing families, take advantage of it. Take whatever the group has to offer, and when you feel stronger, take your leave. While such meetings can be helpful in your transition, they are typically not as beneficial if you use them as you would a long-term support group. You don't want to think of yourself as an "ex anything." And you don't want to surround yourself mainly with other divorced people. You're starting a new chapter in your life. Take the first few steps with help from others in your position and then fly on your own.

For example, you might join a theater group, a hiking or tennis club, or a political action association. Get involved in something you like doing. One woman I know became very active in community planning. This led her to take courses in historic preservation, whereupon she found herself in the center of a large network of interesting people and urban problems. Think about taking courses at a community college or adult education center. Maybe go back to school if you never fulfilled a wish to study some subject that fascinates you. No matter how you feel, try to spend time with people who didn't know you before the divorce. They don't carry any baggage about your former identity. But be sure in cultivating new interests that you're genuinely invested in the pursuit. If you join groups only to meet people and have no enthusiasm for what they're doing, it will probably show.

Finally, try to keep in touch with what's happening in your town. Do you like theater, concerts, or dance? Put up a bulletin board at home and list all the activities that you can attend with your children and those that you and a friend could enjoy.

Remember, in all these endeavors, you are the architect of your life. You create the kind of post-divorce family that you think is best for you and your children. The worst recipe is social withdrawal or isolation. It's time for you to reach out to others. If you keep in mind that you're strengthening yourself and enriching your life and the lives of your children, your efforts will pay off in ways you can hardly imagine at the beginning. You need to build a new home with windows that are open to the world, a new self who is moving on.

PART TWO

*

PARENT-
TO-
PARENT

Chapter 15: A New Kind of Parent

T ime was when people divorced they had little or nothing to do with each other afterward. They didn't have to worry about how to get along. No one told them not to fight. It was fairly cut and dry. One person got the kids. The other was free to pursue an independent life.

In the nineteenth century, when children were regarded as property, fathers usually got custody. In the twentieth century, when advances in psychology and psychoanalysis demonstrated the importance of mother-child bonds, mothers usually got custody—especially for children "of tender age," which typically meant younger than seven years old. By the late 1960s, when divorce rates began to escalate, most children after divorce lived with their mothers in sole custody and visited their fathers according to a court-ordered formula.

Now fast-forward a few years. Beginning in the early 1970s, a million children a year were flung into a new demographic category—minors growing up in single-parent households. Unless or until their mothers remarried, huge numbers of children were living full-time in sole maternal custody and visiting their fathers one weekend every two weeks with an occasional afternoon or evening in between. Although many dads maintained this visiting schedule, countless others disappeared from their children's lives. For a while, this was accepted as an unfortunate fact of life: fathers vanish. Many fail to pay child support. Terrible but not surprising. Even fathers who did meet child support and alimony obligations were not expected to maintain a close relationship with their children.

But no more. With the rise of the fathers' movement and the massive entry of women into the workplace, American culture today assumes that mothers and fathers are equally competent as parents. From the court's perspective they're pretty much interchangeable, in terms of both their parental rights and their ability to raise a child. Once again, advances in child development are keeping pace with social change. Mental health experts recognize the role of both parents in child development and assume that, regardless of custody, children benefit from having nurturant relationships with both their mother and father all through their upbringing.

These changes in societal norms and beliefs have made a huge difference in the nature of the post-divorce family. Nowadays, whether you choose sole or joint custody, you're expected to maintain a continuing connection with your ex-spouse on behalf of your children. This is a new and complex coparenting role that is poorly understood. Many husbands and wives still embrace naïve notions about their relationship after divorce. Some assume they won't have much contact. After all, that's why they're getting divorced. They want the other person out of their lives. Others assume that their relationship won't change all that much. They'll resume life as they knew it, only under two separate roofs. But neither of these alternatives is typically in the cards. The long-term relationship between a husband and wife is inevitably transformed at the breakup and during the years that follow. A new relationship is born, and as strange as this may sound, you cannot at the outset predict its shape by looking at the past. A kind, cooperative, and caring relationship can potentially turn into a hateful, pitiless one. A cruel or desperately unhappy relationship can mellow into a benign truce or even a real friendship.

Let me put it in more personal terms. Your divorce is about to hand you a rude awakening. The person you're trying to get away from, the person you want out of your life, will remain an important presence in the new life you hope to carve out. Since you have children, you're yoked until they're grown. Even then, you have to deal with graduations, weddings, baptisms, bar mitzvahs, and all the other rituals of family life. Parental duties survive divorce by many years. Ironically, some parts of marriage really do endure until death do you part.

You have a difficult problem. What kind of relationship are you going to establish with the person who used to share every part of your world and who is now living a separate life? When you got married, you had a pretty good idea of what your relationship would be like. But how should divorced parents relate to each other? Most people don't have a clue. They go about it in their own way, usually without a plan. Some talk frequently, others don't talk at all. Some consider each other their best friend and others won't be in the same room together. Some continue to share a successful business venture that brings them together every day. Others are livid with rage at the mere mention of the other and spend all their resources and their time in furious litigation. And some divorced people still have sex on occasion when one or both are lonely. What you have is a coparenting relationship stripped of the family that held it in place. It's not a friendship. It's certainly not a love affair. It's not a business partnership. Nor is it entirely adversarial. But it partakes of all those relationships. To be totally honest, it is a love-hate relationship in which the two of you are trying to pull away from each other but are held closely together by your love for and commitment to your children.

So here you are, reading this book, trying to figure out what to do. How do you begin this next phase of your life? Let me repeat briefly what I said at the outset. The first step is to complete the divorce beyond the legal paperwork. You and your ex now live in separate places and you share neither bed nor board. But the real divorce happens more slowly as each of you pulls away from the dreams that you shared and the disappointments that you sustained. This is an inner journey that takes years to complete. The trick is to keep your eye on the goal—a coparenting relationship that protects your children and both of you. To begin to disentangle your lives, you need to overcome the hurts, angers, envy, and wretchedness that go with failure. You need to let go of whatever pleasures were in the marriage. People always overlook the good stuff, as if every marriage that fails was gloomy and miserable. Even unhappy marriages have good moments, hours, or years. These need to be mourned before you can rebuild your life. Both of you have lost something important and need to absorb the loss.

You're also angry. The funny thing about post-divorce anger is that once the crisis has passed, anger can go two ways. It can fade or it can get stronger. If your ex is doing well and you are not, your anger increases. If your ex behaves like he or she always did during the marriage, without consideration or elemental courtesy, your anger increases. If your child support is late or inadequate and you're working like a dog to keep things together, your anger increases. If your child is reluctant to visit and your ex threatens to go to court to show that you are poisoning the child's mind, your anger increases, and so on, ad infinitum. These are very common scenarios that go with the territory of divorce. People stay angry for years, sometimes in court and more often on the telephone with friends, family, and children.

But anger, I submit, gets you no closer to justice and makes growing up harder for your children. Brute that he may be, he is still the father of your children. Cheat that she may be, she's your children's mother. You get no brownie points for being right about the faults or failures of your ex. Nor does your ex get lasting demerits for being wrong. Children get bone tired of a quarrel that has no end. Parents who continue to be angry are a source of amazement and shame to their children, who keep wanting to say, "Get over it."

On the other hand, your anger may diminish. If your ex pays adequate child support on time, you will be pleased. If, during a crisis regarding a child's safety or well-being, your ex rises to the occasion, you feel blessed. If your boss calls to say you need to be in Montreal for a conference and your ex says she'll pinch-hit and take the children, your anger lessens. If your ex informs you that he's getting remarried and wants you to be aware of the changes about to occur in your children's lives, you appreciate his thoughtfulness. One woman I know receives a dozen long-stemmed roses from her ex-husband on every Mother's Day. She loves the message and enjoys the flowers. There are many meaningful ways to show your appreciation, all of which can help create friendship and reduce anger.

So what works? People use many strategies, depending on how angry they are. For example, you can act extremely friendly from the start. You can say, "Let's do Christmas just like we used to," or, "Let's get together for Sammy's birthday." The danger in this behavior is that your children are left wondering if you've lost your mind. If you're so congenial, why did you divorce? Moreover, if your cozy feelings are skin-deep, your true feelings will soon show. It's a hypocritical game that fools no one but you.

Another strategy is to act cold and collected, proper and formal, as if you have no feelings. Clenching your jaw can help protect you from feeling hurt or rejected and help control your anger. But as your children get older, they'll get better at reading your true self behind that formal, cool façade. And if you're always an iceberg, it's not likely you'll get the cooperation you may need someday.

You can also move away, although it's not easy to keep your relationships going over long distances. If your job takes you across the country—or just seventy-five miles away—it will be more difficult to stay active in your children's lives. Or you can get so busy with your new marriage that you don't have time for the children you left behind.

Whatever strategy you start out with, keep in mind that you are bound by your love for your children and by the marriage that failed. Play it straight and honest. No anger, no love, no sex—just forgiveness for yourself and if possible for your ex. Forgive yourself for having been so foolish and for wasting all those years in both your lives. If you betrayed your marriage vows, have the decency to apologize and don't brazen it out. Divorce does not wipe the slate clean when you hurt and humiliated the person you promised to love and to honor. If you've behaved irresponsibly, admit it. Do your best to behave more responsibly from this day forward. No-fault divorce is a legal term. There's no such thing in your mind or anyone's mind. In real life there are faults. If you're at fault, the first step is to say you're sorry. It's hard if not impossible to begin successful coparenting without that step. In many divorces, both partners are at fault. If so, acknowledge it. Say so in a note, by e-mail, on the phone, or in person, but get it across. This gives your new relationship a jump start and gets you moving on the right path.

If you can't forgive, and not everyone can, then for heaven's sake try to forget or at least avoid keeping the sins of the marriage foremost in your mind. Lock them away, out of sight. Every time you find yourself obsessing over what happened, feeling sorry for yourself and getting angry again, give yourself a good talking to and stop. Moreover, guilt is a luxury you can't afford. Just put it away along with righteous indignation, along with hurt. Start building the post-divorce relationship with the father of your children or the mother of your children. You have too much to do to look back at what might have been.

If your ex is dangerous to you or your children or continues to try to hurt you, you may have no alternative than to fight to protect yourself and your children. I am not naïve about the possible dangerous residues of divorce. But I'm also convinced that most people are not dangerous or crazy regarding their children's well-being. I've seen many parents who were locked in battle during their divorce come to a peaceful settlement and take on their coparenting roles with sensitivity and creativity. Perhaps you can, too.

Chapter 16: **You and the Law**

Like most law-abiding citizens, you've probably never come into personal contact with our labyrinthine legal system. Most of what you know about the law you've learned from television shows, movies, or best-selling books about corporate crooks or clever sleuths. You share the widespread opinion that our courts, while imperfect, strive to be fair. Jokes aside, lawyers exist to help solve serious problems, including divorce.

I hope that our legal system delivers what you hope to achieve. But I have to warn you that divorce in America is not a simple matter of walking into a courtroom, stating your wishes, and expecting to walk out a single person. From the moment you decide to end your marriage, you're faced with a maze of options regarding how to divide property, provide for ongoing support, set up child custody or visiting schedules, and otherwise separate your lives legally and permanently. The process of disentanglement can take six months or several years, depending on where you live, what you own, and how you decide to cooperate with each other. Moreover, if you think a judge is going to decide who is morally right and who is wrong in your dispute, let me offer you a wake-up call. That is exactly what the judge will not do. Judges base their decisions on statutes and case law, period. They will consider your rights and the interests of your children in reaching a settlement. But they will not consider the morality of who did what to whom.

Let me say at the outset, I am not a lawyer. I am not offering you any legal advice. My goal is to help you navigate the legal system with your eyes wide open, armed with the kind of divorce-specific knowledge you won't get from watching television or going by your sister's experience.

First and foremost, please don't be in a hurry. You may, as the old song says, "want to wash that man right out of your hair," but you have a lot to learn before you commit yourself to any path. Your decisions at this time will shape your family and the life of each child for many years to come. Take plenty of time to find the right people and the best solution for your children and not anyone else's.

WHO WILL REPRESENT YOU?

One of your first decisions involves whom you hire to represent you. Will it be a lawyer or a mediator? If a lawyer, what kind? How will you know how to choose the right person? Is mediation better and, anyway, what do mediators do? What is this method called collaborative law and what does it offer?

Before we tackle the questions, I want to acknowledge the fact that some people decide to dispense with the legal profession altogether and represent themselves. They rely on books, friends, or information from the Internet to "do" the divorce. Maybe they want to save money or they detest the way the legal system seems to turn everyone into Hatfields and McCoys. All I can say is that if you choose to forgo legal advice, beware of the perils that lie in your path. You may have a pretty clear idea about what you want in the next year or so, but it's not likely that you'll know how to negotiate longer-term issues like who pays for college, how to divide pensions, or what happens when your teenager wants to move in with his dad. You're laying the foundation for your post-divorce family, and to do it wisely, you need expert help. At the very least, run a draft of your settlement by a divorce lawyer. It can't hurt and you may be spared some surprises down the road.

Many parents decide to hire a lawyer. But please don't do what several women I know have done, which is to meet a young attorney at a party or at a bar, find him sympathetic, and hire him without looking into his credentials. You want an expert in family law who is a member of the family law section of your local county bar association. If no one you know can recommend such a person, look on the association's roster for a list of names. Then try to interview two or three lawyers before you choose one to work with.

Each lawyer has a distinct personality and set of convictions. Some take the "hold no prisoners" approach to divorce. They're aggressive in matters of money and property. If you have large assets, ask about their experience with big money settlements and the problems they anticipate.

Other attorneys prefer a gentler approach to negotiating divorce. In what I am pleased to say is a growing trend, many have taken the time to learn about child development and the effects of divorce on children over time. But even here, beware. Some lawyers have especially strong opinions about what kind of custody is best for most if not all children. Others are more flexible. I urge you to find a lawyer who will listen to your life story and who wants to find out as much as he can about your individual children. You need to feel that you're working with someone you can trust, who is tuned in to your agenda and who will be available when you need advice but will not attempt to control the decision-making process.

How much will it cost? Many attorneys require a retainer up front. This can sometimes be negotiated. The price, which can vary a lot, doesn't necessarily reflect talent or achievement. Some people are in high demand so they cost more. The most important thing is for you to feel comfortable with the man or woman you choose to represent you.

WHAT DO ATTORNEYS DO?

If you choose an attorney who follows the traditional adversarial method, you will sit down together and decide on all the things you want her to get on your behalf. Your spouse will hire another attorney who does the same for his side. From this point on, the legal system defines you as adversaries. This does not mean that you are enemies or at war with each other. It does mean that you're participating in a legal system in which the two sides are regarded as opposing parties with opposing agendas and priorities. Don't confuse advocacy with anger.

You need to listen carefully to your attorney's advice. You'll be drawing on her expertise to decide financial and legal issues. She'll ask you to anticipate what you think may happen in coming years, including how your children's needs will change when they get older. You may hire a financial consultant if your estate is complicated. You can seek advice from friends, family, mental health experts, your child's teacher, his pediatrician, or others whom you trust. If your child is old enough, you can talk to him about the plans you are considering for him. Some lawyers will tell you not to talk directly to your spouse because that might give away your legal strategy, but the decision is up to you. Keep in mind that you're in charge. You're paying the bill. Some people record conversations with their attorneys to help them remember and mull over advice. Don't hesitate to ask her why she recommends a particular approach, but again, make up your own mind.

During the negotiation, the two attorneys may seek a compromise resolution for your approval. Again, confer with people you trust and decide if you can live with the settlement. If negotiations break down, you may have to go to court and ask a judge to decide your case. But please be careful. This is a risky and costly method. It's risky because family law cases are decided by one person (a single judge with no jury) who is invested with enormous discretion. It's costly in terms of financial and emotional resources. You may be asked to hire mental health experts to evaluate your child and your relationship with your child. This evaluation can be stressful even if you find the evaluator both pleasant and competent. Going to court is a time-consuming method because court calendars are overcrowded and proceedings occur at a glacial pace. Moreover, each case has only a brief time in court.

ALTERNATIVES TO ADVERSARIAL REPRESENTATION

In recent years, a non-adversarial method called divorce mediation has come into vogue. The mediation process involves the two parents coming together with the mediator around a table in an informal way to discuss their respective agendas and share their concerns. The goal is to arrive at a parenting plan that, after each of them consults with an attorney of their choosing, becomes the official document of their divorce.

Many people choose mediation because it's less frightening and less expensive than the adversarial method. Mediators like to call their method win-win, meaning you both win. Of course, in any fair compromise you both have to give up something, but in a larger sense both sides really can win. By maintaining a sense of working together, which is important for your children, you begin to lay the foundation for the many years of coparenting that lie ahead. When people are asked to evaluate their experience in mediation, most comment very favorably on the fairness and understanding of the mediator; most feel that the experience was very helpful. Some long-term studies of mediation show that child support and other agreements are observed longer and more faithfully when they were arrived at in this manner. This may be because mediation begins with the common ground between parents, whereas the adversarial system begins on opposite poles. Mediation is also a more informal process that can take place in an atmosphere of good will. It can be relaxed, pleasant, and far less threatening than the more formal adversarial system.

Because mediators are not licensed or board certified, choosing a mediator is harder than choosing a lawyer. The profession is new. Training is provided by other mediators in a series of courses and workshops. In most states you'll need to find such a person by word of mouth. When you have a few names, you and your spouse should work together to find out what kind of license each candidate has. Ask about their affiliations in professional organizations. Where were they trained in mediation and how long have they been at it? Do they work by the hour or expect a retainer up front? Many mediators are drawn from the ranks of attorneys. Others hold licenses in one of the mental health professions. Some divorce experts believe that parents should turn to a mediator with a background in mental health to mediate child-related issues and a mediator with a legal background to mediate property. Others believe that a well-trained, experienced mediator can deal with both domains and that he will know when to suggest consultation with an expert in law, mental health, or finance.

In the minds of many people, including leading judges and attorneys, mediation represents an important advance for divorcing couples. It's infinitely better suited to dealing with the subtle, emotionally charged issues of divorce in families with children. Of course, it does not work miracles. No system does. Mediation doesn't necessarily protect children any better than attorney-negotiated settlements. Mediators are not required by law or practice to represent children. It still falls entirely on you to represent each child's needs and wishes. Be aware, too, that mediators tend to concentrate on present issues, arguing that long recitations of past offenses interfere with reaching an agreement.

Some women's organizations object to mediation, arguing that if the man has expertise in negotiating business contracts and the woman has none, the discrepancy in business experience will give the man an unfair advantage. It is true that mediation requires a level playing field to be fair to both sides. But a skilled mediator is aware of this problem and regards it as his responsibility to make sure that the less experienced parent is not disadvantaged. He'll be sure that a woman does not out of anxiety yield more than she intended to give up.

If you feel the mediation is out of balance at any point during the proceedings, you can stop the process and ask your spouse to help you look for another mediator. You can also interrupt the process at any time, opt for a lawyer to represent you, and return to the adversarial system. As always, the choice is yours. You are not committed to any method unless it meets your needs.

You are protected in the mediation by the fact that before you sign the mediation agreement, you bring the agreement to your own attorney for review. This is an important step that you should take very seriously. Raise all of your questions during the mediation and repeat any remaining ones when you take the document to your attorney. Be sure you understand what you are getting and what you are giving up. Now is the time to get all your concerns addressed so you can proceed with confidence. It is usually recommended that the reviewing attorney prepare the formal divorce papers based on your mediated agreement.

If there has been violence in the marriage and you are frightened of being in the same room with your partner, it's possible to divide the mediator's time between you so you don't have to confront each other in person. Mediators have experience and training with domestic violence and should understand your need for safety.

COLLABORATIVE LAW

An even newer method called collaborative law is gaining adherents in various parts of the country. In this legal model, each of you engages an attorney and the two agree to meet in a spirit of cooperation. They also agree not to go to court on your behalf. You, your spouse, and your lawyers talk face-to-face around a table and seek a solution that is acceptable to both of you. Sometimes the attorneys call in therapists to work with you and your spouse. The whole team is dedicated to helping you keep the conversation going constructively. A child therapist may be recruited to assess your child and suggest alternative custody arrangements. The therapists teach you communication skills for resolving difficult issues stemming from your divorce. This kind of coaching encourages each of you to express your concerns clearly and calmly—a skill that is very helpful when you're stressed and worried about the future. If negotiations break down, each of you can hire new attorneys to handle the case in a more traditional, adversarial way.

Some attorneys use collaborative law methods in their regular practice. Some mediators also blend these approaches into their daily practice. Altogether you have greater flexibility in negotiating your divorce than you may have realized.

THINGS TO WATCH OUT FOR

No matter who you choose to help you negotiate your divorce, you'll need to keep a few issues in mind. As I said earlier, it's up to you to convey your child's needs to the legal experts who are negotiating your divorce. Your child has no means for direct participation. She is mute, except for the collaborative divorce team model where a child specialist may be hired to speak for your child. I recommend that you discuss the various options before you with any child who is old enough to understand what's happening. Certainly an eight-year-old can understand and a ten-year-old can deal with schedule issues. An adolescent can critique the entire agreement. You can then bring your child's suggestions back to the negotiating table.

If you neglect to consult your children, they'll have good reason to feel that you're ignoring their interests and that they have no influence in shaping their lives. I'm not suggesting that you allow your children to decide their schedule or that you allow them to veto your plans. But I am recommending that you draw them into the process before it's finalized.

Also keep in mind that what works today for your children may not work a year or two from now (this is a theme I will come back to often). Children mature. They develop new interests and needs. You, too, will change and so will your ex-partner. You may change jobs, move your residence, get a job across the country, or marry a man from Sioux Falls or a woman from Paris. Both the expected and the unpredictable changes need to be provided for or else you'll find yourselves back at square one, struggling over where the children should live and who should pay what. Many mediated or negotiated agreements provide for a review mechanism to deal with such changes.

Be prepared to talk about financial issues regarding how assets can be divided and your rights to child support. Much depends on what you own and whether this includes real property, intellectual property, inheritance, pensions, or trust funds. The law varies dramatically from state to state. In fact, the laws peculiar to your state and judgments reached in former court cases will govern your settlement. Here, too, you will benefit from expert financial and legal advice.

Remember to include payment for college tuition in your deliberations. In most states child support stops at age eighteen, although some states have provisions for support during college. Many attorneys and mediators will not raise the issue unless you insist. They often tell clients that if the child has regular contact with a father who is able to afford it, that father will willingly pay for college. But my studies show that many well-educated, professional fathers who are on good terms with their young adult children and have the means to pay college tuition nevertheless refuse to do so. When I ask why, they tell me that they've done their duty in providing child support. After all these years of making sacrifices, why should they be willing to go beyond what is required by law? This is an enormous blow to children whose family aspirations have always included higher education. Because their mothers tend to earn less money than their fathers and can contribute only a small amount to college costs, many children of divorce take out loans or go to community colleges instead of first-rate universities. Some attend alternate semesters so they can work in between. Others simply drop out. They forgo careers in law or medicine because it costs too much. Many say bitterly, "I'm the one who paid for my parents' divorce."

So be sure that who pays for college is written into your agreement at the outset if this is an important family value. By the time college rolls around, many dads have remarried and have more children. Not surprisingly, they feel that their primary obligation is to the younger children in the second marriage who are living with them every day. You don't want your child's education to be a casualty of your divorce.

IF YOU ARE THINKING ABOUT GOING TO COURT

Before we move to the next chapter on to how to negotiate custody, I want to say a bit more about judges—what they can and cannot do. Unfortunately, many judges find themselves caught in the crossfire between combative parents, each with an opposing Greek chorus of attorneys and mental health professionals. These experts recite long testimony about subtle or gross differences between father-child and mother-child relationships. So it's no wonder that many judges are battle weary with the issues brought before them. While experts disagree on these matters, debating and writing scholarly papers for journals, judges don't read those journals. They have no framework for tilting to one side or the other and depend instead on their personal experiences and their legal training, which often fail to shed light on the complex issues that are brought before them.

I say all this because if you expect that you will have an opportunity to tell the details of your case to the judge and that she will understand the injustice of your plight and set things right, you're likely to be disappointed. The divorce court is not charged with adjudicating issues of justice or abstract evil. So if you've been badly hurt or humiliated by your ex or if you are brokenhearted at the shabby way that you've been treated, the court will not heal your wounds. All too often the court assumes that one parent's concern about a particular child custody plan is rooted in anger at the other parent. And sometimes a genuinely worried parent is muzzled. But judges are people. They're appointed or elected to office from the ranks of practicing lawyers. They lack the time and the staff that they need to go deeply into the issues before them.

I know many judges. Some are extraordinary human beings and others are just getting through a day's work like the rest of us. Some judges choose to sit in family court. But many are assigned and find the emotional impact and complexity of divorce cases to be overwhelming. In many courts judges rotate positions, taking turns. When judges are assigned to the family law bench they often have no background in family law. They are likely, in fact, to be new judges who are given the family law bench as their first assignment. You have no say in which judge you will draw.

Finally, as you put your foot on the first rung of the legal process, keep in mind that all the legal tactics in the country can't win the love of a child who feels that he's betraying one parent no matter which way he turns. Few attorneys and not enough parents understand that time spent with a child, especially court-ordered time, counts as nothing in winning the affection and respect of that child. Only a loving parent and a responsive child can create a loving bond. If you want your child's love and loyalty, you have to create it with her. It can't be ordered from the outside by the court or by anyone else. Nor can anyone take it away.

Most parents are genuinely interested in their children but fail to realize that angry competition between them is harmful to children. They don't realize that it's very difficult for a child to love two parents who are at war. So if you want your child to love you, and of course you do, you have to allow her the opportunity to love her other parent as well. There's no alternative other than having her reject you both. And believe me, some children do just that. Also have some faith in your child's ability to form her own opinions about each of you. All children arrive at judgments about what they got from each parent or what they failed to get. You cannot control what she thinks and feels about each of her parents. You can only contribute to her feeling that you love her and that you did your best.

I remember I once asked a four-year-old what work her mother did. "Oh," said the child sweetly, "she does the best she can." Surely, there is no greater and no more realistic praise for a parent.

Chapter 17: Laying the Foundation for Custody and Coparenting

Your first major decision concerns what kind of custody arrangement you want for your child. Bear in mind that each custody decision, whether sole or joint, and regardless of what you are told, bestows a benefit and exacts a price from each parent and each child. A plan that benefits your children might be difficult for you. Or a plan that benefits you might overburden your children. A plan you like might be unacceptable to your ex. This is heartbreaking, but it goes with the territory of divorce.

At this juncture, both of you need to decide what is best for your child now and how to accommodate future changes. This is very hard to do when your own plans are not firm, you're overwhelmed, and you've no idea of what the future will bring to you in terms of finding a new job, much less a new mate. But keep in mind that a plan you may consider temporary today will, in the eyes of the court, probably become the permanent plan. If you lock in an inflexible custody plan that's supposed to hold until the youngest child is eighteen, you may live to regret it. Of course, you have the freedom to change an agreement at any time after divorce if you both agree. But if one of you balks, you'll probably be facing the expensive and emotionally exhausting move of going back to court, where you and your child may win or lose.

A thousand and one examples come to mind. Now that you're getting a divorce, you may be tempted to take a job that engages your talents and puts you on the career ladder that you always wanted to climb. Perhaps this job demands a move to a distant city. It may require you to work seventy or eighty hours a week or go on many business trips. But this will deprive your children of your company just when they need it most. In addition, you must consider if your ex will agree with your move or might contest it in court. Keep in mind that your impulse to move far away may not be the best plan for you, either. The stress you feel will accompany you wherever you go.

Another option is to stay in the community where your children have been raised until now. This may be the small town of Dullsville that contributed to your decision to divorce or a town or city that you are happy with. In either case, your children may benefit from the continuity and stability if you remain. Perhaps their grandmother lives around the corner. Certainly their friends live nearby. But if you know every man and woman in Dullsville and you're no longer content to be there, your choices in terms of seeking a new partner or a new life will be limited. You have new wings and you want to use them. What should you do?

HOW TO MAKE A PARENTING PLAN

The earlier you put your conflicting interests on the table—before your lives change—the better. You need to try to think of how you'll solve your conflicts when they arise. To begin, assuming enough good feeling remains, you and your ex need to sit down together and start talking. Your attorneys may want to be present, to protect your interests. Consider bringing in an expert in child mental health. Many people do. This conversation is really about how you both, as loving parents, think about ways to protect your children.

Your goal is to draw up a so-called parenting plan. In many states you will be asked to follow guidelines for what goes into the plan—details on medical and health care, insurance, education, residence, and religious training if it is important to one of you. In other states, the plan is more ad hoc. In either case, the parenting plan becomes a legal document when it is submitted to the court. So be sure you give it careful thought. Often coparenting arrangements evolve out of nowhere or by compromise that may not be good for the child. I cannot tell you how often I've heard comments like, "My husband wants Brendan to go live at his house every other week. I think Brendan should stay full-time with me and visit his dad every weekend. So we compromised and decided to split each week." In this "compromise," each parent's wishes or whims are met while no one seriously discusses the initial or long-term consequences for Brendan. Some plans center on only one issue—how many days a child will spend in each home—or are based on what is fashionable in a particular court at a particular time.

A common pattern is for each parent separately to tell each lawyer what they have in mind. The two lawyers then negotiate a parenting plan and custody agreement based on compromise. But this can be a slippery slope. Since your lawyers don't know you, your ex, or your children, they don't have the full story. Their methods are modeled after two faceless leviathan corporations battling it out in court. But your family is not two corporations. You have separate interests that divide you, but you also have strong interests that unite you in your children.

QUESTIONS TO ASK YOURSELF

If you and your soon-to-be ex can communicate reasonably well and you trust each other, begin by meeting on neutral ground and by saying what you both want for the children. You can do this with the help of a mediator or in the presence of your two attorneys. What can you agree on and what can you not? What are your goals for your children? What values do you still share? How important is contact with grandparents and other family members? Do you expect that they will go on to college or graduate school? Do you have a special school in mind? Does your child have special needs in education? For example, does she suffer with a disability that requires special schooling? Does she need medical or psychological care? Is she highly talented in dance, music, gymnastics, or some other specialized field that requires advanced training? Does your child want to continue training with a favorite coach or teacher?

Then talk about the issues that involve the children over the next few years, such as where they will go to school. If they have been in private school, who will pay for it? If they have to change schools, what is the best choice? If you each want to raise your children in a different religion, this is not as big a deal as you may think. In my experience, children adapt to two faiths, saying my mom is this and my dad is that. It may be hard for you to accept, but it is not hard for them. (If you really want to bring up a child as a devout Hasid, don't divorce.) You can also agree on how to make sure that your children maintain contact with both sets of grandparents and other family members.

The nitty-gritty of this meeting is to figure out where your children will thrive. I recommend that you consider several plans and then figure out how each would play out in your life and in the lives of your children. Has one of you been largely responsible for raising the children? Is this an arrangement that you wish to continue?

Consider the workplace. What will happen if both of you have full-time jobs? Who has the more flexible job? Who can be home after school? Can one of you work part-time or work at home? Can you look for a different job that would give you more time to care for the children?

Another set of questions centers on possible moves. Does either of you have immediate plans to remarry? Would this likely involve a move to another part of the country? If you had an intermarriage, consider carefully together how you can maintain each cultural tradition after divorce. It can be done. But it surely won't happen if each of you just goes ahead without considering the influence of the other. All these issues require clarification and compromise, because the spirit in which they are implemented is critical.

At this point, end the meeting by making no promises and no commitments. Both of you look for information about the legal and financial implications of each plan you devised. This is a good time to seek professional help or to consult with your attorney if she was not present at your meeting. You need legal and financial advice. You may also want psychological advice about your child, especially if he has special needs. Because sole custody and joint custody provide different amounts of child support, you need to talk about the pros and cons. Find out the facts. Ask friends and family members what works for their children and what unforeseen problems and benefits they encountered. Heed their experience but don't take it as a prophecy for what will happen to you.

As we talked about earlier, if your children are old enough to attend school, you should gently run each plan by them. Tell them that you had a meeting, these are some plans you have in mind, and do they have anything to add? Did you overlook anything important to them? If there's a difference of opinion about division of time, give each child a week's calendar with three colored crayons. Ask them to fill in how they would want to spend their week—red for Mom, blue for Dad, yellow for time for themselves and with their friends. Tell them you will include their drawing in your discussion and thank them for their very grown-up efforts to help you. But make clear that they have a voice, not a veto.

If you want your children to feel strong, confident, and independent, you need to begin here, with planning the post-divorce family, so that each child is heard and respected. I bring this up because adult children of divorce complain bitterly that no one paid attention to their wishes when they were young. In most intact families, older children are encouraged to speak their mind about how they want to spend their weekends, whether they want to attend summer camp, which activities they want to pursue. If they're required to pay a visit to Grandma when they don't want to, negotiations occur: "We'll visit Grandma and then go to the movies." Americans encourage their children to have opinions and to be independent. Inculcating a sense of responsibility in the child is possible with a parent who listens carefully and respects the child's thoughtful response.

But children of divorce are often told that they must go visit their father or mother on such and such days. It's not negotiable. If they want to take part in the school play and rehearsals and performances require them to be available on weekends, and they have to go to their dad's house on weekends, they cannot be in the play. When children are deprived of a voice in how they spend their time, they end up feeling powerless. They complain, "I'm a second-class citizen just because my folks divorced. My girlfriends can spend their summers at soccer camp or joining a special music program, but I have to be with one of my parents."

Even young children can participate in making plans that will comfort them. For example, one little boy was greatly confused at the end of nursery school each day. He couldn't remember who was going to pick him up, Mommy or Daddy. Finally he suggested that on the day Daddy picked him up he should carry a blue lunch box and on the day Mommy came to get him he should carry a red lunch box. Once this was done, his teacher reported that he was vastly relieved—and his parents realized that he could help them create a parenting plan that met his needs.

COMMUNICATING AND TRUSTING

The key to successful coparenting is reasonably good communication. This goes with some modicum of trust. Is your ex boring as a husband but trustworthy as a father? Is she a nag of a wife but a reliable mother? Do you trust this person's commitment to your children? If you have reason to trust, you're in clover and can proceed. But do so with caution and only with legal guarantees. Feelings often change rapidly after divorce and especially after remarriage. So can a sense of commitment that's sincerely felt at the time of the breakup. The essence of this trust is not related to marital fidelity but to the other person's commitment to be a good parent. Be advised that they are not the same, but they are not entirely unrelated.

If few good feelings have survived the breakup—you feel she's capricious or he's erratic, both of you feel that the other is unreliable or delinquent and that you can't believe a word this person says—you need to decide your bottom line. What are you willing to sacrifice and what is not negotiable? And how best can you protect your child?

If you don't feel comfortable coparenting with your soon-to-be ex, there's a middle ground called parallel parenting. Some couples are able to handle an agreement that calls for minimum contact between them. Each of you conducts your own relationship with your child and arranges programs fully on your own time and turf. You do not consult. But you are able to work side by side without intruding on each other's turf. This can work if people are consistent about schedules and are able to abide by the rules. In a way, parallel parenting is more like a business relationship that safeguards your independence.

The disadvantage of parallel parenting is that it will be more difficult to address differences in your two homes when they arise. If you and your ex are not talking regularly, your children may have trouble adjusting. You may need to bring in therapists and mediators more often.

If you feel that you cannot communicate about mundane details like when to pick up your child without one of you flying off the handle, then you need a legal agreement that holds you both to a clear schedule. The children get picked up at five o'clock on Friday and dropped off at five o'clock on Sunday. Such an agreement, which can be negotiated by attorneys, mediators, or ordered by the court, provides the external controls that you and your ex-partner may need.

Sometimes the act of negotiating or mediating such an agreement raises or clarifies issues that one or both of you may not have considered. For example, what happens if a parent is called away when the children are scheduled to be with him or her? How is time off from school handled? Some jobs do not have predictable schedules. How should changes in the schedule be handled? And most of all, what if one parent fails to show up as expected? All of these issues need to be built into the arrangement so that backup plans are worked out before an emergency occurs.

A strict agreement and adherence to parallel parenting can not only help limit the amount of time that you come into contact with each other but also help the children know exactly when each of you will arrive and depart. This arrangement can help a partner who was a doormat in the marriage not get walked over in the post-divorce family. It can require a former Napoleon to obey the rules. It can provide an opportunity for a parent who was absent during the marriage to take a more active role in the post-divorce family. For all of these contingencies you need to inform your attorney so she knows what is a priority for you. But even in these strict agreements you have to allow flexibility for change as circumstances change or the child gets older. The best way to protect your child is to consider his needs as he grows.

Keep in mind that all schedules including court-ordered or mediated schedules are regularly breached. Inevitably people come late or early. They are delayed by business or traffic. Or a parent may deliberately violate an agreement to vent anger at the restrictions that the schedule imposes. People who are angry at the breakup are likely to be angry at the schedule and whoever they think devised it.

If your spouse is late or does not call or does not return your children at the agreed-upon time, try your best to allow for human error before you conclude that the delay is deliberate. And even if it is deliberate, you can't go back to court each time the children come home late. You can expect to feel tensions when your children are picked up and dropped off. This is part of the post-divorce experience. It occurs in every custody arrangement. It may be a terrible nuisance but it's probably unavoidable. Unless your child is in danger of being harmed or kidnapped, there is little you can do or should do.

THE CONTINUING NEGOTIATION

As I mentioned earlier, many parents expect that the custody plan they have chosen will define their post-divorce family for many years. Facts show otherwise. Seventy-five percent of divorced men remarry, many within one or two years of the divorce. Around 50 percent of women remarry, although it generally takes them longer. Moreover, second marriages break up at the fearsome rate of 60 percent. So the custody arrangement that you set up now may be entirely unrealistic at a later time. Considering the financial and emotional cost of making all these arrangements, this should give you pause.

For this reason, I suggest that when you decide on custody, you set a time to meet again to review changes that have occurred in your family. If you have a baby or toddler, I think you should meet after two years. Young children change so fast that what you decided for a two-year-old may not work for a three-year-old. While your two-year-old may have had trouble separating from you, he may at age three be ready to charge into preschool with hardly a wave good-bye. While he was more comfortable living solely with you at age two, now he might benefit from spending a couple of nights each week with his dad.

If your children are older, you should plan to meet every four to five years to reexamine custody issues. Four years roughly coincides with significant developmental change. A nine-year-old has different priorities from a thirteen-year-old, and so on. You can safely invite any child over age twelve to sit in on your custody update meeting to get her view of what is and is not working. It's important to respect the stability of the post-divorce family. I'm not suggesting that you change custody every few years. Rather I am saying that you should consider changes in your children's schedules. These kinds of changes happen automatically within intact families.

The risk of such a meeting is that it will reopen old wounds. The resolution that you and your former spouse hammered out might disintegrate. But if you confine the agenda to look at how the schedule is working or not working and how each child is doing, you'll go a long way toward helping your children. If you think it's a good idea, include the mediator or attorneys who helped you at the breakup. Or bring along a mental health professional whom you both trust. In some families, one child might be fine in the custody arrangement while a sibling is suffering. Children have different needs to be with one or the other parent at different times during their growing-up years. You are not bound to have the same schedule for each child. Your youngest child might temporarily need a different schedule than her older siblings. Consider the needs of each child individually, but realize, too, the value of keeping brothers and sisters together if you can.

With the risk of sounding like a broken record, I want to stress that you really need to think about the fact that after a certain age, your kids don't want to spend their free time with either of you. Your eleven-year-old wants to go to the mall with her friends. She wants her mom's credit card or a ride from her dad but doesn't want either one of you in tow. She's hanging out. That's the joy of being eleven years old. The dating scene, school activities, sports, and music consume her time and interest at age fourteen. She doesn't want to spend all that time with you dictated by visiting or joint custody orders. She certainly doesn't want to spend a whole summer with you when she can do much more interesting things with friends. She wants the freedom to be an American teenager, the envy of the world. Few children growing up in intact families spend lots of time with their parents unless they're together as part of a family outing or attending a particular event. Kids hang out with kids, not parents.

One more thing bears repeating: as good parents, you can renegotiate schedules at any time. You don't have to wait one year or four years, and you don't need to go to court or even to a mediator. The two of you can just meet. You can sit down with a friend, minister, rabbi, or relative you trust. You can turn to a therapist to discuss your needs and your children's needs if you can trust each other. You're not obligated to do what other people say unless you are fighting. Parents who fight relinquish their power as parents. Parents who work together maintain their power as parents.

Chapter 18: Custody

One of the most important decisions you are about to make—what kind of custody to choose for your children—is also one of the most confusing.

To begin, you need to understand two key definitions in describing custody. Physical custody refers to where your child lives; it can be with one or both of you for whatever division of time you determine. Legal custody refers to who makes the major decisions in your child's life; it can be one or both of you for all major decisions or it can be both of you only for certain major subjects. That said, hold on to your hat. Judges, lawyers, and parents tend to mingle and mangle the definitions in ways that confuse even the most seasoned experts.

For example, in some courts sole physical/legal custody where the child lives most of the time with the mother is called joint custody because the father visits. Strictly speaking it is not. In joint legal custody, a child can live full-time with his mom and rarely see his dad, who may live in a distant country. In another joint legal custody home, a child can live with his mom and see his dad every day. People make of these custody labels whatever they want.

One reason for the confusion is that we're witnessing a quiet revolution in America in which parenting roles are getting blurred. Fathers from intact and divorced families are more involved than ever in raising their children. One small sign of this big change, which many women don't know about, is that men's rooms all across the country now have diaper changing tables. More about changed roles later.

The fact is, many families start out with one form of custody and then, as the children grow older and have different needs, schedules change while the custody label remains the same. One major study found that a third of children in physical joint custody—meaning they lived part-time with Dad and part-time with Mom—gravitated to their mom's home within two or three years after the breakup. Again, in most of these families the custody label did not change.

One key thing to keep in mind at the outset is that you don't need to go back to court to change custody if all you want to do is rearrange your child's schedule. You can change the living arrangements any time you agree to do so.

Let me try to sort out the confusion about custody by describing the most common patterns. In the end, you'll shape one of these arrangements to the needs of your child and to your liking. What matters is what you decide, not what you call it.

SOLE CUSTODY

In sole custody children live primarily with one parent after the breakup. Traditionally this has been the mom. Dads visit according to an agreed-upon schedule. Many women expect to have sole custody of their children because it continues the kind of child-rearing that was in place before the divorce. Some men want their children to be raised by their ex-wives. Others don't want children underfoot or don't feel able to provide a real home for their children. Others just assume that the mother is the child-raising parent. Of course, some men spend a lot of their time traveling for their work or going to places in the world where it would not be suitable to bring up children. And finally, many have selected new partners who do not welcome the former wife's children in their homes and are eager to limit the contact.

Nevertheless, a growing number of men are raising children in sole custody and are doing a splendid job. They make the same kinds of sacrifices that single women have always made—coming home tired after a day's work, preparing meals, putting children to bed, doing the laundry and other necessary household tasks, and falling into bed. They suffer with similar complaints such as exhaustion and sundry physical symptoms including joint and back pains. One dad I know groused that the kids' clothes were not returned or came back dirty from visits with what he called their "good-time mom." But single-parent dads also speak with excitement and pride about their children. Single parenting is, by any standard, a triumph no matter who does it.

In traditional sole custody, one parent is primarily responsible for setting the overall climate of the child's upbringing, including residence, schooling, discipline, medical decisions, and the like. The sole custodian can, of course, consult the other parent regularly as she sees fit. The visiting parent gets to spend a lot or a little amount of time with the child—it's really up to both parents to decide—and can have certain rights in making decisions that are usually specified at the outset. This might include religious training, some aspects of education, or diet— whatever the couple agrees on. In many families fathers are routinely invited to parent-teacher conferences along with mothers who have sole custody.

Children raised in sole custody enjoy many benefits, including a stable home, a constant group of friends in one community, and a greater sense of continuity in their daily lives. Because their routines are not interrupted as often as children who shuttle between two neighborhoods, they have more opportunities to pursue activities and interests that require uninterrupted presence, such as certain sports, music, and drama groups. They can develop close and loving relationships with their dads on visits. In fact, the schedules of many children in sole custody overlap with those that are termed joint custody. Sole custody does not mean that a father never gets enough time to be with his children. Visits can run as long as you both decide, and the children can spend as many overnights with their dads as you decide is appropriate.

Fathers who manage to make their visits interesting and enjoyable for their children and themselves say that they're very content with sole custody. To help in this, they speak with their ex-wives frequently to get updates on each child's life or they're in direct touch with older children via phone or e-mail. What movie would Maya like to see? Does Alex want to go to the ball game and bring his two best friends? Should Mom or Dad get tickets for the circus? I know one dad who helps his daughter with her math homework every night via AOL instant messaging. Another takes his children hiking on most Sundays. Others get absorbed just sitting on the floor playing with their younger children, telling stories or going on trips to the playground, swimming pool, or zoo.

The main danger in sole custody is that fathers, unlike those with joint physical custody, tend to drift away. Some can't figure out how to bring off the role of visiting dad. How does one maintain a relationship with one's children outside the family structure? A father can become uneasy about who he is and how much authority he has—especially if there's a stepfather in the home. He has a hard time figuring out whether his job is to entertain the children, to involve the children in the routines of his own household, to assist with homework, or what. Despite the fact that fathers have been encouraged to maintain their relationships with their children after divorce, they've received very little guidance from anyone about how best to do this. Educational programs for parents rarely address this important issue. When fathers remarry— and three out of four divorced men do, with new children arriving— maintaining the role of visiting dad becomes more demanding. How to divide time between two families is confusing and difficult to manage. Finally, some fathers blame their ex-wives for discouraging the children's interest in their visits.

My advice to all you fathers whose children are in sole custody with their moms is fairly straightforward. Being a father outside the structure of the family, especially when you and perhaps your ex-wife are remarried, requires redefining your paternal role. You are neither Santa Claus nor a playground director. You do not need to fall all over yourself to entertain your children when you see them. Nor are you a favorite uncle or pal. Try to relax and enjoy your children. Greet them warmly. Do fun things together. Teach them skills they can use on the playground. Build back-yard structures together. But keep in mind, first and foremost, you're their one and only real dad. Your task is to serve as a model for their present and future behavior. You are responsible along with their mother for teaching them right from wrong and how to learn to obey the rules of the games they play and the greater rules of courtesy and civil society. As a dad, you want to engage them to tell you about their schoolwork and friends. If they have troubles, you want them to consult you. You want them to think of you as being available and a very good listener.

More suggestions: Encourage your children to bring their homework along on visits so you can look at it and help. Tell them about your own work and how you, too, have deadlines like the ones they have at school. Your children should be able to observe you at work, not only at play. They should know what you do. If your children are school age, encourage them to bring along best friends during visits, especially if you're going someplace special. Enjoy all the kids and realize that the friend's parents may reciprocate one day by inviting your child to join their family on a special outing. During the first few months after your divorce, try not to invite an adult friend along for the visits. You want your son or daughter to think of their time with you as special and privileged, devoted just to them. Children of divorce who feel they have priority in their dad's eyes are greatly protected. If your daughter tells you or her mom (because she wants to spare your feelings) that she would prefer to go to choir practice or even to the mall with her girlfriends, or your son tells you that he wants to practice his drums for his new rock combo or has to work on a delayed school assignment on the days of your visit, don't act rejected. Don't give them a hard time about it and don't blame their mom. There is, I submit, no child in America who is always eager to spend time with his parent, either his dad or his mom. By the same token don't encourage your children to complain about their mom. If they have complaints, be sympathetic the way you would if you were still married, but encourage them to take the issue up directly with their mother.

If you're a mother with sole custody, you will feel that you have greater control over your children's lives. The disadvantage is that you're fully responsible for what happens to your children and that you're on duty most of the time. During the expectable crises of your child's growing-up years, you must often act alone. If you remarry, you have greater latitude in many states to move away or make other changes in the family. But you're still bound to assure adequate time for visiting with their dad. In other words, in sole custody, mothers and fathers are freer to go their separate ways and to build separate, new lives. If one parent is a troubled person or just a disinterested parent, sole custody with the healthier or more committed parent can better protect children from being physically or emotionally harmed.

I discuss how to think about choosing custody in Chapter 20 but can say here that generally speaking, sole custody is better for the kinds of vulnerable children I talked about earlier. It may be too much to ask a disabled child to negotiate two different homes and two different environments. Any and all change can be exhausting and baffling. A stable arrangement with either father or mother is much more comforting and is more likely to provide a consistent environment. The custodial parent will of course need periodic relief, which the other parent can provide. But it's better in these situations to maintain the stability of one home. Sole custody may also be preferable during vulnerable periods in a child's life.

JOINT LEGAL CUSTODY

Parents with joint legal custody agree to share equally in decisions regarding their child's education, religion, place of residence, health, and any other issues specified by their parenting plan. In some jurisdictions all divorcing couples are routinely assigned joint legal custody. In other places both parents must request it. In still other courts, one person's request is sufficient.

Joint legal custody by itself has no bearing on where the child lives. It only refers to how the decisions affecting the child are to be made. As in sole custody, the children in joint legal custody can divide their time between Mom and Dad in many ways.

Interest in joint legal custody reflects the conviction of many people, including some judges and attorneys, that if a father and mother have equal authority for making decisions about their children, the father is more likely to pay child support regularly, in full and on time, and stay more involved with the kids. Actually, studies differ on this point. Some find a connection between payment of child support and joint legal custody; others do not. In general, payment of child support is related to whether a father holds a full-time job, whether he has the funds to pay, and whether there are effective enforcement methods in place.

JOINT PHYSICAL CUSTODY

Joint physical custody, also referred to as dual residence, is a relatively new family form where the children live in two homes, one with Dad and one with Mom, shuttling back and forth within any given week, month, or year. Typically both parents are expected to share equally in the rights and responsibilities of parenthood. The popularity of joint physical custody varies across the country. In some more affluent areas of California, 20 percent of children are in this custody arrangment. In other states, the number hovers around 5 percent. Figures are difficult to come by because there are hardly any studies that compare incidence of different forms of custody in different states across the country, and the courts don't keep complete records. Based on informal conversations with mental health colleagues, lawyers, and judges, my sense is that this form of custody is growing more popular, especially among two-career couples.

While it's not a substitute for a reasonably well-functioning intact family, joint custody does more closely approximate the intact family by providing ongoing contact with both parents, although separately. What's more, it captures the new wave of fathers who appreciate how important they are to their children. Many men truly love being fathers and fully expect to continue their close relationship with their children after divorce. This may be one of the most beneficial outcomes of the divorce revolution. Thus joint custody is built on the contemporary view that men and women are interchangeable as parents and that the growing child benefits from the continued contact and nurturant relationship that occurs from living with both parents. Some people go even further, arguing that divorce hurts children entirely because they lose contact with their fathers. If that loss can be avoided, the only threat that divorce poses to the child will be eliminated. By and large, studies do not support this sweeping opinion, although losing a father is a severe, potentially lifelong blow for any child.

There is no scientific evidence that the general psychological adjustment of children is related to any particular form of custody. According to studies done at our Center that followed children in sole and joint custody for two years, and other studies done elsewhere, the amount of time spent with either parent is not relevant to the child's well-being. Rather, the psychological health of the child and of both of the parents, the quality of the child's relationship with each parent, and the relationship between the parents are key factors in the child's emotional and social adjustment after divorce. In general, more affluent families tend to ask for joint physical custody. It costs more to support a child who divides her time between two homes. Also it may be easier for professionals to arrange their own schedules than it is for hourly workers. Thus these children, compared with many youngsters in sole custody, may have advantages of wealth and education and more reliable child support. These are important to the child's welfare but they are related to social class, not custody.

In any case, what affects "most" or "many" children may not be relevant to the decision that you make. You need to consider what suits your child, your family, and you. You need to think about your child's age, inner sense of security, attachment to each of you, temperament, flexibility in adapting to change, and social adaptability—and, if he's old enough, his preferences. As for you and your ex, you need to think about your respective jobs, schedules, availability, and interest in parenting, the attitudes of your respective new partners, your ability to communicate and cooperate with each other in the details of your child's life, and the geographical distance between your two homes.

Another reason for increased interest in physical joint custody needs noting. In California and some other state courts, child support is calculated according to how much time a child spends in each parent's home. Since most child support goes from fathers to mothers, a time-sharing policy has financial implications. When a child spends a substantial amount of time in his father's home, the amount the father pays monthly is reduced. This is regarded by some as an incentive for fathers to request joint physical custody.

How does joint physical custody work? For starters, joint custody does not mean that your child's time will be divided precisely in half—three and a half days with Mom and three and a half days with Dad. Sometimes it works that way, but more often a child's time is divided by a two-thirds to one-third formula—twenty days with one parent, ten days with the other. This division of time works well for two-career couples who need to accommodate their work schedules with parenting. Indeed, many parents tell me this is the main reason they chose joint custody. You can also divide time according to months or years. January with Dad, February with Mom, and so on. Or 2003 with Mom and 2004 with Dad. The principal idea is that both of you remain equally responsible for your child's schedule and for all decisions taken on his behalf. When joint custody works well and a child is asked where he resides, he will ideally say, "I have two homes," giving preference to neither.

Joint physical custody requires careful planning by both of you. You want your child to feel that he has two homes, not just two places to sleep. He needs your help to make this happen. He needs a safe, permanent place to keep his all important "stuff" so his toys and hobby supplies don't get tossed out or raided by other people in the household, especially stepsiblings who live there full-time. He needs clean clothes and a closet in each home to store seasonal changes. He appreciates a wall or part of a wall for posters of rock stars or athletes. He needs a reasonably quiet place to do his homework, a desk to store his work, and access to a computer. As he gets older, he may have even more expensive equipment—a bicycle, a tennis racket or other sports gear, CDs or a stereo. In sum, the joint-custody child needs space in each home where he feels comfortable and where he can return without having it violated. The goal of providing protected space that is used only part-time may be difficult to achieve in crowded households or where one parent has a huge house and the other a tiny apartment.

Transportation is another problem. Some items can be carried back and forth. Others, like bulky musical instruments, may be too heavy or too unwieldy for a child to carry, especially on a bus. If your child is expected to practice the piano every day, you'll need two pianos. This means that joint physical custody can be expensive unless you can find a place where your child can practice conveniently. Children want and need two of everything that cannot be schlepped back and forth. And when a kid leaves his winter jacket at one home for the seventh time, it may be easier on your nerves to buy him a second one for the second home. It beats trying to get him to remember.

If you've agreed to joint physical custody, I recommend that you engage your child as a partner in setting up his special place in each home. Obviously a preschooler can participate minimally, but even young children should have some role in selecting a part of the new home. You want him to feel that he helped create it. An older child will likely be pleased and flattered to be consulted. Pets are a problem that you should take seriously. Obviously, you can't expect your child to carry a rabbit back and forth. One of you has to take care of the rabbit when your child is away. But then it behooves you to assure your child that the pet is in good hands. Many children are sleepless with worry that the animal will be forgotten or neglected or be dead when they return. Problems like these go with the territory of providing two homes for your child.

You can help in other ways. At least one of your child's new homes may be in an unfamiliar neighborhood. Finding new playmates in a strange environment is a formidable and even terrifying challenge for many children. You can help by scouting out the neighborhood first. Mosey around and find out where families with children live and how old the children are. Talk to neighbors. Where do the children play? Is the community safe for children? Is traffic a problem? Is there a park? Is there a community center with after-school programs? Are there Little League games or Cub Scouts or Brownies? Is there an ice cream store or a grocery? Where is the bus stop? How far is the school and how does the child get there and get back? Walk around the neighborhood yourself and then with your child in a leisurely way, pointing out what you've discovered. Your child will find your sensitivity to his concerns reassuring and immensely helpful.

And, of course, talk with your child. Discuss his current schedule and how it might change. Will he be able to continue his activities if he lives in two separate homes? Will he enjoy living with each of you during one week or would he prefer changing his residence every other week or perhaps not at all? He'll have many questions. You should welcome them and encourage him to raise his concerns now, before you sign the legal agreement.

Finally, for joint physical custody to get up and running, you and your ex have to talk with each other relatively comfortably. Consider sharing a babysitter to make for greater continuity. I knew a couple with a fourteen-month-old baby who hired a nanny to move back and forth between homes along with the baby. Set up an easy-to-follow schedule. Children can get confused about which home to go to after school. Make a wall chart. Remind your child in the morning where to go in the afternoon. You have to be willing and able to accommodate your own preferences to create a relatively harmonious environment. You don't have to set each household up as a clone of the other, but you will need to set up guidelines that include the following issues and then some.

A child cannot have an eight o'clock bedtime in one home and a ten o'clock bedtime in the other. His sleep will be disrupted. A child cannot have all the junk food he wants in one home and be kept to a rigorous diet in the other. He will refuse to eat the good food. A child cannot have unlimited TV in one home and strict limits in the other. You will never hear the end of it. A young child cannot be toilet trained at age two in one home and at three in the other. He will be totally bewildered by the mixed messages. A child cannot sleep in a parent's bed in one home and in his own bed in the other. He will be up all night.

To avoid conflict in joint custody, you need to agree ahead of time what the rules will be in each home. Sometimes you can compromise. Sometimes you can't. Often there is no halfway. Moreover, there's no way to anticipate the many new situations that will arise. For joint physical custody to work, you need the willingness and the capacity to bow to each other cordially or even gracefully to maintain the dual ongoing household that works for your child and for each of you. Can you cooperate with each other without anger? Can you capitulate without loss of face? If you cannot communicate or learn to do so, then joint physical custody is not in your child's interests or yours. In a nutshell, it provides endless opportunities for hurtful confrontations.

Joint physical custody will keep you more closely connected to your ex-partner than sole custody. This could be painful if your jealous, angry, or loving feelings for your ex are still unresolved. Even without asking, you'll overhear your child's innocent chatter about what goes on in your ex's household. If your former wife is dating your best friend or if your former husband is involved with a person you distrust, you'll hear all about it. I recall one mother whose patience ran out when her young daughter described the nudity in her father's household. In joint custody there is greater opportunity to relive the pain and grief of the breakup, more stimulus for flashbacks to the pleasures and disappointments of your marriage, more room for rage and jealousy to rise. Joint physical custody may keep you more closely connected than you can stand. Since your emotional comfort is important to your ability to raise your child well, think about these issues before you cast your vote.

Like sole custody, joint physical custody has advantages and disadvantages for each family member. If you take a look at children who are thriving under this form of custody, they say that they prefer it because they get to spend time with both parents. They enjoy lots of contact with Mom and Dad and feel integrated in two families. These kids are fortunate when they have moms and dads who set aside time for them when they come home. They especially love an arrangement that enables them to bike back and forth easily on their own. By and large, children who like joint custody attend only one school and have succeeded in establishing a circle of friends in both neighborhoods. Often their parents live within a few blocks of each other. Some children handle twice weekly bus or subway rides with aplomb and are rightly proud of their achievement. Others are fortunate in being driven around by familiar sitters. When I interview these contented youngsters, I'm struck by their independence and maturity. They say honestly that although divorce was not their first choice they're willing to put up with the sacrifices of going back and forth because the rewards are so high. They recognize the sacrifices made by each parent. One ten-year-old told me, "It's not the best. But it's the best they can do."

The downside for children is difficult for many adults to grasp, especially those who idealize the arrangement and have not talked candidly with children. The truth is that for some children, joint custody is burdensome. They feel disorganized and scattered with their clothes and books and assignments spread between two homes. I know several preschool children who, upon returning from a visit to their father's home, went around their mother's apartment touching each object to make sure it was still there. They touched their bed, their bureau, and the toy animals they left behind. They had worried that the home they left behind might disappear. Sometimes school-age children have a hard time settling down after their return. I have talked to teachers who say they can always tell when a child has made the transition between two homes. It takes the child at least a day, sometimes two days, to be able to concentrate again, resulting in lost schoolwork and the danger of falling behind. Others complain that they're pushed out the door in one home and welcomed without much interest in the other. "I never see my dad," an eight-year-old told me. "The only people at his house are my stepmom and her kids." Very young children often feel they're being sent from one home to the other because they've been naughty.

Sometimes the two homes are so very different that children feel cared for in one home and deprived in the other. Looking back at her childhood, Joanna, who is now twenty-five, said, "I felt forced and co-erced as a young kid. I felt kicked out of my mother's home to go to Dad's where I was frankly miserable. Dad set up temporary quarters in a garage he promised to rebuild, but it soon became our permanent home and I hated it. It was cold and cramped. My sister and I slept in one bed. Dad slept on the sofa when we came. We lived with promises he never delivered."

I was surprised to find that some children internalize the constant going back and forth into their personalities and literally have a hard time dealing with a stable environment. Caroline said, "When I came to college it was the first time that I ever spent the night in the same bed for more than five consecutive days. I didn't know how to handle such stability and clarity."

The most difficult challenge is having to make friends in two separate neighborhoods. For some children this is more than they can manage. They feel lonely and isolated in at least one of the neighborhoods. Be-cause they move back and forth so much, children can miss out on the activities in each neighborhood. One eight-year-old told me sadly, "Kids don't have appointment books like grown-ups. My friends in my dad's neighborhood forget all the time when I'm coming back. I come and then I have no one to play with. Or they forget about me totally and I don't get invited to the sleepovers, or birthday parties, because their parents don't remember when I'm coming."

This loss of continuity in friendships and participation in group ac-tivities and team sports is one of the most serious drawbacks of two separate residences. Children who have a hard time making new friends or who hang back from joining in group activities may feel uncomfortable for a very long time. But even a good joiner may miss out on the fun and games of spontaneous activities. One eight-year-old avid baseball player told me plaintively, "My coach said, 'Son, you are a good pitcher but I can't let you pitch unless you're here.' " Teenagers, of course, have an even more demanding schedule of activities. If the two homes are reasonably close by, these issues can be managed, especially if the teen has a car. The best option is to make it a priority to live reasonably near each other while your children are growing up.

Parents in joint custody enjoy special benefits. When your children are at the other house, you're free. You can spend uninterrupted hours doing what you like best. You can take courses. You can have a social life. You can have a sexual relationship or attend educational or cultural events without worrying about a babysitter objecting to late hours. If your work demands travel or late-night meetings, you can try to fit these responsibilities into the days when the children are away.

A downside for joint custody is that you may find it hard to shift gears. You're fully attuned to being a parent when your child is with you and then suddenly the house is too quiet. You're lonely and not sure what to do when you come home from work.

A very wise judge told me, "For joint custody to work, you need a joint custody child, a joint custody mother, and a joint custody father." Joint physical custody works best for a flexible, socially competent child who can cope with different environments. It requires vigilant parents who are reasonably in touch with their child's thoughts and feelings and who can cooperate with each other on the child's behalf. You need to keep a very close eye on how your child is coping with the many frequent geographic changes and psychological readjustments that joint physical custody demands. Some children can mature as they rise to the challenge and others lose their psychological footing and begin to show slippage in learning and anxiety in their relationships with peers. I think of one four-year-old who, after a year of going back and forth, got increasingly tense. One day she refused to get in her car seat, in either home. She couldn't articulate her distress the way an adult would have, but she made it perfectly clear that she couldn't do it. Traveling between two homes was too much for her. In this situation, I suggested that the parents maintain a single primary residence for the child for a one-year trial period to see if their little girl calmed down. She did. Her parents then gradually reintroduced the original plan and found a much more receptive, more mature child who could deal with the frequent changes.

As you consider these options, get the best legal and psychological advice you can. A mental health professional can be especially helpful in shaping your decisions. Consider all your options carefully and take a long-range view. Replay the pros and cons I've just laid out. You know your children best. You know yourselves. Given the right information, you can make a wise decision.

MOVING AWAY

A final caution. Whatever custody agreement you have—joint, sole, physical, legal, visiting, once married and divorced, never married—if you meet a wonderful new person who lives far away or you get offered a dream job in a distant city and you want to move, you may be blocked by the court. So-called move away policies vary from state to state, so be sure to talk the issue over ahead of time with your attorney.

The problem in a nutshell is that your freedom to build a separate life for yourself after divorce can be limited. If a mother wants to move to a different community to remarry, take a better job, or be closer to her parents, she may not be able to do so because her ex-husband, who shares joint physical custody or visits, does not want to lose the same pattern or ease of access to his children that he and they enjoyed. He may argue in court that her move will disrupt his parenting in ways that will be detrimental to his child. After all, the visiting or custody arrangement was designed to keep him actively involved in his child's life. Why should that be taken away now just because his ex-wife wants to move?

These cases shed light on a clash of values inherent to our modern divorce culture. Mothers and fathers both want to parent their children. When one person wants to move away, the other parent argues, "No way, that's not what we agreed." Typically it is fathers who go to court to prevent mothers from moving by requesting that the court transfer custody to them if the mother moves. As a result, women have been torn between their wish to remarry or otherwise rebuild their lives and their wish to have their children reside in their homes at least part-time. Sometimes fathers have claimed that an ex-wife's interest in moving is motivated not by realistic needs but by a vindictive wish to take the children away. In checking with legal experts I found no instance where the father's wish to move was contested.

Courts have responded in a wide variety of ways. In some states, judges have told mothers that they're free to move, but if they do, they cannot take their children. Custody is given to the fathers. Obviously, this has deterred many women from moving. In other states, judges have permitted the mother to move if she agrees, at her expense, to continue the child's regular visits with the father. And in still other places, judges have allowed women to move away as long as they demonstrate that the move will benefit the children. In many courts, mothers are required to show that their move is not dictated by a wish to block the father's access to his children.

The upshot of these cases can be tragic for mothers, fathers, and children. Torn between love for their children and love for their new man, some women have given up the man. Others postpone moving in with a second husband who lives some distance away until the children leave home. Other women live part-time with their second husbands. I know several mothers with advanced academic degrees who could not find work where they lived with their children; to take jobs commensurate with their training in a different community, they lost custody. Many courts refuse to listen to what children and adolescents say they want when these cases come before them. I know of courts where the letters to the judge from the adolescent children have been returned unopened. And many fathers are deeply saddened when their children move away; their contact lessens and they suffer.

Moving away is a serious issue that you need to anticipate in negotiating your custody arrangement. Find out from your attorney about court rulings in your area. Then choose a custody arrangement that gives you as much flexibility as possible if or when your circumstances change.

I want to offer one more word of caution. Under the stress of the breakup, many parents get exasperated with the slow tempo of the legal or mediation process. Fed up with the struggle to find solutions that please both parents, they settle for custody arrangements that end up being detrimental to their children. For example, some parents agree to put their young children on airplanes unaccompanied to visit the other parent. I've known frightened children as young as age five clutching their dolls or stuffed animals flying alone to distant cities. Even when they get to their destination safely, they're glassy-eyed and exhausted by efforts to contain their anxiety. The airlines carry about 7 million unaccompanied children between the ages of five and twelve each year, many of whom are children of divorce following custody agreements. The burden of your divorce falls squarely on their little shoulders. As every parent knows, air travel at best is subject to hazards. The best arrangements break down, planes park at the wrong gates, the weather suddenly changes, the person expected at the other end has an accident on the freeway. But even without mishap, children have a right to your protection. They should not be placed in terrifying situations because you could not agree on a custody plan that would protect them or because you felt pressured to come up with a plan. Keep in mind that neither the courts, the mediator, nor the attorney will protect your child. That's your job. It's your most important job. Don't yield to pressure. If the plan is not right for your child, don't do it.

Chapter 19: High-Conflict Divorce

I f you're among the minority of tormented parents who can't stop fighting in the courts over your children after you decide to divorce, I want to offer my sympathy and what I hope is good advice to help you through your ordeal. I have come to think of your continued suffering as reflecting an inability to finish the divorce. It's like you're stuck in a pipeline that was supposed to lead you out of an unhappy relationship and into greater freedom. But it's not working and you're paralyzed. You can't go forward and you can't go back. If you try to go back, you come face-to-face with your grief. You may have been stunned by your spouse's decision to break the marriage and you feel hurt beyond what anyone should ever endure. Who can blame you for your rage? If you try to go forward, you feel frightened and humiliated. Why should you hope or expect that you won't be hurt again? You may feel too weak to rebuild your life or to protect your children. So here you are, unable to move forward out of the morass, finish the divorce, and put that life chapter behind you.

As I noted earlier, I wish I could tell you that the court will help you achieve the sense of moral justice that you desire. But I doubt it. The court process is not only costly in terms of money and time but it takes a heavy emotional toll as well. It will leave you drained. It's not designed to mute your anger, help you close the door on the divorce, or move on with your life. The court's adversarial system may even increase your anger because it tends to polarize people.

If you're among parent combatants fighting for custody, I want to offer candid advice. The fight you're having over your child may have less to do with your concern for your child and more to do with your own distress at your partner's behavior toward you. This is something to consider carefully before you go full speed ahead with the trial. Also, while it may take two to tango, it does not take two to continuing fighting over a child. You may be fighting for vengeance over a divorce that you did not want or expect. Or you may feel helpless in the face of a continued emotional assault from your ex and feel that your only recourse is to fight back. By the time your case gets to court, the judge may not be able to distinguish these motives and will likely assume that both of you are equally locked in conflict over your child.

You should bear in mind that the impact of your conflict on your children is likely to be very serious and long-lasting. High conflict between parents not only causes children immense suffering, it causes serious problems in their development. They soon have the sense that they cannot trust any adults. Since each of you has opposite views, they learn to believe no one. They're likely to withdraw from friends as well because they don't want anyone to find out how bad things are at home. They're ashamed of you and your behavior. Perhaps the most serious effect of parents' quarreling over children is that the kids learn that feelings are too painful; they teach themselves not to feel pleasure or pain. In the battle between you, they learn to be polished diplomats. They'll tell each of you what you want most to hear—not because they're liars but because they want desperately to soothe each of you, to calm you down, to reduce their fears that you'll become enraged. They're afraid of your anger, they pity you, and they want you to feel better.

This is not a good time to put children in the middle and ask for their preferences regarding the post-divorce family. If you're fighting, this is the worst time to ask children who they want to live with, Mom or

Dad. They're much too scared and worried about you to think clearly. Whatever you do, don't lobby your children. Your job is to keep them out of the firing line.

What if you believe that your former husband or wife poses a genuine danger to your child? What if your worry is justified according to an independent measure—for example, a psychiatric diagnosis or criminal record? I wish I could tell you that you'll carry the day, but life is more complicated. Many parental behaviors that threaten a child are very hard to prove using legal standards. Typically there are no witnesses to sexual molestation. Emotional abuse and threats leave no bruises A little child's testimony is inadmissible in many courts because, it is argued, little children have a hard time separating fantasy from reality—which is sometimes true, sometimes not. The best attorney may not be able to convince the court that your child is in danger if he or she has unsupervised visits with your ex.

If you're caught in this kind of high-conflict divorce, you may be inviting even more trouble than you realize. If you're intensely angry at or frightened of your ex (or vice versa) and this anger is at the forefront of your every interaction, your mutual rage will set the tone for how others perceive both of you. And if you go to trial to settle matters, you stand a high chance of having a joint custody settlement imposed by the court—something neither of you want. This happens because judges often feel bewildered by parents whose every statement is contradictory. Each of you claims that the other is endangering your child. Each of you claims that you love your child. It's likely that you're telling the truth, but it is the truth as you perceive it. Your perceptions may be entirely different from those of your spouse. As far as the judge can figure out, both of you may be telling the truth, one of you may be lying, or both of you may be lying. Bewildered, judges fall back on a modern solution—joint physical custody—that can be beneficial to many children but is a disaster for children from high-conflict homes. As in King Solomon's court, the answer is to cut your child in half. But unlike the biblical story, no one rushes in to rescue the baby.

Studies show that a child who is ordered into going back and forth between two homes occupied by intensely angry adults feels safe nowhere. Your concern for your child may remain unaddressed. Your child, who is already severely stressed by the conflict between you and by your pre-occupation with litigation, is in no condition to cope with the difficulties of negotiating two homes and mastering the transition between them. Her mental and physical health are likely to deteriorate further. This is not speculation. Studies of such children show striking negative effects in their psychological health. Schoolwork suffers. Boys become more ag-gressive. Little girls become seductive with their fathers. Boys and girls show a higher incidence of physical ailments, including asthma, stom-achaches, and other stress-related symptoms.

The custody arrangement likely to work best for you is called parallel parenting. Your contact with your spouse should be minimal. Decisions about your child should be detailed and precise. It's better for a child in a high-conflict family to live in one home with definite arrangements for contact with the other parent at clearly specified times. Issues of schedule and daily routines should be decided in the presence of a mediator with a degree in psychology and additional background in child development. This kind of expert can help you settle child-related issues on the basis of general knowledge of children caught in these situations. If you both agree, she can also spend several hours with your child and base rec-ommendations on her understanding of your child's needs, including how your child is responding to your ongoing distress. While I recommend flexibility for most children, as a general policy for divorced parents in high-conflict families, the less flexibility the better. Clear, consistent, and absolutely fair rules are more helpful to everyone. Your child will benefit from strict enforcement of the agreed-upon schedule to assure the pre-dictability in her life, something she may not have seen much of after months or years of chaos.

Why do some people engage in such seemingly irrational behavior? You'd think they'd see their child's suffering and realize that all the money they're spending on lawyers could be put to better use in raising their child. No one ever wins this kind of contest. Divorce can be a terrible blow, but most people gradually recover and move on to love again. Those who are not able to recover remain suspended in time, deeply wounded and preoccupied with their hurt and anger. Sometimes the rejection of the divorce kicks off a series of earlier rejections from childhood—reminders of pain suffered from long ago. This history of past losses and abandonments helps explain why some parents can't relinquish the presence of their child for even a few days. It also explains their dependence on the child. I've known parents who walk from room to room, weeping, during the days that their son or daughter is with the other parent.

Other factors keep the struggle going. Many parents who litigate are supported in battle by a chorus of attorneys, family members, and even therapists, all of whom take sides in the fray. When an interracial, interfaith, or cross-cultural marriage breaks up, whole families can become involved as if it were a tribal war with the child's soul at stake. Remember the crowds rioting in Miami and Havana in the custody battle over Elian Gonzales, the little boy who lost his mother at sea on their ill-fated voyage to America and was taken in by Florida relatives who claimed him? That was an eruption of the intense passions aroused when people cannot agree where a small child should live and with whom. It's an excellent example of how issues unrelated or tangential to the child fuel the battle over the child.

What should you do if you're caught up in a high-conflict divorce? If you're convinced that your ex-partner is not fit to be a parent, you may ultimately decide to raise your objections in court. The judge may then order a psychological evaluation of you, your ex, and your child to get a clearer picture of the situation. He will summon a psychologist, a psychiatrist, a clinical social worker, or in some states a family counselor to do the evaluation. Depending on the jurisdiction, either the court will choose or each party will choose a separate mental health expert or agree to the same person. This expert will interview each of you and try to work out a custody plan that will be acceptable to everyone.

If you and your child are ordered into evaluation—and if you have a say in the selection of the evaluator—you need to find out the background and training of this person. Many otherwise well-trained mental health experts have very little or no competence in examining children, especially young children. If you have an infant or a young child, you need to learn whether the evaluator has special training to work with babies and toddlers. You can find out by asking for a résumé and running it by a recognized expert in the field of mental health. After checking the evaluator's credentials, you also need to find out whether this person is truly unbiased. Does she have a history of tilting toward sole custody or joint custody? Does she show more sympathy overall to fathers or to mothers? Does she undertand about substance abuse and how it can impact the parent-child relationship? This you can learn from your attorney or by asking around. You may have to be clever in ferreting out these facts, but they're important to know beforehand. You might ask her to describe the outcome in her last ten evaluations. Were the solutions always similar or did they vary with each family? Has she done much work with children the age of yours? You want someone who will make recommendations based on your individual case—not from her preconceptions about what people should do.

If you find the mental health expert lacking in some important way—for example, she has no experience working with children or she has only limited knowledge of substance abuse and this is your major concern about your spouse—you may, depending on the rules in your local court, have the right to reject her and tell your attorney why you found her lacking. Even if she has a Ph.D. from a major university, it doesn't mean she's the right person for your family. You need to work with someone whose judgment you can trust.

Once the evaluator has been appointed, do your best to cooperate. You might ask her how to prepare your child. If you don't get an answer, try a conversation something along these lines: "A nice lady whose name is Dr. Smith understands a lot about children and wants to ask you some questions. She wants to know what you think about our family. There's no reason to be scared. Dr. Smith is going to help us. You can help by answering all her questions honestly. Dr. Smith may want to play some games with you, maybe with some dolls or drawings, and I think you'll enjoy that. I'm going to take you to her office at 11:00 tomorrow morning. I'll be in the waiting room right outside her door. When you're done talking, we can go have lunch and do something that would be fun for us both." You want your son or daughter to be ready and relaxed for this interview. Make sure each child has slept well the night before. A fatigued child may look very tense to a person who has never met her before. If you're nervous, your child may pick up on it and feel frightened. One additional note. Do not coach your child on what to say or what to avoid saying. Evaluators are especially alert to behavior or statements from children who have been coached. Efforts by parents to influence the evaluator are easily detected and will count heavily against you.

If you have an interview with the evaluator, hold on to your composure. This is not a time for angry feelings to erupt. Speak calmly. Answer questions carefully and thoughtfully. Don't cry. Ask your attorney for his detailed advice, but try to think ahead of time what you want the evaluator to understand about you and your child. Let her draw her own conclusions about your ex-partner. Come prepared to talk about your child's school record, her successes and failures, your concerns, and your hopes for the future. State your concerns clearly and give specific examples, the more specific the better.

It's especially important in a high-conflict divorce to have an attorney who is experienced in custody cases that go to court. Keep in mind that the advice you receive is only as good as the person who provides it. Specifically, ask your attorney if he is knowledgeable and experienced in preparing himself and you for the court evaluation process. You absolutely need to work with someone you fully trust and who will be available during this stressful time. You may find that you're overwhelmed with anxiety and that a therapist who is familiar with the court process can help you learn how to stay in control. A court evaluation will tax you to the limits of your emotional equilibrium. Try to maintain your exercise schedule. Eat healthy foods and get enough sleep. You need to be alert and able to make rational decisions on behalf of yourself and your child.

In the end, you may win. You may find a judge who agrees that joint physical custody is not the best outcome for your child. He may even order that visits with the other parent be carried out under supervision, which means a third party is always present. If the judge orders supervised visiting, you can ask that the person doing the supervision have adequate training. In most states, no training is available for supervisors. In some places an excellent nonprofit organization known as CASA, or Court Appointed Special Advocates, can provide trained, educated laypeople as volunteers. Ask if you can have a meeting with the supervisor to explain your child's special needs. Explain that your child may be frightened and anxious about meeting the other parent in a strange place and ask her to provide whatever help she can.

If your ex remains volatile, you need to be on guard if you think your child is in danger of being kidnapped. Consult your lawyer and get advice from her on what you need to do. Make sure that your attorney knows where your ex might flee in the event of abduction. Learn what you can about local and federal laws regarding parental kidnapping. The police are better trained than they used to be about the dangers of kidnapping in divorce disputes. Make sure that the proper authorities have been warned, including your child's school. Check that they're taking appropriate action. Take appropriate safeguards in your home such as having alarm systems and escape plans. Make sure, too, that your child memorizes your telephone number and address. Explain that all children should know these things.

If by some great misfortune your ex is making violent threats or you are being stalked, take action immediately. Talk to the police captain in your neighborhood. Get your lawyer to obtain a restraining order. Make sure that you're not alone. Do whatever is necessary. Violence following divorce is a serious threat.

Unfortunately, many children who witness violence or are themselves abused—physically, verbally, or sexually—identify with the aggressor. Unless they get help from a therapist, many daughters of abused women seek out abusive men when they grow up, having internalized the image of victim. Sons of violent fathers often seek out vulnerable women, having internalized the image of aggressor. Children who have been sexually molested are drawn to repeat the behavior with other children. Tragically, the courts don't understand that removing such children from the threatening parent is not enough. You need to seek professional help for your son or daughter without delay. Don't wait until your child is older. Find a competent mental health expert who can start working with your child right away. You may need treatment for yourself as well, or at least good advice on what you can say or do at home.

On the other hand, you may lose in court. If your child is ordered into joint physical custody and you are expected to interact with your former spouse on a regular basis, you have no choice but to work out ways to reduce your anger and to protect your children, even if your ex continues to rage. Frequent contact by itself, I assure you, will not diminish your anger at each other. All of you—your ex, your child, and you—need help. You need help to hold on to the reality of what's happening and to separate this reality from your partner's accusations and distortions. You need help with your own distortions of reality, which occur even if you pride yourself on your clear thinking. Most of all, you need long-term, uninterrupted therapy for your child to maintain an oasis where she can express her feelings without fear of retribution, where she can maintain her sense of herself as a whole, balanced person. Children whose parents fight bitterly often feel desperate. They're convinced that they're the guilty ones. After all, if they'd never been born, if they were not there in the middle, Mom and Dad would soon stop their fighting. They're also very aware of how vulnerable one or both of you are. Many children tell me sadly, "It's better not to have feelings." As they clamp down on their fears and sorrow, they also clamp down on feelings of pleasure. The stark reality is that ongoing conflict between parents can effectively destroy the joys and safety of childhood.

Find a therapist who is well trained to work with children and has had experience working with children in divorcing families. Be careful in your choice. You want someone who understands how to help high-conflict families. Be sure to ask. Also try to get your ex-partner to agree to the therapist who seems best qualified. He or she can block the sessions if things don't appear to be "going right." He or she can belittle the therapist to undermine your child's trust in the process. Once your child is in therapy and becomes attached to her therapist, you don't want the meetings to stop suddenly. If you're worried about such interference beforehand, talk to your attorney or mediator to negotiate how to handle disagreements over continuing the sessions.

When you meet the child therapist, describe the family situation candidly. Explain that you're concerned about your child's suffering. You want the therapist's office to be a safe haven, a place where your child won't be afraid to express feelings, where he can learn to not blame himself for his parents' troubles. Tell the therapist that you understand she won't reveal your child's confidences. But also say that you hope she'll guide you in ways to handle difficult situations that may arise. Keep the therapy going for several years if you can. Finally, arrange to meet with the therapist at regular intervals so you can talk face-to-face.

If you cannot mute your hurt and rage, try your best to get some perspective. Otherwise these feelings will dominate your life. Even your best friends will tire of hearing the same old complaints. Ask yourself honestly, what broke up my marriage? Did we ever build anything together that was worth fighting for? Did our marriage fall apart from within because of problems between us, or did some outside force—an illness, job loss, death of a parent—ricochet in and upset our lives? Once you understand, you can begin to work on your own recovery. Can you put your anger aside and concentrate on your new opportunities to be a good parent and to enjoy new relationships? If you're blocked, get help for yourself. It's very serious to be overwhelmed by hurt and anger. You need professional help from someone you respect so you can rescue yourself.

If your ex-partner continues to behave horribly as you share custody, try your best not to respond in kind. Consider it a triumph when you can quietly end a provocative conversation and not bang down the phone. The less direct contact that you have with your ex the better. You can inform each other about important events with letters that are neutral in tone and end with polite phrases, like "I trust you are well." If your ex threatens you, be sure you can reach your attorney quickly for advice. You can never know for sure when an angry person will become violent.

If your child must visit or live several days a week with an ex whose morals you abhor, it does no good to call him an idiot. If he waves a Nazi flag when he comes to pick up your six-year-old daughter, you can either rush to court and await the next provocation or you can say to the child, "That is really funny. Your daddy does things I never dreamed of. He and I have very different views." Your child will get the point. If your ex-wife drinks a bottle of wine every night but is not so impaired that a judge would call her an unfit parent, you can discuss alcoholism with your child and what it does to people. Be clear about your own morals but don't put your child in the middle. All you can hope is that your morality wins out over your ex-partner's immorality. The example that you set is more important than the court order forbidding Nazi flags and excess drinking.

One of your most difficult tasks will be to carve out a place where your child is free of your anger. You want her to love you, respect you, and admire you. You love her and want her to be a loving person when she grows up. Granted, you've been hurt to your core by the divorce, but your child needs to feel that she's safe with you. She shouldn't be afraid that you're going to explode any minute. It's up to you to teach her how to control her own anger and not be afraid of strong feelings as long as she's in control of them. As she matures, you'll have many opportunities to show her that a relationship between a man and a woman does not have to be like the one she observed.

Children caught in the flames of a high-conflict divorce have been referred to as "children of Armageddon"—victims of the final war on earth. They are true casualties. Parents trapped in mutual anger often become heedless of anything else. I urge you, despite your perhaps very justifiable rage, to try to protect your children from being placed in the middle. Fight over money, property, or whatever matters to you, but do not fight over your children.

Take your anger to the arena of long-term therapy to rid yourself of the misery that's destroying your life. Your children probably also need long-term therapy to restore their sense that it's okay to have feelings and that the world is not a chaotic place where aggression rules. Rather, it's a place where there can be peace, love, and good will. It may take a long time to believe this, but with changes in you and the proper help, it can be done.

Chapter 20: How to Choose the Right Custody for Your Child

I 've given you a lot of information about different forms of custody, but what choice will work best for you? How do you know what makes the most sense? To explore this further, let's take three hypothetical examples—three-year-old Tommy, nine-year-old Karen, and fourteen-year-old Melanie. Let's say that each is an only child and you're the parent. Your goals are to safeguard your child, to enhance his or her development, and to try to create a post-divorce family in which your child benefits from a rich relationship with both parents. How does that translate into custody choice?

Please keep in mind what I said earlier about how the labels used in different forms of custody are mixed up and that different courts call the same arrangement by different names. Whatever definitions are used in your community, don't let anyone pressure you into joint custody or any other kind of custody without considering the needs of your individual child. You have a unique opportunity to make a choice that works for your family. Children of divorce come single file. Now let's walk through the decision process with your children in mind.

The first step is to sit down alone or together with your ex-spouse and think carefully about your child's needs, strengths, and limitations. What are the challenges and protection that each form of custody would offer him?

How old is he? Where is he developmentally? Can he walk or ride his bike between two homes? How much care will he need during the next few years? Obviously, a young child will need a more protected environment. An older child may be able to handle his own transportation. On the other hand, a preschool child's schedule is more flexible than that of a school-age child who has a circle of friends and activities that you need to respect in choosing a custody plan.

Then ask yourselves a series of questions about your child's temperament. Is he on target developmentally or does he have special problems? Was he a difficult or easy infant? How does he respond to change? Has he ever spent the night away from his mother? From his father? How did he respond to the separation?

If he's in day care or nursery school, does he like it? How does he interact with other children? Is he a fearful child? Is he a finicky child with food? Does he nap at nap time and sleep when you put him down? Is he frightened when you're late? What was his response to the breakup? Is he still distressed? How does he show it? Is he a clingy child? An independent child?

Answers to these questions will help you decide whether your child is likely to be comfortable moving back and forth between two homes after an initial adjustment or whether he would be more comfortable in one home. Could he comfortably manage two sets of playmates or would he end up withdrawing into his own solitary world? Is he very attached to one parent, crying inconsolably when separated, or does he embrace the world fearlessly?

Now ask yourselves another set of questions. Are your two homes going to be reasonably similar in providing your child with a comfortable space and room for his toys? His computer? His musical instruments? Or will he have very different arrangements in each home? Are there other children within each neighborhood? How far apart are your two homes and how much of your child's time and effort will be spent in getting back and forth? Who will provide that transportation? Will he be ex-pected to fly back and forth unescorted? Are there other children or other adults in one or both homes? If children, what are their ages? What are their attitudes toward your child? Will he be an intruder on their space or welcomed as a new friend or playmate?

Finally, what is your child's relationship like with each of you? Is each of you available for the rigorous demands of parenting? Who has been the primary parent? How much have you both joined in parenting? What are your work obligations and schedules? How invested is each of you in parenting? How much traveling do you each do and can you fit that into a joint custody schedule?

Let's hypothesize further. In one home Mom is an executive at a large department store, which takes her on buying trips and business conferences all over the country. Dad is a consultant with flexible hours and can be at home any time he's needed. In another home both parents are attorneys and their child will spend most of his days in child care centers and with sitters until seven in the evening. In a third home, Mom is a teacher and can be home in the mid-afternoon. Dad is a car-penter with regular hours. In a fourth home Mom is a journalist who works largely at home. Dad is an athletic coach at a local high school.

Now let's run through a profile of each child, starting with three-year-old Tommy. Let's say you conclude that Tommy is a timid child who cries easily when other children are aggressive. He's been very distressed by the divorce. He clings to his mother and wets his bed. He likes having routines, especially at bedtime, in a special sequence that he dictates. Only then can he sleep comfortably. He spent a night away from his mother only once and it was difficult for him. His mother is a teacher who will be available in the afternoons and evenings and has no business travel. His father is a carpenter who is able to visit during the week and the weekend. The homes are different in that the father has a six-year-old child from an earlier marriage living with him half the time.

You decide that Tommy is a sensitive child who reacts anxiously to even minor changes. He would benefit, at least for now, from living in a calm, relatively undemanding environment. You're concerned about the regression to bed-wetting and clinginess. These might get worse if you place more demands on him. You also think that Tommy's living half the time with a six-year-old stepsibling might work out well or it might be stressful—you really can't predict. Given these factors, you conclude that Tommy would be better off, at least for now, living in sole custody with his mother with lots of visits from his father. You plan father-and-son daylong outings at least once or twice a week and evenings where Dad puts Tommy to bed, if Tommy permits it. You discuss your decision with Tommy but you give him no choice because he's too young to decide.

Your profile of Karen is different. At nine, she's a lively, outgoing youngster who is mature for her age. Karen has many interests and makes friends easily. She should be able to find playmates in two neighborhoods. She's very fond of both her parents, but her life is centered at her school and around her extracurricular activities. Given her busy life, which acted as a buffer to problems at home, she took the breakup in stride. Karen is devoted to singing in a choir that practices once a week near the home where she grew up. She has been to choir camp and is looking forward someday to touring with the group abroad. She's active in the Girl Scouts and wants to continue. Next year she hopes to go out for soccer. She's a stellar student who can handle all these outside activities. Both of Karen's parents are attorneys. They lead busy professional lives and she is used to seeing them both at or after supper.

Karen's parents opted for joint physical custody, splitting each week in half. Karen thinks of it as an adventure and is happy to continue seeing both her mother and her father. She worried about getting to all her after-school activities until her parents found a reliable high school student who wanted a job chauffeuring Karen in the afternoons. The two became fast friends.

Your profile of fourteen-year-old Melanie is also very different. Melanie has been depressed since the breakup. After considerable reluctance, she agreed to go into treatment and is developing a relationship with her therapist, someone well known for her rapport with difficult adolescents.

The therapeutic relationship is in its early phases and still shaky. During this last year, Melanie's grades dropped steeply. She has been getting into minor troubles at school, including truancy. Once she came to school drunk. It's clear that she needs a lot of parental attention and supervision. It is unlikely that having two homes at this time would provide that protection. Both parents agree that Melanie should continue her therapy. Both also realize that since entering adolescence Melanie has been in greater conflict with her mother. She accuses her mother of being "narcissistic and uncaring." Melanie's father has been a more benign figure. He's working at home at this time and has no plans for extended trips. Melanie's mom, on the other hand, has a busy, stressful life as an executive.

This family agreed that Melanie would benefit from being in sole custody with her dad, who worked closely with the school to make sure his daughter attended therapy. Melanie's mom came by one night a week and took Melanie home for weekends whenever her daughter was amenable. This was no time to ask a troubled youngster to adjust to living in two homes. As plans were discussed, Melanie acted lethargic and indifferent, as if they were talking about someone else.

Obviously, all of these conditions are subject to change. Custody plans put into effect at the breakup should not be thought of as lasting. I'm convinced that a child's post-divorce family should be respected and that custody should not be changed unless the initial choices are shown to be harmful. But any child's schedule can be adjusted to his changing needs and interests. Tommy may brighten up when he goes to elementary school. He may loosen his dependence on his mom and seek more time with his father, in which case you might reconsider having him spend several days a week at his father's home.

Karen may suffer a series of setbacks at school. She might enter young adolescence like a tiger with a delayed reaction to the divorce. She may need a lot more supervision and control than the present arrangement provides. One parent may even need to take time out from work to be more available to her. She may need to live in one home for a time.

Melanie may recover fully and go on to seek a closer relationship with her mom while still living at her dad's house. She may want to try spending one or more days a week at her mother's home before she leaves for college.

Every parent's life is also likely to change with new love affairs, new jobs, new pursuits or layoffs, demotions, and transfers. New children and adults may enter the family with second marriages. Lives change. And because lives change, I recommend that you arrange to reevaluate your child's schedule at regular intervals. Every four years seems a good rule of thumb considering how fast children grow and change. You may wish to review each child's schedule more frequently. This can be put into writing with your mediator or attorneys at the breakup. Obviously, not every change in your child requires a change in his schedule. Stability is very important. But there may be times when you and the children would benefit from a different arrangement. It might even be detrimental to rigidly maintain the early custody arrangements. Other times you will want to maintain the status quo. My goal is to protect your child's growing-up years by providing her with the same benefits that children in intact families take for granted.

I realize that in some states child support is based on where your child resides, and so you may need to rejigger financial arrangements when your child's life changes. However, research shows that sole and especially joint custody is rather fluid. One large study showed that a third of children in joint custody gravitated to their mother's home within two to three years after the breakup. As I'll talk about later in more detail, teenagers who get into trouble are often sent to live full-time with their father by moms who've "had enough." The moms hope that a man will be better able to keep tighter control. Parents and children decide on these changes informally outside of any legal framework. In other words, you and your ex can fine-tune your child's schedule at any time as long as you agree on what is good for your child and consider her changing interests. You can make necessary financial adjustments with the help of a mediator. Obviously, this is the best outcome to divorce for your child and for each of you.

PART THREE

·

THE
POST-DIVORCE
FAMILY

Chapter 21: **Take Another Close Look at Your Children and at Yourself**

L et's assume that several years have passed. It could be three, four, five, or more years since you signed the divorce papers and went your separate ways. This is a good time to take another close look at your children and at yourself. How is the new family working for your children and for you?

First, how are your children? By this time their early responses to your divorce should have subsided. They should have made their peace with the changes in the family and, however reluctantly, come to accept those changes. And they should have resumed their journey up the developmental ladder. This means that your little ones are not afraid of separation and that early regressions like bed-wetting have disappeared. Your older children have come to terms with the divorce and muted their anger at both of you. All the children should be doing reasonably well at school and with their friends or playmates. They should have mastered the challenges of visiting or joint custody, which means they can go back and forth without fear of being lost or losing contact with you. Your teenagers should have more or less settled down.

If you had to move out of the family home after divorce, how are your children adjusting to their new surroundings? Have they made new friends? Are they happy with their new school? Or do you have the sense that they're not fitting in? Are they gloomy or sad or angry? Are they still preoccupied with returning to the old neighborhood?

If you and your children are doing well, congratulations. Your hard work has paid off. I hope you'll share what worked for you with friends who are going through their own divorces. Your guidance is invaluable.

But if you're like many parents, you may find yourself struggling with the challenges of creating and living in a post-divorce family. You're not happy with how your children are doing. You expected that they would be recovered by this time but they are not. You're surprised and worried. Where do you go from here?

In the first place, it's not realistic to think you should be completely out of the woods by now. Divorce is not a minor crisis in your child's life. In middle-class families, it's usually the biggest crisis a child will face while growing up. The notion that children are resilient and quickly recover from divorce is simply misleading. But don't despair. Rather, be prepared to accept the fact that it takes years for children to master divorce. As I explained earlier, divorce is not a sudden event like a minor earthquake that you recover from once the house is put back in order. Divorce is a long-term process that ushers in a new kind of family that is different from the intact family. It requires continuing adjustment, for years on end, and that's not easy for many children and adults. You need to be patient and realistic. Give your children time to adjust, but keep alert to symptoms that can lead to more serious trouble.

For example, your child's initial reaction to your divorce does not predict how he or she will cope with it down the road. Severe temper tantrums are often not too difficult to extinguish when they have been in place a few weeks. After a year they are much harder to treat. Sleep disturbances are common at the breakup. By comforting your child right away, you can restore the sense that he's not been forgotten. But if the sleep disturbance lasts over a year, so that your child cries out for you several times each night, your child needs help beyond what a devoted parent can provide.

On the other hand, some children show mild initial reactions to your divorce. They shrug, go back to doing their homework, and carry on as if not much has happened. But don't be fooled by their apparent nonchalance. Many children show delayed reactions to divorce that get them into serious trouble years later. Sometimes they develop fears that their parents will get sick and disappear. Or the depression that was carefully hidden may surface. Now that the acute crisis has passed and several years have gone by, they may feel freer about showing their distress. Or they may find it difficult to concentrate in school. Or they may act out on the playground.

If you're worried about your child several years after divorce, I suggest you start with a face-to-face conference between you and the teacher or school counselor or both. Don't try to catch these people on the run but call and ask for a meeting. Explain that you're eager for their impressions about your child. Give them some time to collect their thoughts and to confer with other teachers at the school. While many teachers today are too busy to get to know all their students well, they tend to be excellent observers and often have a perspective on your child that's a lot different from yours. Your child's teacher is likely to welcome your interest and feel relieved to share her concerns. Or she may be happy to tell you how pleased she is with your child's progress.

Things to look out for: Does the teacher call your son a "bright underachiever" because he doesn't do as well in school as he should? Does your daughter avoid children her own age, preferring to play with dolls or younger children or be at home alone with you? Is your teenager into chronic petty theft or truancy? Has he been smoking pot or drinking? Is she socially isolated? Do your children feel hurt because your new partner really doesn't want them around and you don't know how to solve this problem?

After you've talked to people outside the family, sit down and have a long talk with your child. Make a date so you have a reasonable chance at not being interrupted. Say that you're enormously pleased with how well she's doing and that you know it hasn't been easy. Make it an "awards" day for things that are going well.

If you are concerned about her, say that you realize she's been having a hard time. Ask if there are things she'd like to talk to you about.

Explain that your lives have been busy and you may have missed something important to her. Can you help fix any problems? If your child is worried about a burglar entering your home and your being unable to cope—this is not uncommon after divorce—show her that you have very strong locks on the doors. If someone did try to break in, you'd call the police. If you find out that your child is worried about money, explain that you're not in danger of starving and that you have plenty of money to feed the family, including her dog. If she's sleepless, ask whether she has a particular nightmare or troubling thought she can tell you. Try to get at the root of all these worries and clarify the reality. Her fears may be unrealistic but they are never groundless. They start somewhere, even from things seen on television or overheard on the playground. You can often help dispel these fears by finding the source and making assurances that you can handle everything just fine.

You may want to consider getting a therapist for your child—not to deal with the crisis at the breakup but to help with the sorts of problems that show up after several years. Introduce the idea by saying that you don't think it's fair for children to have so many worries and not have as much fun at school and with friends. You would like to get some help from a person who understands children. If your child doesn't object, find a licensed therapist who treats children the age of your child. Ask where they trained and for referrals. Ask your pediatrician or school counselor for names and check with friends whose children have been in treatment. If you can afford to do so, interview two or three therapists before making a selection.

The person you select would probably want to see you first, then see your child, and then offer an opinion on what approach to take. If therapy is recommended, find out what your insurance covers for your child and for you. If your insurance doesn't cover mental health counseling, see if your ex will share in the expense. Grandparents on both sides may be forthcoming. Most communities have family agencies that charge on a sliding scale and offer good services.

When you interview the therapist, make sure that he helps you understand why your child is suffering and what kind of treatment is recommended. You can't know ahead of time how long the therapy will last, but the therapist should be able to give you a broad estimate. Also find out how you and the therapist will communicate. Will you talk on the phone? Will you meet at regular intervals? Will he want to see you and your child together? Does the therapist want to talk with your ex or have regular meetings with your ex? All of these plans should be clarified at the outset to the extent possible.

A word of warning. Parents often disagree in the matter of how well their child has recovered. Not surprisingly, I've found that the person who initially sought the divorce tends to report a fully recovered, well-adjusted child, and by the same logic, the parent who resisted the divorce sees a troubled child who is suffering with troublesome symptoms. I don't think that one parent is necessarily lying, although that can happen. But I do think that a parent's perceptions are influenced by what he or she needs to believe. Also it's possible that a child behaves differently in each home. If that child is more relaxed in one home, he or she may show symptoms more clearly. Conversely, if the child maintains tight self-control in the other home, he or she may not show those same symptoms. But symptoms that persist at the one- to two-year mark no longer reflect an early response to the divorce. They reflect a disturbance or a worry that is becoming ingrained and has a good chance of not going away without good treatment.

Another word of warning. Children who continue to have difficulty in learning may be mistakenly diagnosed as suffering with attention deficit disorders. Your child may have this problem but could also still be suffering the effects of the family breakup. The teacher or pediatrician who made the diagnosis may be unaware of your child's history. Many excellent educators and physicians are not familiar with the many ways that divorce can disrupt a child's learning. They need you to fill them in on your divorce, especially if the breakup was marked by high conflict or violence.

Now a harder truth. Your child's problems may reflect your own misery. If you remain depressed, angry, defensive, or otherwise joyless, how can your child separate and move along a normal developmental path? How can he not worry about you? You need to treat yourself with the same consideration that you offer your child. If things are going badly for you, take this occasion to review your decisions of the past few years. Suppose at the five-year mark you haven't put your life together. Suppose you're discouraged, lonely, depressed. Do you gaze at some of your happier friends and feel envious? Do you ask how they got so lucky or so smart? Where did you fail? Perhaps some major decision you made in the aftermath of the breakup did not pan out the way you wanted. Maybe you took the wrong job or the first job that came along. Suppose you've been slaving away at several jobs to make ends meet, or you're in a job like selling real estate that takes away your weekends and crimps your opportunities to meet new people or accept invitations. Or you were studying for the wrong degree or you were wasting your time with a boring lover who was convenient but didn't make you happy. Now is the time to stop, look, and listen to yourself.

If any of this sounds familiar, now is the time to consider changing. I also recommend that you consider therapy for yourself. A good therapist can help you exorcise the ghosts of your failed marriage, understand why you picked so poorly, why you paid no attention to danger signs on your radar screen, and, very importantly, what you contributed to the failure so you can be prepared to do better next time. Pick the therapist carefully. Don't assume they're all the same. They come out of different disciplines and have different levels of training. Although most states have license laws, a license does not tell you enough about that person's competence. Nevertheless, find out where they went to school, what license they have, and how long they have been in practice.

The three main disciplines in mental health are psychiatry, psychology, and clinical social work. Many states also license marriage and family counselors who generally receive less training than specialists who have Ph.D.s or M.D.s. Licensure and training are important; also ask what experience each person has. Over and beyond training are the intangibles of compassion and human understanding each therapist brings to each individual. For therapy to work, you need to find good chemistry between you and the therapist. So ask around. Learn everything you can. Go to a first interview with an open mind and make a preliminary judgment. If it doesn't feel right, go talk to someone else. Many men and women whose histories I know well have been enormously helped and supported through a very difficult time with the help of their therapist.

Remember, you are doing this not only for yourself—which is reason enough—but also for your child.

Chapter 22:   The Overburdened Child

After your divorce, you'll find that the experience of being a parent is radically transformed. Your children will find that the "job" of being a child is very different from what they've been used to. Divorce alters the two-way street of child-parent relationships in ways—some good, some bad, some obvious, some subtle—that may surprise you for years to come.

For example, you may develop a special closeness with your child. Before you know it, she becomes your advisor, confidante, and best friend. She's always willing to listen when your other friends are bored with hearing your complaints. No one in the world is more loving, loyal, and helpful than this devoted child who gives you full priority. In fact, she may be the only one who knows that the strong façade you show to the rest of the world has a vulnerable, tender underbelly. She's wonderfully empathic.

In most families, this reversal of parent and child roles is more or less temporary. The exchanges are kept to a minimum and familiar patterns of parenting soon return. There's nothing wrong with leaning on

your child in the aftermath of divorce. She may benefit from added responsibility and enjoy her status as mentor.

But leaning on a child for advice is a slippery slope that can cause
serious problems in the post-divorce family. Some parents lose perspective
and ask what to do about a lover, how and where to live, whether or
not to remarry, and whom to choose. I was startled when Sammy, who
was four, comforted his grieving mother whose lover had just left by
saying, "He shouldn't quit in the middle. That's not right." One father
told me that he revealed all his business and personal plans in Castro-
like lectures to his five-year-old who "understands everything." Actually
the boy didn't understand anything his father said. His play consisted
almost entirely of a noisy Mack truck that ran repeatedly over a little
car, reflecting his feeling of powerlessness in the face of his father's
lectures.

More insidiously, children can take on an overly protective role without your knowledge or encouragement. They become confidantes because
they like feeling important, needed, and all grown up. Your child may
seem amazingly insightful, but be aware that there's a high potential for
you to overestimate her competence and ability to understand you. The
truth is, her brilliant perceptions may be built on sand. Your ten-year-
old has no emotional or intellectual scaffolding to give you advice about
your adult relationships. Although she can understand your loneliness,
she can't understand your need for sex or your financial worries. Even if
she did, she wouldn't have the knowledge or experience to give sound
advice.

Adolescents very quickly become a captive audience. They can be
disarmingly helpful, sympathetic, loving, and comforting at all hours of
the day and night. But don't be fooled. Although they speak with greater
self-confidence than their younger siblings, their knowledge is shaky.
Don't make the mistake of thinking that a teenager who carries out all
sorts of adult responsibilities intelligently and competently also fully understands the complex emotional issues of your divorce. Some parents
tell and retell their teenage children the intimate, lurid details of the
breakup, including sexual details of impotence, frigidity, and infidelity.

They mistake the sophisticated adolescent façade for true maturity. One sixteen-year-old told me, "Every Wednesday night for the last year, my dad takes me to dinner and talks and talks about his sexual frustration with my mom, how she never said yes and all that. I smile back at dinner but I get depressed and angry for days when I get home. Why does he think I want to hear all this? I don't want to hear any of it. He needs to talk to a girlfriend, not to me. But I don't know how to stop him without hurting his feelings."

When parents really lose perspective and begin leaning heavily on their children for emotional support, children become deeply worried. They say or think, "Mommy, are you okay?" "Daddy, what I can do to make you feel better?" Soon a kind of tracking falls into place where your child watches your every move, attending to where you go, what you do, and what you say. Focused on taking care of you, she gives up thinking about her own needs. After waiting up for you when you come home from a date, she turns to you and says in a sweet motherly tone, "Now, tell me everything that happened."

In this self-sacrifice, the child walks a fine and dangerous line. On the positive side of the ledger, she learns compassion and how to take on a caregiving role. She becomes a sensitive human being who is skilled at helping others. She also learns to be self-sufficient—a trait that will help her when she's an adult. In fact, one of the major findings from my long-term studies of divorce is that children of divorce use these compassion and negotiation skills to succeed in highly competitive careers. Andrea, a successful young businesswoman, expressed what so many feel when she said, "I've had to become independent and strong. I can work well with change. When things get chaotic, I don't lose my cool. I learned at an early age to think for myself and to rely on myself." Others speak proudly of the strength they acquired in having to do things on their own. "Because my parents were so different I learned to navigate my own way in the world," said Jerry, a thirty-one-year-old stockbroker. "I've learned to use my head and my heart. I'm not afraid of what comes along."

On the negative side of the ledger, a child can take on the role of being the parent, literally. She crosses a line into becoming a martyr who sacrifices her own needs for yours. I see this mostly in oldest girls in families with two or three children, but I also see it in young adolescent boys. These so-called overburdened children take on a very complicated job in the post-divorce family. In extreme cases, I've met children who are convinced that they're keeping their parent alive. Such children pull away from friends, stay home from school, and place the center of their universe on the doorstep of the troubled parent who may not be able to sleep without their child in the same bed. These youngsters can run a household and take full charge of younger siblings as they cook, clean, and get everyone ready to face each new day. This may be the norm in some parts of the world but it is not the norm in a country like ours. Moreover, in immigrant families where children do take on greater responsibilities for raising siblings, the parents remain in charge at the level of making more important decisions.

WHAT TO DO, WHAT TO SAY

My advice is that when you ask more of your children, keep asking yourself, "Am I going too far?" One sixteen-year-old boy I know was the only member of his family available to go to the hospital to attend to his younger sister who was in the emergency room with a broken ankle. The parents, who were both at work, could not be located—a not uncommon situation. The boy was terrified. The hospital would not continue treating his sister without a responsible adult to sign her in. But he couldn't reach them. Always make sure that you have plans worked out for what to do in emergencies. You may be in a meeting that no one dares interrupt or on an airplane with your cell phone turned off. Everyone in the family needs to have phone numbers of where to find you at all times. The school should have this on record.

To avoid overburdening your children, check in every now and then. Ask if they're okay with what's expected of them. Are they doing too much? Too little? Do they want more time with their friends? It's okay to lean on a competent child in a crisis, but you need to watch for signs that you may be expecting too much. If your twelve-year-old son withdraws from social activities, hangs around the house, and takes on chores over and beyond what is required, you need to sit down with him, thank him for his help, tell him you are going to take care of things, and send him back to his ordinary pursuits. If your ten-year-old daughter finds pleasure in giving you intimate advice about dating, she's over the line. She may be able to tell you which dress looks best on you, but a child this age does not understand adult male and female relationships. If you're getting this kind of advice from your child, stop it now and look elsewhere. There's got to be someone who can take his or her place.

Only you can draw the line. Only you can limit your child's devotion. I'm not talking about vacuuming, shopping, or fixing dinner. I'm talking about an emotional dependency that you need to make sure diminishes as you all get on with your lives.

If your child has stepped over this line, you need to say, "You've been wonderful but now I'd like to see you have more fun with your friends." Your goal is to gently nudge your child back into the world of childhood, to his friends and schoolwork. Make clear how grateful you are for his excellent help and advice but make it clear that you expect other things. If he objects, overrule him.

If your child takes on the role of being the parent to your ex-partner, you face a different challenge. If there was ever a time you needed good communication with your ex, this is it. I remember a girl who was in joint physical custody from the age of six. By the time she was thirteen, in addition to spending three days every week in his home, this child called her depressed father on the telephone every day, having taken on full responsibility for his problems. On the days she spent with him she did his shopping, cleaned his house top to bottom, and cooked meals for him to have during the days that she was at her mother's home. Her sad, needy father had become the central figure in her life. Her mother couldn't erase the fact that her daughter had become his full-time caregiver and housekeeper, but she could undertake efforts to improve the situation. First, she called her ex-husband and told him of her concerns. She offered to locate a housekeeper from the local family service agency. She also spoke at length to her daughter, commending her for her loyalty to her father and her compassionate concern, but reminded her that she needed to attend to her schoolwork and spend time with her friends. She discussed the fact that the dad needed professional help and promised that she would try to help him find a good therapist. When the mother called me to discuss her strategy, I commended her for handling what could have been an explosive situation. The daughter easily could have accused her mom of trying to separate her from her dad. I thought that it was especially wise of her to praise her daughter while taking steps to help her troubled ex-husband.

If your child is taking too much responsibility for the other parent and you can't get the point across to your ex, be advised this is not an issue you can expect to take back to court and win. No court will limit a child's contact with an unhappy parent. Your best route is to keep trying to get your ex to realize what he or she is doing, perhaps by asking trusted friends and family to intervene or by intervening yourself. Do whatever you can diplomatically to convince your ex to let your child go back to being a child. Or you can try to coax your child into having other interests. Be very careful about criticizing your child's benevolence. It is greatly to her credit and you should be proud of her compassion.

Caregiving that involves too much self-sacrifice for the needs of others is poor preparation for happy choices in adult relationships. Children who are "parentified" or overburdened often encounter serious problems with intimacy in adulthood. Many children of divorce reinstall their wish to rescue a parent into their adult relationships by getting involved with troubled partners who have a hard time being adults. One lovely young woman from my long-term study of divorce spent her whole childhood taking care of both parents. Years later, after finishing college, she moved in with her boyfriend. She sadly described their relationship. "He has no ambition, no life goal, no education, no regular job. He's going nowhere. But he loves me. He would be devastated if I ever left him." It took her a long time, and some therapy, to realize that she wanted a man who could stand on his own, not a replica of her relationship with her parents.

My advice is twofold: do your best to create a close relationship with your children, but keep your distance so that you can be an effective parent. Encourage them to help you but to spend time with kids their own age. This is a tricky business that draws on your diplomacy. The issue of using an older child as a built-in babysitter can be very seductive to a mother or father. A wise, caring parent will know to limit this kind of help and to make other arrangements to provide the youngster with relief. Protect your child from doing too much, even if it's offered with love and generosity.

Chapter 23:   Parent-Child Alignments

I want to warn you about another pitfall in parent-child relationships after divorce. In an intact family, parents often have favorites. One child is daddy's little girl or lifetime baseball buddy. Another shares an interest in music, animals, or science. While these close relationships may lead one or more siblings to feel less loved, they are often fleeting and usually kept within reasonable bounds. Few children are treated as badly as Cinderella.

Children in intact families often have strong preferences for one parent over the other. Maybe they find Mom boring, surly, or rigid or too serious and maybe they seek out their dad's company because he tells funny stories, has interesting skills, or is just a more sympathetic person. These natural alliances also shift as children move through different developmental stages and as parents change.

But in a divorced family, the tendency to play favorites can assume a darker cast. The relationship between child and parent can reflect the anger between the parents. In the worst cases, a parent and child form a battle team that attacks the other parent so that the fight can end up in court, where the weary judge is expected to make judgments about family issues that would tax the knowledge of Dr. Freud.

In many divorced families, these alignments fall along gender lines— mother and daughter or son and father take on the opposition. For example, some moms may feel especially close to their daughters, a relationship that intensifies after the breakup. They find that their daughters are more responsive to their problems and help out more around the house. Their sons, on the other hand, may remind them of their exhusbands. One woman I know said with irritation, "My five-year-old son looks like his dad, talks like his dad, puts dirty dishes into the refrigerator like his dad, does dumb things like his dad." You should do your best to guard against this kind of thinking. Ask yourself honestly, are you treating your son with the same warmth as you did before the divorce? Are you pushing him away because of some real or fantasized resemblance? Your child can't help having that gorgeous smile, the freckles, the funny little cowlick, or that stubborn streak.

I have watched men praise their little boys to the skies and neglect their daughters after divorce. One four-year-old girl came back regularly to her mom's house in tears after each visit, saying that her father ignored her while he played with her brothers. The dad criticized her constantly. "She's stupid, just like all women, just like her mother," he told me. The mother offered to let her girl stay at home during these visits, but the child insisted on going in the vain hope that her father would change. Tragically, this child suffered low self-esteem well into adulthood. Although she grew into a very attractive young woman, she expected men to treat her with disrespect and unconsciously sought out men who humiliated her.

In happy intact families, resemblances between parent and child work in the opposite direction. You see in your daughter the beauty that attracted you to your wife and you're delighted with her. But after divorce these connections can be full of pain or anger for you. If your beautiful daughter now reminds you of her beautiful mother who walked out on you, don't push your daughter away.

Children are especially vigilant after divorce as to how you treat each of them. You need to be especially fair. They're extrasensitive and can quickly feel hurt. After all, they've just seen you reject their mother or their father. They're worried about who you might reject next. So go out of your way to treat your children alike. Keep in mind that whenever you smile at one, you should do something nice for the other. When you praise one, do the same later for the other. Whenever you spend time with one, offer to spend the same amount of time with the others.

A serious problem occurs when a child and parent of either sex joins forces in an outright alignment against the other parent. The goal is simple: to engage in practices that hurt or humiliate the other parent. The psychological pattern is clear: an embattled parent, who is often disturbed or certainly very angry, convinces the child that he or she should join in criticizing or rejecting the other parent. The request falls upon fertile ground if the attack is launched against the parent who sought the divorce. It's a duel and duet in which aggression between the parents spills onto the child. But for the child, it's more often a fight to punish the parent who left. The child's unrealistic goal is to restore the marriage. In families caught up in this kind of conflict and anger—which happens in unhappy intact families that may or may not end in divorce—the child becomes an active participant in the conflict.

If you're tempted to use your child as an ally in upsetting your ex, think carefully about what you're doing. It's humiliating for a child to be used as a messenger. When a child is instructed to say, "Mommy said to tell you that she needs money to buy me tennis shoes for gym class," the child feels demeaned and wretched. When a child is used as a spy—"Look in Daddy's dresser to see if you find ladies' lingerie"—that child feels that he's being used to hurt his dad. When a child comes home from visiting his mom and his dad asks, "Does Mommy have a boyfriend?" the child feels like he's betraying his mom. He cannot stand it.

Children quickly get trapped by such requests. They're anxious to please but are caught in the middle by their loyalty to both of you. If you're not careful, you can lead your children into playing out the anger between you and your ex in a whole range of minor and major roles. Children who acquiesce in these "games" are usually very ashamed of their behavior and can be conscience-stricken for years. Martin, a twenty-two-year-old college student, told me with great anguish how he used to lie about visiting his father because he thought it would help his mother feel better. He would say that he didn't want to visit his dad or he would hide when his father came to get him. His mother was truly desperate to restore the marriage and he was frightened by her pain. Although Martin was only seven years old at the time, his agony was evident years later as he almost broke down in my office, repeating, "I lied to him. I lied to my dad. How will he ever forgive me?"

Not all children can be drawn into these kinds of alignments. Many of them who are approached this way flatly say no. These tend to be psychologically sturdy children who have friends, interests, and high self-esteem. Children who succumb to a parent's blandishments or persuasions to engage in behavior they know is wrong are often youngsters who are worried, have felt deprived or unloved, and find themselves, for the first time, in the center of one parent's interest. These needy, insecure children can be drawn into battle because they confuse a parent's attention as love. Many find their new, important status irresistible. Others are persuaded to participate by their pity for the parent who makes the request. "My mom was so sad after my dad left that she pumped us about whether Dad had a girlfriend. She wanted to know what the girlfriend looked like and what she wore and whether Dad kissed her," a nine-year-old confessed. "I told her. I couldn't bear to disappoint her, she was so upset."

Nine-, ten-, and eleven-year-olds are particularly prone to fall prey to such behavior because they are not only eager to undo the divorce, they have the illusion that they can do so. Any target, including a parent they love, will do. Dazzled by sudden attention and flattery, they're happy to do battle, although parent and child are fighting under the same banner for different reasons. The parent wants to punish a person who has hurt him or her. The child wants to restore the marriage or to punish one parent for wanting a divorce. The child also wants to retain the attention that is newly focused on him. What's shocking to the adult mind is to see how quickly children will turn on a parent they love in their vain hope to bring back the marriage. Actually, youngsters at this age have little understanding of how hurtful their words can be for adults. Nor do they understand the real-life consequences of their rude behavior.

Although the parent under attack may feel like the problem will never end, I've never seen an alignment last through adolescence. During adolescence, relationships with both parents change capriciously. Parents who were adored yesterday fall off their pedestal by morning. By the same token parents rejected earlier are suddenly sought after. Children tend to move on, losing interest in their parent's quarrel as life at school gets more interesting. Parents who go to court to end such alliances by requesting changes in custody would probably save a lot of money if they kept their peace and just waited calmly in the wings.

But this hasn't stopped lawyers and others in the legal system from stepping in. They have a term for it—parent alienation syndrome or, sometimes, child alienation syndrome. It means that a child refuses to visit a parent for no reason that the rejected parent considers sensible and about which he is willing to launch a court battle. This behavior is wrongly called a syndrome—that's a medical term requiring professional consensus, which in this case has not occurred. Nevertheless, attorneys for parents who feel under attack have claimed in court that the child has been "brainwashed" to engage in hostile behavior and have requested that the child be moved immediately to live full-time with the parent he rejected. In some cases, they have won. One mother I know was chastised strongly by the court for "brainwashing" her son. The courts removed the boy from her home and did not allow mother and child to visit each other.

The problem is that judges in these cases tend not to explore the child's motivation—which may be entirely separate from what either parent believes. Fortunately, many divorce and mental health experts have stepped forward to question the court's use of a concept that has no scientific support. While a child's behavior may be "alienated" and is painful to the victim, it can hardly be labeled an illness. Moreover, what seems irrational to an adult who is highly indignant and greatly enraged at being rejected by his child may be entirely rational and age appropriate for the child.

Children refuse to visit a parent for many reasons. All roads do not lead to the mother inciting a child against the father or vice versa. Many young children have difficulty separating from their mothers. Kindergarten teachers see this all the time. And it can surely extend into the early school grades in a child after divorce. Sometimes one parent really is difficult to be with, or is boring or unpleasant, or asks the child to do things he doesn't like. This is not at all uncommon. Parents whose children object to visiting are likely to be the architects of their own predicament. Some children refuse to visit because they're genuinely worried about the parent left alone. Or they may be highly critical of a father's behavior during the marriage and divorce without having been influenced at all by the mother. Children have a moral sensibility and a capacity to think that is not a product of propaganda by a parent.

I recall one highly principled twelve-year-old girl from Illinois who refused to visit her father because he insisted that she join him in shooting birds. The child felt that she was committing a crime and had nightmares about dead birds. The case went to court. Unfortunately, the judge ruled against the girl, insisting that her father was within his rights in directing his own child even if the child took it to be a gross violation of her morality. But this child had impressive courage along with principles. She stood up to the judge and said, "You are making the biggest mistake of your life." He countered by ordering the little girl into detention. In describing this deplorable case before the chief justices from all fifty states, I asked them to consider if this child, as a consequence of the judge's intemperate order, might grow up to turn her back on a society that she felt had betrayed her.

Fortunately, many judges are beginning to realize that they can't solve complex psychological issues like a child's refusal to visit by changing custody or by punishing one parent. But if you find yourself being drawn into this kind of battle, talk to your attorney and find out how a child's resistance to visiting is understood in your community. Can you expect your local judge to understand that children in intact and divorced families often have wishes and preferences that are not in keeping with those of one or both parents? Many children in our society are raised from an early age to think for themselves.

Important lessons can be drawn from all these unhappy stories. First, try your best not to involve your child in your anger at your ex. Your job is to protect him. He can't bear the notion that you're fighting, especially over him. If he becomes embroiled in the battle, he will suffer that much more. Avoid the temptation of co-opting your child's loyalty and of trying to convince him that your version of what went wrong in the marriage is the correct one. You may be right. Nevertheless, it's a temptation you should resist with all your might. You may sometimes feel that the only ally you have in the world is your faithful child, but don't make him take sides. It's a no-win situation for everyone in the post-divorce family.

As a wise parent you should trust that your child will come to his own judgment about what was right and wrong in your marriage and divorce, regardless of what he may have been told in the heat of the conflict. It's foolish and self-defeating to ask the court to order your child to spend time with you against his will. I'm very opposed to forcing a child to visit in these circumstances. It will only quadruple his resentment and strengthen his refusal to visit. Think carefully. You don't want to drive your child into becoming a runaway. You can force a child's presence, but you surely cannot force his love and loyalty. You may win the battle and lose the war. What's more, there's no end to a child's ingenuity. I recall a nine-year-old who, in accord with a mediated agreement, spent long weekends with her father against her will. Years later she confessed, with a mischievous smile, "I would pretend to myself all weekend that I wasn't there. After I reached eighteen, I never called him."

It's a far better idea to sit down with your child and discuss frankly what's wrong and how you two together can improve your time with each other. If your child refuses to see you, try a letter or an e-mail. Or talk to someone she respects, like a minister or favorite teacher, to intervene on your behalf. Some children feel more comfortable visiting if they can bring along a friend. Put your vanity aside and ask yourself whether a child would really enjoy the schedule you have arranged. If you force the visits, you'll be losing the opportunity to enjoy your short time together. Children grow up fast. Before you know it, they're the masters of their own time and will decide on their own whether they want to spend time with you.

Before we leave this topic, I want to give you an example of how one rejected father won back his daughter's affection. Marianne was thirteen when her father met another woman on an overseas trip and decided to leave his unhappy marriage. Marianne had been her father's favorite child. She was a star athlete and an excellent student. He had great ambitions for her to follow in his footsteps. She, in turn, idealized her father as an honorable, trustworthy man. But this was too much. She refused to speak to him, saying he had fallen in her esteem. "He taught us all these values and commandments and he betrayed them," she said. "I don't respect him anymore." The father's reaction was intense. Marianne was central to his life and he couldn't stand her anger. Fortunately, before he went to court to accuse his ex-wife of inciting Marianne's behavior—and requesting that the court order his daughter to live with him—he came to seek my advice. I told him to write to Marianne, apologize to her for breaking up the family, and also explain his behavior. She returned his first letter unopened. He re-sent it. She opened the letter the third time it came and agreed to meet him for one hour. She finally agreed it was a fair request. The father explained that he understood how dismayed she was at his behavior and how worried she was about her mother. He explained that she was old enough to understand that there are two sides to a marriage and to a decision. Marianne was silent but listened carefully to his message. He suggested that they meet again for a second hour. She agreed and the relationship gradually resumed. He encouraged Marianne to take care of her mother and promised to provide for them both. He wanted her to know that he was neither a villain nor a saint—merely a human being who had been unhappy.

Think how different this would have been if this father had gone to the court to force his daughter to visit. It's not likely that she would ever have forgiven him. As it turned out, they developed a good relationship that grows stronger each day.

Chapter 24:   A New Kind of Teenager

Since an estimated half of the children in divorced families are six years old or younger at the breakup, a majority of children of divorce enter and live through their adolescence in the post-divorce family. So let's take a close look at what this means. Is adolescence qualitatively different because your parents split up years ago? Or do teenagers everywhere pass through the same developmental gauntlets, regardless of their parents' marital status?

The answer is yes and no. Many of the challenges you face in raising teenagers, as a single or remarried parent, are familiar to all parents. Teenagers confront similar growing pains in every family. But you will also face additional challenges stemming from your divorce. Children of divorce tend to enter adolescence earlier than peers from intact families. They tend to persist in adolescent behavior longer than those same peers—sometimes well into their late twenties. It's even likely but not a certainty that the teenage years will be stormy. But take heart. There's a great deal that you can do to help.

First, I'd like you to step back and take a deep breath to get some perspective. It's fashionable to think that teenagers are crazy, capricious, maddening, hysterical, and mysterious. But let me offer you a different and more cheerful way of thinking about them. You certainly don't have to live in dread of all the "awful" things that will happen. While the adolescent years are fraught with dangers, it's also a period of moral and intellectual growth. As goofy as your teenager may appear, he has a new capacity to think, question, formulate his own opinions, aspire, love, and suffer. He's really in the midst of a most exciting, important time. Think back on your own first love, how you cried when you thought that the other person hardly knew you were alive, how you jumped sky-high when you—not the most popular kid in the class—first got asked out. Think of the rapture of your first kiss. And think of how powerful you felt because you were the generation that was going to show the world, because you knew so much. Adolescents are exasperating, funny, and fun. The more you can approach this period with a sense that teenagers are full of potential and that they'll get through it, the happier you'll all be.

Teenagers in divorced families have an extra task in this period, one that involves some serious thinking. Because you divorced, they feel compelled to think about family relationships, about you and your ex, about why your marriage came apart, and who if anyone was to blame. They feel a need to think about right and wrong in human relationships and whether they can avoid the turn that you and your ex took somewhere along the road. They want to understand what happened from beginning to end. While other teenagers think about their future and what they want to achieve, your teenager's ruminations are more urgent and fraught with anxiety.

Adolescence can be particularly stormy in divorced families. All teenagers confront issues of sex, male-female relationships, and what to expect in the future. But children of divorce deal with these questions within a matrix of experiences related to divorce. First, they witnessed your marriage fall apart. Second, it's certainly possible that many have been sexually excited by seeing new lovers (yours and your ex's) coming into the household. They've seen romances blossom and crash, observing your highs and lows, your delirium and disappointment. These experiences tend to propel children into adolescent behavior sooner than their peers whose parents, in their minds, remain sexless.

In Chapter 8, I described how eleven-, twelve-, and thirteen-year-olds can, at the time of the breakup, enter adolescence early, especially when there is less structure and discipline at home to protect them from the voices of the street. The children I am talking about in this chapter—who were much younger at the breakup and later stand on the threshold of adolescence—face the same dangers. While the post-divorce family presumably now has some structure, rules, and expectations, the fact remains that many children of divorce are not as well supervised as children who have two biological parents at home who spell each other and support each other when their teenager is nowhere to be seen at midnight curfew. Teenage children of divorce take advantage of having less supervision and are more likely to press limits and boundaries. Nationally, girls from divorced families are more likely to engage in early sexual behavior, which in my experience can be as early as age twelve. Boys tend to engage in delinquent behavior at an earlier age—"just try to stop me" is a phrase you will hear a lot.

You can help your teenager every step of the way. In fact, it's imperative for him and you that you do so. First, you need to be vigilant without being ultrasuspicious. Please don't give your youngster the impression that you anticipate trouble. When a parent expects a teenager to stray, it easily becomes a self-fulfilling prophecy. The best strategy is to stay in close touch with your teen, to express genuine interest in what he's doing at school and with friends, and to respond thoughtfully to the questions he raises. This way you'll get a quick sense of when his life begins to change and you can intervene early. This may call for quick, strong action on your part. One woman I know, whose fifteen-year-old defiantly announced that she was going to spend the night with her boyfriend and departed in a huff, went to the boy's unsupervised house at midnight and insisted that her daughter come home with her, pronto. When the girl refused, the mother said, "You are fifteen and in my care. If you don't come, I will call the police immediately." As the girl realized that her mother wasn't bluffing, she howled in protest but agreed to return home. The next day mother and daughter had a long, sober talk about the daughter's behavior and why it was not acceptable to casually spend the night with a young man. The daughter, who years later admitted she was relieved by her mother's action, was more conciliatory after the showdown.

Sometimes there's no alternative to in-your-face, aggressive parenting. Sometimes you need to state your values clearly to prevent your child from getting into serious trouble. What you may get in return is a temporary cooling of your relationship and all sorts of threats, including classic riffs about running away from home. You need to remember that your child's judgment is seriously flawed by adolescent impulsiveness. It's your job to prevent him from acting out when he's likely to harm himself. But here's the rub. You need to be able to distinguish between normal acting out and harmful acting out. Teens everywhere experiment with marijuana and alcohol, usually without hurting themselves. But if they start using drugs and alcohol every day, it's a different story. If your son decides it's cool to dye his hair green, you may all have a good laugh. But if he dyes his hair green to be accepted by the gang that deals cocaine, it's no laughing matter. Adolescent girls are foxy, attracting boys their own age and the glances of older men. If they date boys from school, it's appropriate. But if they want to date much older guys, you have a problem. Apart from the dangers of sexually transmitted diseases, pregnancy, and abortion, sexual activity at a young age can devastate a girl's self-esteem.

You won't be able to distinguish what's normal from what's harmful unless you're connected to your child's life. You need to know what's going on so you can know when to intervene. If your teenager starts to get bad grades or begins hanging out with a peer group headed for trouble, sit down with him, explain why you're concerned, and ask what you can do to help.

You may be surprised at what this kind of heart-to-heart conversation can produce. Linda was one of those wild sixteen-year-olds who flaunted her pseudo-independence and hung out with a motorcycle gang. One day, after she'd had a blowup with her leather-jacketed boyfriend, her stepfather sat her down and said, "You're wasting your life. You're much too intelligent to go on this way. If you stop hanging around with those losers and get yourself to class and study, I'll pay your college tuition." The message got through. I remember her saying several years later, "You know, he meant it. He put his money where his mouth was and sent me to school." Linda graduated with honors.

The key to this kind of intervention is to mean it. Show genuine interest and follow through. Don't be put off by your child's gruff manner and don't wait too long. If you and your ex can work together, all the better. Teenagers are often rather surprised to learn that their parents really care what happens to them, even when they are not in trouble.

Teenagers can be excellent manipulators. All of them do it, but children of divorce have more to work with. Chances are they'll take advantage of the fact that you seem like an easy mark, compared to the more forbidding image of two parents waiting up when rules are broken. The truth is, you are weaker. Even if you have a successful second marriage, a stepparent does not have the same authority—or the same obligations—as the biological parent. You're going to be the lone legitimate adult enforcing your rules in your house. I say this not to scare you but to help prepare you for what typically transpires between the ages of thirteen and seventeen in our modern American culture.

Some parents fall for their child's sob story because they fail to communicate. Another sixteen-year-old boy I know was told by his mother that he could have a car if he kept his grades up. His school year started off very well and she bought the car. But when his grades dropped badly a few months later, she took away the keys. This enterprising boy called his father, who lived in another state, and told him that his mother had taken away his car for no good reason. He added that he wanted to come live with his dad, who sent $2,500 by return mail. The boy went to live with his father and stepmother for six tumultuous months. During this time he totaled his father's car in an accident for which he was entirely to blame. He quickly left his father's home and went back to his mother.

Some adolescents have ulterior motives for behaving badly. They learn fairly quickly that if they get into trouble, they can get a parent, who is otherwise occupied with a new marriage or second family, to come running. My favorite story is about a very enterprising youngster named Jonathan who got involved in a series of petty robberies when he was thirteen. Many years later, he told me, smiling broadly, "I went to the biggest jewelry store in the mall and stole a watch with the security camera right on me. My mom had just said, 'One more episode of trouble out of you and I'm sending you to your dad.' She called my dad that night and he drove six hours straight to our house. When he got there at midnight I was up waiting for him with my stuff packed ready to go. When he opened the door I said, 'Dad, what took you so long?' I'll never forget the look on his face."

Some boys get into serious trouble without being conscious of the fact that their behavior will bring their dad to the rescue. One very mild-mannered sixteen-year-old boy was apprehended by police with a gun he had picked up illegally in a pawnshop. His father, whom he had not seen for over a year, flew in from a distant city to put up bail. When I spoke to the boy he seemed unaware of the seriousness of the charge. He was all smiles. "My dad came to put up bail and see me!" he said happily. "He really cares about me."

Many children of divorce ask to change their residence during adolescence. It can be a good idea or a poor one. But if you decide to follow through, be sure that both you and your ex plan the move carefully. You don't want your teenager to think no one cares where he lives and that he's free to wander like a nomad.

If your child insists that he or she wants to go live with his father, it's a good idea to call and discuss the possibility with your ex-husband. Don't wait for your child to get into trouble to reach his or her father. Offer to sit down and discuss the idea, if it is realistic. If you're a mom and your son persists in disobeying you, to the point you throw up your hands and decide to send the boy off to his father, please don't make the move impulsively. While it's true that some fathers are better able than their ex-wives to handle a recalcitrant child, a father needs time to prepare his home for his son's arrival. I know many instances where fed-up mothers put their teenage sons on planes, buses, or trains and then sent a message: Bobby is arriving at such and such a time. That was it. The children arrived on their father's doorsteps but there was no place for them to sleep other than the couch. If you decide to move your child to his father's house, make a plan that involves all the parties, with certain conditions attached.

If your ex is not able or willing to take your child into his home, ask him to tell your child the reasons why. You should not carry this disappointing news. Nevertheless, your child may accuse you of having foiled his plan. One mother, who had serious doubts about her exhusband's interest in their son, called the father in the boy's presence to find out his plans for his son. The boy was taken aback at her forthrightness, confessing that now she had made the call, he was not sure what he wanted to do. The mom encouraged her son to discuss plans with the dad and come back and talk with her. As the situation developed, the boy decided to stay put. Airing the discussion took the rebellious wind out of his sails and he settled down.

If your teenager plays these destructive games, you and your ex should be talking frequently, not just when a blowup happens. If you have a new lover or spouse who's not sympathetic to your problem, you need to choose your priorities. Sure, your son or daughter may seem like an unwelcome intruder—some children show up on a parent's doorstep ten years after divorce—but this is your child and you are the parent. It's better for you and your new partner to be prepared for this possibility.

Many drug and alcohol treatment programs are designed for high school students. You can also set down a new set of rules concerning curfews, grades, and other expectations. Whatever you do, don't give up. Your child may appear to be ignoring you when in fact she's looking over her shoulder to make sure you're paying attention. You have more influence than you realize. Your words will be long remembered.

If your child continues to get into trouble, what can you do about it? First, it's important to distinguish a real crisis from a minor skirmish. If your child is using dangerous drugs, missing school, or sleeping around, call a family meeting. Get your ex to come in person. It's an emergency. Be sure to include the siblings and perhaps grandparents if they're close. The format should not be accusatory but rather focused on how the assembled family members can help. The goal is not to confront your child but rather to convey genuine love and concern and willingness to make sacrifices on her behalf. One mother called such a meeting when her sixteen-year-old daughter announced that she was dropping out of high school. She said, "What are we going to do that will help you?" Without hesitating, the girl said, "I want to be able to go to college but no one in this family gives a damn. So why should I try?" The mom responded by mortgaging her home to pay for college tuition and arranged counseling for her daughter. The dad agreed to pay for the therapy but wasn't able to pay anything toward college. Within months, the daughter's behavior changed dramatically. "I can't believe what my folks did," she said. "I'm really lucky. And I'm not going to disappoint them, ever."

What if you call a family conference and your child just glares at you? State your concern and your willingness to help and set another date. Don't lose your temper and don't accuse her. If she threatens to run away, tell her that you would miss her very much and that you hope she is not that desperate. Tell her that you want her to leave when she is ready and able to take care of herself. But that is not now. I don't need to tell you that there isn't a remedy for every adolescent crisis. Sometimes life has to take its course. But the power of a family meeting in handling a real crisis is that your teenager will be deeply, if silently, impressed by the attention. And she will remember your concern.

If your child seems irrationally angry at both of you, the feeling could stem from an earlier time. Preschool children of divorce often feel abandoned as Mom and Dad are preoccupied with getting their lives back on track. The anger they feel at this betrayal can smolder for years, until it's acted out in the drama of adolescent defiance. These children come to adolescence feeling hungry for the nurturance that got interrupted by your divorce. And when adolescents are depressed, they rarely sit in rocking chairs. They're more likely to be out in the street disturbing the peace or getting into trouble at school.

It's become unfashionable in many circles to talk about morality. Some parents find it easier to be a buddy to a teenage son or daughter. But we make life more difficult for children when we refrain from telling them what we believe in. If your child laughs at you for being old-fashioned, don't worry. A child's developing conscience is helped by having a parent who has standards of right and wrong. You can think of yourself as an antidote against the popular stimuli in rap music, violent movies, movie star images, and ceaseless advice from adolescent peers who think they know everything. You can't deprive your children of popular culture, but you can provide a balance against the intense sexual stimulation and violence they see by holding to the standards you set within your own home. And when they pretend not to hear, they are probably listening.

If you're worried about your daughter's sexual activity, talk to her, ask her. If she denies she's sleeping around, tell her that you love her and you respect her. You don't want her to feel less respect for herself and her body. Explain that sex within a loving, caring relationship is an entirely different experience than sex with strangers. Then tell her that she's too young to be having sex and there's no way that you can permit it. It may be very difficult for you to be strong enough in this regard. Daughters are especially adept at invoking guilt in their mothers, as if guilt were floating around in the air and they could grab hold of it whenever they want. Keep in mind that all mothers feel "guilty" with or without cause whether they're married or divorced, whenever a child is in trouble. My advice, knowing full well how difficult it may be, is for you to hold on to your moral position, concern for your daughter's self-respect, and insistence that she follow your rules. In setting these standards, you need to be clear about what you believe is right and wrong and to draw on your own convictions. What a neighbor says or thinks is not relevant. As a parent, it's your decision. Since it relates to your moral values, it's your decision. Your second husband may strengthen your position or provide excellent advice, but you are the one who goes face-to-face with your child, as many times as it takes to get her to listen.

If your child is depressed and has no friends, you should take it seriously. Adolescence is a necessary prelude to growing up. This is the time you learn about getting along with other people and home in on the kind of life you'll have in the near future. If your child avoids social contact, has an eating disorder, or hides out in his room complaining of chronic boredom, first talk with the school counselor to find out how your child is doing at school and then consult with a mental health professional to get advice for you and help for her. Fortunately, there are in most communities professionals who are especially trained in work with adolescents. If money is a problem, try a family agency. They are likely to have well-trained people on their staff and they usually have a sliding scale.

Obviously, you need to stay on top of what's happening in your child's life. You can say directly, "You know, I don't know why you're having such a hard time. Please tell me. I'm concerned about you. I want you to do well in school and in life and I don't believe for a minute that you don't care about your grades at school." Don't let your child throw you off base and please don't buy into the argument that you're guilty, that you've deprived your son or daughter of guidance, love, or whatever. If you can manage it, stand up straight, hold your ground, and repeat your expectations. You are being pushed to the limit to maintain your adulthood and to control your temper. You may feel like you're on quicksand. But if your child hurls an insult that hits the mark, do your best to stand firm.

At the same time, you need to be reasonable. After establishing rules of conduct for your household, you can provide privileges that your child earns by showing responsibility and grown-up behavior. If your son won't follow the rules, you can withdraw his permission to drive the family car. If your daughter promises to graduate with her class and follows through, you can reward her with something she wants. Special perks like a camping trip with friends, a set of skis, a mountain bike, a special outfit, or whatever your teenager values and finds challenging are surprisingly successful. One mother told me that her daughter found the promise of a car on her graduation irresistible enough to give up a long-standing pattern of truancy.

If you can find a way to involve your child in the real world, help-ing in adult roles, the experience can be transformative. Look for pro-grams that take teenagers into new environments. One mother I know asked her sullen fifteen-year-old daughter, "What are you going to do this summer?"

The girl shrugged and said, "Hang out. Go to *Rocky Horror*."

"How would you like an adventure instead?" asked the mom and described a public health program in Latin America that sends teenagers into remote villages to build latrines and vaccinate animals against rabies.

The daughter, who needed to face something bigger than herself, jumped at the chance. She wrote home, "Dear Mom, I cry when I watch how the people in my village take care of each other. America seems impoverished by comparison." When she got home later that summer she said to her mom, "I know who I am now. I like myself."

If you ever thought that parenting would get easier when your chil-dren got older, think again. Powerful voices from the street call to your teenager from countless sources. Raising a teenager requires more time, more supervision, and better than ever listening on your part. You need to be vigilant about schoolwork, the acceptability of what your child wears (does the school allow bare midriffs?) and whether adults will be present at the next and the next and the next party your child is invited to.

While I'm not suggesting that you become the militia, any rules and curfews that you impose at this time are very important. Often children from divorced families have never even heard the word "curfew," a fact that astonishes their friends from more traditional intact families. If you find that your rules are lax because you're simply too exhausted to do much about it, I strongly suggest that you counter this feeling with the understanding that the stakes for your child are high. Now more than ever, it's time for you to be the kind of parent who's in full control. This is the time to maintain distance between yourself and your child, even though it's tempting to treat your daughter like a sister or your son like a buddy. If your ex treats your child like a comrade in arms, with weaker rules to boot, you still need to hold to your own moral standards.

A final word of reassurance: In recalling your own adolescence, you may remember some hair-raising episodes that you never told your parents about. But also remember that you probably came through it wiser or at least unscathed. It's impossible to prepare for adult life without adolescence. You can be sure your children will do the same, only perhaps with more resources and perhaps with more imagination. While not all teens get into trouble, few go through adolescence without some risk-taking, and it's best to be prepared. Keep things in perspective and hold on to your sense of humor.

Chapter 25:   A New Kind of Father

Divorce transforms the experience of being a mother or father. If you think back on your marriage in happier times or can imagine how everyday life runs inside a reasonably good intact family, you'll recall how much men and women rely on each other to nourish the parent-child bond. But when this tie is broken, the fundamental nature of parenting and the very experience of being a mother or father is forever changed. I say this not to scare you into thinking, "Oh no, what have I done to my children?" but to help you move into this new role with your eyes open. I'm not talking about a drop in income or the difficulties of juggling two homes but rather a profound cluster of psychological changes that accompany your new role as a parent in the post-divorce family. These changes are different for men and women.

First, the dads. When your marriage ended, nobody warned you what it would feel like to be a father in a divorced family. All of the print flowing out of fathers' groups and popular media fail to make any distinctions between a dad in an intact family and a dad in a divorced family. But there are differences that you'll need to understand if you're going to enjoy being a father in this new chapter of your life. This doesn't mean that you can't be a wonderful father who enjoys his children or an influential father who provides a moral compass for his children, but it does mean that you have to expect more static and interruptions in navigating a road that is less predictable than you ever imagined.

Fathers and children need each other after divorce. But all of a sudden, you're confused about how to go about being a good father. Part of the reason is that when you're married, you're always the father even if your business takes you away from home frequently. You call from distant cities and your children tell you about their activities that day. You make it a point to remember to pick up a small gift on your return to show your child that you remembered him while you were away. You always knew exactly who you were and so did your children. But in a divorced family, you are only the father when it's your turn with the kids, regardless of how often that occurs. You are part-time. What kind of role is that? How can a parent be part-time?

Fathering is also difficult in the post-divorce family because you don't have the supports that you had in your marriage. A happy wife is an enormous support to her husband; a harmonious home supports a father in his role. Each parent complements and nurtures the other. At the end of every day you bring each other up to date on what is happening with your child. But after a divorce, you're in a vacuum. Suddenly your relationship with your child has to sustain itself with less communication or help from anyone. There are a thousand and one experiences in a child's daily life about which you don't have a clue. And so you ask yourself, like millions of other fathers, Who am I? How central am I? What does being a divorced father mean? What does being a coparent mean? Am I a playmate? A Dutch uncle? A friend or a guy who helps with the math homework? Who sets the discipline? Who sets the goals? How important am I now that my ex-wife is remarried and the kids have a stepfather? How do I divide my time after my own second marriage and my new wife has children, or we have children of our own? How do I continue to feel that these are my children?

Every divorced dad I know faces these questions. Divorce calls for a total redefinition of who you are as a father and challenges you to come up with a plan for how to maintain or surpass the relationship you had with your children during your marriage. Unfortunately, there are no guidelines for divorced fathers the way there are cultural norms for fathers in intact marriages. In the intact family you didn't have to define your role. Everyone knew who you were, even your youngest children and their little friends. You were Daddy. But now you have a whole new role that our society has yet to define. Let me help.

Let's say you're a dad who was very close to his children during the marriage—you regularly put them to bed, played with them, and took an active part in helping them with homework. All those good activities may continue. You'll have to negotiate an agreement with your ex-wife that enables you to continue this closeness. Also be aware that a year or two from now, if either or both of you remarry, your lives may change in ways that demand redefinition and flexibility. But I guarantee that if you're able to continue taking care of your children, you'll be rewarded in countless ways, including the fact that you won't feel like you're losing them.

If you've been an absent father—and many dads in unhappy marriages are just that in the years prior to the breakup, some going out of their way to stay away—then you may feel confused about what happens next. You may think that your children will hardly notice the difference. But that's not true. Preschool children with absent dads—men who say the kid won't know I'm gone—can show some of the most severe reactions to divorce, including a kind of listlessness that breaks your heart. At the point of the breakup, even if you've been away for days at a time every week, children cry, "Where's Daddy?"

After divorce you need to think about what kind of relationship you want with your children. Are you going to bow out? Some men do, especially those who themselves were abandoned by their fathers. Others, who suffered that hurt, decide to become steadfast fathers for their own children. Whatever your background, you have that choice. In the first few years after your divorce, you have a new shot at fatherhood. But be aware that this role takes time, effort, and a willingness to stick it out. Despite what your attorney may say, your relationship with your children is not dependent on how much time you spend together based on the divorce settlement. The extent of your influence is not measured by units of time. You can spend hundreds of hours watching TV with your son and not get any closer to him. Your relationship is only measured by how much your child feels your love, your commitment, and what you're able to bring to that relationship—a world that's different from what his mother brings. You're not a Mr. Mom. You're a dad. A friend of mine likes to quote an Indian legend that says the father's job is to carry the child to the top of the mountain and face the child away from home toward the bigger landscape. That's poetic but it's only true if the father carries the child carefully and does not drop him on the climb.

Once you decide what role you want to play in your children's lives, you have to organize your life so that you give the plan priority. You can't squeeze your role as a father into a time slot that you attend to after other responsibilities have been met. And you need to be aware from the outset that your children's desires, needs, and friendships will change as they grow older. What works today, when they're little and your decisions govern the relationship, will probably not work a few years from now.

These logistics aside, your new role as father outside the intact family involves losses that you will, I'm sorry to say, have to face and accept. A father and mother under the same roof are not the same as a father and mother under separate roofs. Parents in every reasonably good intact family carry on a daily dialogue about children. When a new family moves next door, they discuss their impressions of the new neighbor's children and whether that child might be a friend to their kids or whether they're better off maintaining some distance. When the teacher says that Emily is being bossy on the playground, parents talk all the way home about why the teacher fails to see Emily's leadership qualities but what might be done to teach Emily some tactfulness. When Grandma says crossly that the children's manners could improve, they discuss at length whether to correct the children or ignore Grandma. But once your marriage ends, you and your ex-wife no longer carry on these kinds of conversations. When your children go back and forth between your two homes, you're only getting a part of the story of what's happening in their lives and you can't count on your children to fill you in. You have much less opportunity for shaping their lives. How would you like to run a company with only half of the sales receipts available for you to see?

Mothers, more than fathers, tend to be the interpreters of what young children want inside an intact family. Call it a biological epiphenomenon, a cultural artifact, or what you will, but the fact is that mothers often play the go-between between young children and their fathers. They often hold the key to how the child feels and what he or she wants, and they carry messages to that effect. In countless homes it's the sensitive mother who says to you, "Tommy hasn't dared mention his wish that you'll go along on the scout camping trip. He's dying for you to go." Or, "Becky was really sad all week because you went out of town. I know you're busy but you should try to make it up." In many homes it's still the mother who says, "You have to go to the father-daughter dinner at the elementary school next week. I know you have to be in Toronto, but if you catch the earlier flight you can be here in time."

Developmental stages in your child's life do affect the tenor of your relationships. Young girls, especially as they reach adolescence, feel safer in the house if their mother is present. This is not because men are sexual predators and will commit incest at the drop of a hat. But it's a fact that when young girls are struggling with their own sexuality, they want their moms around. The things they're interested in can be shared more readily with their moms, and for a temporary period, they may need some distance from you. If this is happening to you, your daughter is a normal kid. Don't blame your ex-wife.

The fact that you may lose access to parts of your children's world because their mother no longer shares a home with you is one of the expectable losses for fathers after divorce. The only fathers I know who can avoid this feeling are those who have sole custody of their children.

In that case, men can and do move into the mothering role, often with great sensitivity and heroism. But even they have to maintain a distance from their daughter's intimate life as she moves into adolescence. At this stage of development, a girl needs her dad to protect her but not to intrude on her privacy. It's okay to take your adolescent daughter hiking, but not dancing. Men need to understand that teenage girls need to withdraw from too close a relationship with their dads. When they're seventeen or eighteen, if you have kept up your end, they'll be happy to reestablish a closer relationship.

I believe that a highly motivated father can acquire the sensitivity to read a child's wishes—even when these wishes are stated obliquely. You can master the language, but bear in mind that this skill will not pop into your nervous system overnight. You'll need to observe your children carefully. Instead of filling every moment you're together with television, computer games, and other forms of entertainment, you need to spend simple "downtime" just talking and laughing together, letting feelings emerge naturally. Don't make the mistake of thinking that it will happen automatically or that it can be legislated by time. You'll be loved. You'll be rejected. Your wisdom will be mocked and valued. Sometimes you'll be right, sometimes wrong. To function alone as a parent is different from any other role you've ever had. And to do it with no backup is really tough. If you're the kind of guy who thinks he's always right, you're in for a surprise. I can assure you it'll be hard in the beginning. The path zigs and zags. But it's extremely rewarding if you hold on.

What mistakes can you make? The most common one is that you can give up too soon. As an experienced father, you may not want to admit that you need new skills and that you can't rely on "just being there." I'm sorry to say that I know a lot of men who made no changes in their schedules after divorce. They expected their children to fit into their lives and spent time together in the easiest way possible—watching rented videos or football games on TV with one of their buddies. One man I know figured that he could visit his son while playing tennis with friends. He couldn't understand his son's disappointment.

On the other hand, I've seen fathers who've been extremely creative in forging meaningful ties to their children. Their shared activities have results—like building a tree house or playhouse in the backyard, hiking the ten biggest peaks in the state, volunteering a weekend to plant trees, or working in a community garden. Children are intensely interested in what their fathers do and are flattered to play a real part in a man's world.

If you never had a role model for this kind of fathering, your job will be a lot harder. You can figure it out or you can watch a friend you admire spend time with his children. If you were abandoned, you may be tempted to give up. But regardless of your fathering, you're going to have to make up the rules de novo—for your own individual children and your own life circumstances—as you go along.

What defeats many fathers is their thin skin. Some men find that they are able to be good fathers, however they define it, as long as their lives are running smoothly. But when they suffer a defeat—lose their job, fall ill, or experience crises in other realms—they quickly become discouraged and back away from the fathering role. Their discouragement leads to a sense of being useless to their children: "I have nothing to offer" or, "My child has a better father in her stepdad."

This is not true. Your child's need for you is in no way diminished by external setbacks in your life or by his having a nifty new stepfather. If you lose your job or fall ill, as hard as it is, try not to let this translate into a loss of the relationship with your children. Your children are a priority in your life that cannot sustain compromise. Children never confuse their father with their stepfather. They have a separate slot in their heart for each of you and different expectations.

So far I've talked about how a father can build a close relationship with his children and avoid feeling hurt by the vicissitudes of post-divorce parenting. But is what I've said enough? If you follow my advice will you feel as connected to your children as you might have, had your marriage been loving and creative?

In talking with fathers individually and in focus groups over many years, I fear the answer is no. Many fathers try to stay close to their children in whatever ways they can, only to experience a feeling of loss.

I recall one episode from a focus group of fathers whose children were in their teens or young adulthood. After each man had finished describing his experiences, I turned to the group and said, "I think you're saying that despite your great efforts, you all share the fear that no matter what you did, no matter how hard you tried, you still felt in danger of being marginalized."

An audible gasp went round the room.

I had hit a raw nerve. As we talked further, the men explained that despite doing "everything right," they were still afraid of being left on the periphery. The security of the "man of the house" role in an intact family could not be recreated by being a good father in a "joint custody house" or one "visiting house." These external measures did not and cannot undo the father's inner sense of loss.

This is a very important realization for all divorced fathers. If the fear of being marginalized intrudes too much into your life, you may be led into ill-advised attempts to withdraw or to stake out a greater claim to your child's time, love, or interest or even foolishly use the courts to assert your claim. And we agreed, such efforts are bound to fail in the long run.

Sadly, many fathers choose another route: they bounce in and out of their children's lives every few years. Some return to court to assert their parental rights and blame their ex-wives for the fact that the children are frustrated, disappointed, and tired of visiting. They fail to see what the child sees: a disaffected father who never explained why he was not available for years on end. If you've done this to some degree, you owe your children an apology and an explanation of why you failed to visit. Most of all, you need to start rebuilding a relationship with your children that takes into account changes in their development.

Start at square one by getting to know them all over again. Help them to gradually become reacquainted with you. Understand that for a long time your children will expect you to disappear again. Be gentle with them. Don't demand that they spend several days a week with you in your home without knowing their usual schedule and preferences. Talk to their mother about their interests, activities, and medical and school history. Visit the school to learn more about your child and how your visits can help her.

The greatest gift you can give your child is the sense that you're a "forever father" who's deeply committed to parenting. You're also a realistic father who recognizes that children both need you and need to grow away from you. The main purpose of parenting is to help children grow into independence. Recall that children in intact families sometimes seek their moms to lean on and sometimes want Dad to help them. You can expect your children to do the same. If they happen to lean on Mom for something important to them, you shouldn't automatically interpret this as rejection. As they go back and forth, and especially as they move into adolescence, you need to keep in mind that your centrality in their development never diminishes, but your time with them sure does. You have to take on faith that you're a central axis in your child's life, around which his or her character and conscience develops. Trust me, it will fluctuate month to month, year to year.

The father-child relationship in both intact and divorced families serves as the template for a daughter's view of men. Her expectations and hopes for adult love and commitment are based in part on her relationship with you. Are you trustworthy? Are you loving? Will you protect her? Are you willing to make sacrifices for your relationship? Do you respect her ideas? Do you have confidence in her abilities? Have you told her how proud you are to be her father?

Similarly, fathers provide their sons with a template for what it means to be a man. Will your son say, "I learned a lot from watching my dad about what a good father can be and I want to be like him," or will he say, like one young man I know, "I learned from my dad how not to parent." You can be an example of a moral, hardworking adult who struggles manfully with the complex issues of family life. The choice is truly yours.

You need to feel good and sure about how important you are in your children's lives. If you have trouble believing this, you can look to our changing culture for support. Twenty-five years ago, it was not unusual for divorced fathers to drop out of their children's lives. No one thought much of it—society expected it. But nowadays, society recognizes the importance of fathers in their children's lives. Children grow up with thousands of memories of their dads, out of which they shape their hopes and expectations of themselves. You have no more challenging or more important task in life.

Finally, keep in mind that your role does not disappear when your child reaches adulthood. In many intact families fathers and sons grow closer, especially when the father retires and the son has children of his own. My own work shows that this does not happen as easily or as frequently in divorced families. But there is good reason to think that adult sons would welcome a closer relationship with their fathers. Bill had lost touch with his father after mid-adolescence. But he always remembered how together they built model airplanes, a hobby that influenced Bill's decision to become a pilot. When Bill turned thirty, he called his dad and invited him over to work on a model airplane kit that he had bought for the occasion. This broke the ice and the two resumed a friendship that lasts to this day.

Chapter 26:   A New Kind of Mother

I still remember the first time I talked to Joanne, an attractive forty-five-year-old teacher and mother of three children. I asked her how being a mother was different before and after the breakup. A look of surprise washed over her face and then she threw back her head and laughed. "Do you remember the little singsong we recited as kids?" she said mischievously. " 'First comes love, then comes marriage, then comes the baby and the baby carriage.' Well now we can add a few lines. 'Out goes love, out goes marriage, you still got the baby and the worn-out carriage!' "

Everyone likes to talk about the changing roles of women in recent decades. The news media are preoccupied with stories about how professional women bump their heads on glass ceilings or jockey for positions in corporate, political, or academic life. But the role of the mother who assumes full responsibility for herself and her children after divorce doesn't make headlines. No one notices it, even though most divorced families by far are headed by single women.

While fathers are lauded for showing an interest in their children, no one praises moms who walk the floor all night long with a fretful child and then go to work the next day with reddened eyes. I still remember how startled I was fifteen years ago when I gave a speech to about a hundred mostly male judges in which I noted that my research had found how very important fathers are to their children. I got a standing ovation. I couldn't understand what I had said that so excited these usually restrained and dignified judges. Of course, things have changed since then. There are more female judges and seeing a father push a baby carriage no longer attracts attention. Nevertheless, the prevailing assumption remains that mothers are expected to care for their children. What could possibly be new about that?

But I submit that motherhood after divorce is a very changed role. Your life, your view of herself and your children, the kind of care you provide, and the strains and stresses you find yourself under is a whole new ball game.

Let's examine this more closely. Some parts of being a mother have not changed. If I were to tap you on the shoulder at any time of day or night and ask where your children are at this exact moment, chances are that you'd know. You know when it's recess and when soccer practice ends. You know when the next dentist appointment is due and that Susie's gym shoes need replacing. Maybe you don't know the precise whereabouts of your teenager, but who does? To be perfectly honest, you won't know where any child is every moment of the day. But you still feel in control. The fact is that your children remain an integral part of your psychological makeup long after their birth.

A good marriage supports your feeling of being a mother who is in control. When your children are off with your husband, you have a sense that they're continuing in your care. When they come home and tell you about their day at the zoo, you get a full report from them and from your husband—what went right or wrong, who said what, and, Mommy, do you know what the elephant did?

But after divorce that sense of knowing where your children are—and feeling secure in that knowledge—is a lot harder to maintain. When your children are off with your ex, they might as well be residing in a black hole. Sometimes the children will tell you what they did, but not always. You don't get a full report. Because you don't want to coach them or nag them for details, you mostly won't know what they did. You certainly can't ask them to tell you what your ex did with his girlfriend. Their dad is not likely to tell you, either. Anyway, what happened on Saturday at Dad's house is history by the time they see you on Monday. If your child comes home distressed, you may never really know why. You can guess, but you don't really know.

You feel bad because you can't give your child the full-time supervision and protection that goes with your inner vision of what a mother should do. Had the marriage stayed happy or at least functioning well enough, you would be providing a different level of care and protection. You'd be there when your daughter falls off her bike. You'd sense that your four-year-old is coming down with a cold. You'd know that your nine-year-old needs drilling on the multiplication tables. You'd make sure that your eleven-year-old shopped for the parts he needs to make his science project. For a mother that makes a world of difference. This loss of feeling in control can really shake you up. How can you be privy to just a partial view of your child's life?

A second big change is that you're often lonely or disoriented. One day the children are with you and you know who's in charge. Then suddenly they're gone. It's not easy to shift gears to being alone. It's all very well to say you now have time to see your lover or to write a new Broadway play. But the truth is that when you're used to having the kids around and they leave, it gets lonely. The house seems spookily silent. And then, just when you may feel relieved to finally have some time of your own, they stampede their way through the door and you're back on duty full-time. It's a dizzying pace.

The third change is perhaps the most difficult. Who fuels you as a mother? Who takes care of you when you need to take care of the children? Divorce leaves you stranded.

If at one time you experienced a good marriage, you and your husband loved and protected each other. Each child was a product of your love. During the many challenges of parenting you had a partner who had confidence in you, who was grateful for how well you took care of the children, who loved you for all that you did for the family; even when you were physically apart, you were never alone. Even if your marriage was not so good, you may have maintained an alliance on behalf of your children and appreciated what the other did. This is precisely what keeps many unhappy marriages afloat.

But now you're alone. After divorce, when you put the children to bed after a hectic day and they seem so calm and angelic in their sleep, no one is there to put his arm around you. No one says, "You did great." Or, "Sit down, let me get us a drink." So where do you get the courage, energy, love, and hopefulness to keep going? The answer is simple and undeniable. It comes from you and no one else. All of your mothering comes from inside you. What keeps you going is your own dedication, endurance, and love. That's a big part of what makes mothering so hard in a divorced family. If you're lucky, you have a mom who thinks you're doing a great job or a dad who praises you. You have friends who support you. Your boyfriend or second husband may help. Or he may not. Your ex may help a lot with the children. Or he may not. But even with these supports, the motivation, push, and amazing perseverance for raising your children comes from within you. You replenish. You're also replenished by the progress you see in your children. That's your reward and it doesn't make headlines.

Given these incredible challenges, is it any wonder you sometimes lose your temper? Maybe you even scream or slap on occasion. In your worst moments, maybe you feel that you've not done well by your children, that you've failed them or even hurt them.

Or is it any wonder that in the rising passion of a love affair you give your lover priority? Sometimes a love affair can trump everything in a person's world. If you temporarily neglect your children, forgive yourself. Despite these lapses, you were there when they needed you.

A fourth challenge is bittersweet. Despite the challenges and obstacles of the post-divorce years, some of the hardest moments come when your children leave home—especially the youngest boy or girl. Separation from the "baby" in the family is a turning point in all families. Social scientists often call this the empty nest syndrome and describe it as a time of grieving for both parents, especially the mom.

But as many people in intact marriages describe the phenomenon, life gets better. Couples turn to each other in new ways and develop new shared interests. Being childless brings them back to an earlier stage of the marriage when they were freer. This is also a time when people look at each other across the breakfast table and discover that they no longer have anything in common.

But in a divorced family with no lasting remarriage this transition from kid at home to empty nest is much more difficult for mothers and children. You face living alone—really alone—for the first time in many years. Your youngest child is acutely aware that she's leaving you alone and possibly lonely. It breaks her heart.

Your task, as difficult as it is, is to let her go. Encourage her to take the job she wants or go to the college she chooses. Tell her how proud you are of her achievements. Make it clear to her that you have other supports. She may not believe you but try anyway. The truth is that once again you have to put your child's needs ahead of your own.

After she leaves, try your best to fill your life with other people and interests. You've been here before. You're an old hand at reconstructing your life and filling the gaps. If you're wise, anticipate this departure. Before she goes, take some classes, start a business, make travel plans, grab whatever help you need to move on as well. This goes with the territory of being a good mom and you know it. And since you are still a young woman, you have much to look forward to in the years ahead.

Let me help you understand all these feelings at a deeper level. Mothers after divorce seem to acquire an infinite capacity for guilt. I have seen this time and again. They feel guilty when their children stumble in the dark. Women feel everything is their fault. They blame themselves for divorces they're responsible for, for divorces they're not responsible for, and for every mishap in their child's life. Even women who escape violent marriages by the skin of their teeth feel guilty, saying that their children "need a father." In Jewish tradition, the woman is responsible for *shalom bayit*—the peace of the home. That's her job. If the home is not peaceful, it's her fault. When the marriage fails, it's her fault. Since you have no one who says, "Hey, honey, you did the right thing" whenever you have a confrontation with your child, you're going to be harder on yourself. You may slip into the role of being your own hanging judge and executioner.

These feelings of guilt can last decades. One woman whose divorce occurred twenty-five years before we met said sorrowfully, "I'm afraid that my twenty-eight-year-old got lost in the shuffle. I thought I was doing a good job, but now I think I wasn't really there when she needed me."

Let me say emphatically, enough already! For all you moms out there with guilt nipping at your heels, I have some advice. Now is the time to bring down the curtain on your divorce by forgiving yourself. It's true that divorce has long-term effects, but it doesn't follow that divorce is causing all the problems you're seeing in your grown children. The guilt that you feel for everything bad that happens to your children is an unfair burden. Surely you deserve forgiveness if you made some dumb mistakes or lost your temper on several awful days.

Lighten up. You would have made mistakes if you had married Prince Charming or if you had stayed married to Satan. You'll do a lot that's right because you love your children. Try to forgive yourself for your real and imagined sins of commission and omission. Try to be a gentler person with yourself. Take pride in the enormity of your accomplishment. Whatever your aspirations, you can't do it all. Give yourself a break from your self-accusations.

PART FOUR

*

SECOND MARRIAGE

Chapter 27: Dating and Sex

At some point—perhaps the end of the first year or when you feel comfortable with the idea—you may say to yourself, I need to break out of this loneliness and get a social life. You're right. There's no best time to start dating, although there are better and worse times for making a new commitment. I'll get to that later. But now that you're ready to date and eager to start a new life, what do you need to know? What will happen if you find someone you really like? How will you handle sex? And where will you have it? How can you find out if he or she will get along well with your children? How do you feel if this wonderful new person has children from a previous marriage? And, hardest of all, can you really trust your judgment this time?

Say someone from your office or a new neighbor calls and asks you out. Or it may be an old flame who just found out that you've divorced and by coincidence is also divorced and who is really quite attractive (you'd be surprised at how often this happens). These days women ask men out as freely as men ask women, so I'm assuming both moms and dads will have similar experiences. It's a first date. You haven't dated for millennia. If you're a woman, it hits you: How do I look? What should

I wear? Should I pay my own way? I don't know how people handle that anymore on a first date. And I'm sure that I'll blow it. Should I expect that he'll call for me? If so, do I invite him in to meet the children? Should I invite him in for a nightcap? Am I supposed to kiss him good night? What if he expects more?

If you're a man it hits you: How much money should I spend? Should I take my car to the car wash? Should I offer to pick her up? What will we talk about? Will I bore her? Will she bore me? Should I talk about my divorce? Should I mention my kids? Would a show be better because then we wouldn't have to talk? Will she expect me to make a pass? Do I really want to? What if she has kids? What the hell will I say to them? Should I pretend to be carefree?

My first piece of advice: don't talk about your divorce on the first couple of dates. You can mention it but not the gory details. If you're out with a very sympathetic person, you may be tempted to pour your heart out, but my advice is, resist. If you get a direct question about your children—maybe this person is also divorced and has kids—you can give a very brief description of each and how old they are but then move on to other topics. Don't rave about their achievements. If the person you are with has no children, I suspect the reason you'll get a question about kids is to learn whether they live with you or not. Definitely don't go into problems you're facing. A litany of woes is likely to scare the other person away. Keep it light until you know where the relationship is going and until you're reasonably sure that you want to pursue it. Your purpose is to enjoy the evening. That's all for a while.

Suppose you like each other and you begin to go out more often. What do you do about the children? When and how do you make their presence known and vice versa? These are serious questions that you and your new friend may find bewildering and maybe distressing. Moreover, they are questions you never had to face before.

If you're dating casually you can introduce your friend as being just that, a friend. If you're a woman and your date leaves you at the door or comes in for a drink at the end of the evening, your child may or may not get upset. Little children are less likely than teenagers to take note of your new relationships. But don't count on it. You may face a series of interrogations. Who is he? What does he want? Don't even be surprised if you get asked by a young child, "Is he going to be our new daddy?" or by a young teenager, "Is he your boyfriend?" Be prepared to explain enough to allay your child's anxiety. "Jim works with me at the office," or, "Jim and I went to school together a long time ago," or, "No, dear, he is not my boyfriend. We are just friends." Keep in mind that children really have no idea how adult relationships develop. When they "met" you, you were already married to their father.

The notion that your children will behave in a civil manner when you first start to date someone regularly is often misleading. Some will. Little children especially may be happy to meet a kindly new adult who is attentive and brings along a small gift to please them. They're willing to sit on the stranger's lap and play if that person is amusing, will read a picture book or admire beloved possessions brought for inspection and approval. Older children who foresee that your new friend might be in line for stepfather or stepmother are a different matter. I talked to one eighteen-year-old boy who was beside himself with rage when his mother's date put an arm around her waist. The boy had to restrain himself from pushing the guy outside the door. A teenage girl had a similar reaction when her mother invited a casual date in for a glass of iced tea. The daughter had a royal temper tantrum: Who is this man? What is he doing in our house? Even your little one may give your new friend a hard time. A three-year-old who had long been toilet trained picked the occasion of her mother's first date to wet her pants and drip urine all over the living room carpet. A four-year-old pushed his mother's date in the crotch as he shouted, "You're not my daddy!" One child I knew well was asked by her father to sit on the lady's lap right after they met. The little girl cried and cried and wouldn't be comforted. Her father was startled that she did not find his new love as adorable as he did.

So what you think will be really simple—after all, you're not getting married again or anything so radical—turns out to be more complicated. What's going on?

The first appearance of a new adult in the wings is a major statement that the divorce is for real. It foretells the fact that big changes lie ahead. Children who have been dutifully told about the divorce and understand perfectly well that you are living separately are suddenly struck with the reality. My mom is dating? Another man can put his arm around her waist? My dad is taking out a strange woman? Another woman can hold my dad's hand? I remember one ten-year-old who took one look at her mother's date and screamed, "It's too soon! It's too soon!" and rushed to the telephone to call her father. The mother just stood there, immobilized and profoundly embarrassed.

To avoid these kinds of reactions, it's better to tell your children in advance about your plans to date so that they're not surprised when it happens. If you've met somebody that you like and you're planning to go out for the evening, tell them ahead of time. If you invite this person into your home to briefly meet the children, tell them that you expect them to be on their best behavior. Make it clear that you expect them to show proper manners.

If you start dating frequently, tell the children your plans so that they gradually come to understand that you have a social life that is different and separate from your life with them. Realize that this is a major departure from the expectations in an intact family where children are often included in outings. Explain that you and your new friend are getting to know each other and that takes time.

If the relationship seems to be developing and you're into your fourth or fifth date, and it looks like it's going somewhere and you really like this person, then it's time to really introduce your children. If it's the first person you've been dating since your divorce, I can tell you that whoever it is, that person will not be entirely welcomed by your children. They may keep their feelings hidden or they may act out. You can do a lot to smooth the way for both parties.

First, it would be enormously helpful if you could prepare your date with some information so he or she can connect with the children. Often the new man or woman would appreciate being clued in. They're probably as nervous as you. Many adults have trouble talking to children. Fill the person in as best you can. How old is she? What grade is she in?

What television programs does your child watch? Are they into the same sports? Do they like computer games or horseback riding? Coach the other person so that he or she can speak to your children with some knowledge and respect. You're looking for friendly points of easy connection. Most people don't do this because they're anxious about how the children and new adult will get along with each other. If you spend a lot of time dressing up your children to make them look nice, they'll feel stiff and anxious. Better to spend time telling your children about the new person's interests and accomplishments. But do not make the mistake of thinking that your children will accept the splendor you see in this stranger. If he's a good tennis player with a fine serve, your children might be impressed. Or if he plays a cool saxophone and you think they'd like his taste in music, tell him to bring the sax over and play for the children. But if he's a stockbroker who made a killing in the market, this will get him no brownie points. However wonderful, interesting, or beautiful your view of this person, from your children's point of view, this is an interloper. Be sure that your children understand you're not asking them to show instant affection. Conversely, your friend should not presume to think that he or she will be liked instantly by your children. It takes time to develop a friendship with anyone, and children are no exception. An adult has to earn a child's trust and affection. This happens gradually over time.

Your children may be worried. They know from your manner that your friend may turn out to be very important in their lives. At the same time, they're still struggling with the permanence of the divorce. Many are hoping against hope that you'll reverse your decision or they'll wake up and find the family back together in some magical way.

Tread lightly at first if you've met someone who looks like a serious candidate for cohabitation or marriage. Gradually work up to spending time together in some activity that the children like—going to a ball game, the beach, a movie, and the like. Be true to your interests and the children's interests. This is not a time to pretend that all of you really like bowling if you've tried it before and no one can stand the game. It's a time to cultivate the kinds of activities that families do together. At the same time you should be spending important time together as a couple. Courtship is courtship, and it doesn't go with children or anyone else as chaperones.

If the person you like has children, you can prepare each family to meet. The timing for this depends on how the relationship is progressing. Some relationships move at glacial speed and others take your breath away. The families should meet when it is getting serious between you. Perhaps an average of three to five months after you have started to date would work out best. Here the recipe is the same but the play has more characters. Find out about your friend's children and after you have met them sit down with your own children and describe the meeting. The children from your two families may like or dislike each other instantly. There's no way to predict this. Convey that to your lover so he won't be too anxious.

This is the time to be cool, not overeager. You can ease the meeting if you provide some activity that involves all of you. If your children are close in age, getting together outdoors with some exercise followed by a snack is a good bet. Going to a new movie or sporting event followed by refreshments would be good for older kids. You're not a blended family yet, so you don't have to pretend that everyone is going to live happily ever after. Depending on the personality and ages of your children, it can work out well. An adolescent from one home and a kindergartner can get along beautifully. If you're lucky, the older child may take a real interest in the younger one. The younger child is flattered and it can be lovely.

As the new relationship develops, enjoy it but keep in mind that you have just come out of an unhappy time, you're lonely, you may feel unloved, unappreciated, and sexually deprived, and you may be tempted to exaggerate the pleasure of his company and sweep some of your doubts aside. Use the courtship time to observe the new person carefully. How is he with his children? How is he with yours? Is he an honorable man? Is he a bore? Can you rely on him? Where does he fall short? How important are these flaws? Keep a running diary in your head of all of your observations and try to make a thoughtful decision that balances virtues and drawbacks. Think about what it would be like to live with him. What changes would the relationship demand of you? What changes would it demand of your children? In brief, slow down to think. If you only see blue skies, you may be in love and that sometimes works out. But it may not be realistic for your children or for his. There's a great deal worth considering, and this is the ideal time to do so.

SEX

If you're in an uncommitted relationship and you're thinking about having sex or you get carried away by passion, I would strongly advise that you do not bring your sexual partner into your home. Don't rip each other's clothes off on the couch. Get a hotel room. It's much better to tell your children that you'll be away for the weekend and that they'll be staying with your ex-spouse or a babysitter whom they know. Another benefit of coparenting is that you will have opportunities to pursue an active love life on the days and nights your children are not staying at your house.

It's not a good idea to let your children see you get involved in sexual relationships without a sense of commitment. I don't mean that you can only have sex with someone whom you plan to marry, but any relationship should have the possibility of being one that endures. After an unhappy marriage in which there is long-term sexual deprivation, men and women can be tempted to have lots of lovers. Some feel that they need a man or woman to get them through the night. It's true that nothing restores self-esteem faster after divorce than having someone exciting think you're desirable. But try to shield your children. You want them to value commitment and not think that relationships between men and women are easy come, easy go. Children of divorce are inevitably worried about the stability of male-female relationships because yours did not hold up. For this one very important reason, you want to give your children the example of someone who takes relationships seriously. You may have to bend over backward to convey this message.

It's normal for teenagers in intact families to think of their parents as being sexless. This belief helps them maintain control in their struggle with their own powerful sexual impulses. They become excited and anxious at the thought of you enjoying an active sex life. If you're dating, this excitement is inevitable. But it's easier for them by far if you're discreet and keep the sexual part of your relationship behind closed doors. Take care to block all "windows." Several children I know confessed to me how they spent their evenings watching their mom and her lover through a keyhole in the bedroom door.

When you're ready to take a chance on someone new, don't ask your children for their permission or advice. Tell them firmly but gently that inviting this new person into your life is your decision. You hope that they'll become good friends. Many people ask their children, but this isn't a good idea. Your child has no wisdom to impart. If you're afraid of making another mistake, discuss your doubts with another adult whose judgment you trust.

If you decide to invite your lover to move into your home, prepare your children carefully. Make sure they've met this person many times before and have spent time together. Explain why you would like him to join the household; for example, tell them you don't feel lonely when he is here and you enjoy his company. Redouble your efforts to make them feel assured that they will not lose you. You are the key figure in helping the relationship develop between your new friend and the children. You can't sit back and let things fall where they may. Both need your encouragement and praise to develop a friendship.

Set household routines that accommodate your new partner and the children. Try not to disrupt the children's customary schedules. Your new partner should know that your children are used to certain routines. If you like to spend Sunday morning with the children and your lover wants you to stay in bed a while longer, plan ahead for how you'll handle this conflict. You can arrange for a later family breakfast and make it extra special, or you can tell him it's not possible because the children will be upset and suggest that you and he go out for lunch to someplace special. Keep a balance wheel in mind. If your children lose out in one part of their lives, they need to gain something in another part. You can expect that your children and your lover will try to please you while you bend from one side to the other. You may feel like a pretzel, but as the new relationship gets established, you'll have new routines in place.

Your children will inevitably feel tense as your relationship unfolds. They'll watch you both carefully and be on the lookout for any difficulties between you. After all, they saw their parents having problems and they are not sure how a happy couple interacts. They may also have seen other relationships of yours or their father's crash and burn. So they walk on eggs wondering about the outcome. If the relationship continues, you may need to institute some of the family meetings that I describe in the next chapter on remarriage.

On the other hand, your attempt at a serious relationship may fail. Adventures of the heart can always end in a blind alley. Others will break your heart. Or you may feel relieved. But since all these relationships start the same way—on a rising sense of hope—your children may end up feeling bewildered, distressed, and of course, like you, sometimes relieved. If they genuinely grow to like or even love the person you've invited into your lives and that person disappears one night, it's another loss. It's frightening when people disappear and it's awful to feel rejected. If, on the other hand, they never liked your new friend because they found him unfriendly or just difficult, they may rejoice at his departure. Or their reaction may combine both elements of sadness and relief. In any case, they may be happy to have you more to themselves.

If this happens to you, tell your children exactly how you feel. If your heart is broken, say it. If you think the relationship was not going to work out, tell them why in ways that they can understand and store as useful information for themselves. You can use this opportunity to comfort your children and yourself and to teach them about relationships. You thought this one would work out. You're disappointed that it hasn't. This experience might be especially helpful to share with your adolescent daughter. You could tell her what you learned and how she might make use of your experience in her own life. It's never helpful to say that if someone leaves "it doesn't matter." It does matter. You want your children to learn how important it is to choose wisely and to pay attention to what people need and deserve from one another. If you're depressed or agitated because you deeply cared for the person who left, you have no choice but to tell your children the truth: it's terrible to lose someone you love. But of course you and they will recover. Try to do something pleasurable to cheer up all of you. If your friend established a long-term good relationship with your children and the two of you are still friendly, call and suggest that he write the children a note saying his good-byes and that he will miss them.

Sadly, children sometimes maliciously and deliberately wage war to drive away a new lover. They want you to themselves or they don't like the new person and they try almost anything to get rid of the threat. The best way to handle this is to see it coming. At the first hint of trouble, call the children together and say, "Sam is going to live here. I don't expect you to love him before knowing him well, but I do expect you to behave." Treat it seriously and firmly. Their bad behavior is unacceptable. If your children tell you, "Daddy said Sam is a fool" and you're on speaking terms with your ex-partner, call and explain what's happening. Make sure that he or she has not intentionally or carelessly encouraged the children to reject your new love interest. Ask for help in calming the children and getting them to accept this change. Don't assume right off that there's nothing you can do about this. Many times an ex-husband or ex-wife will resent a new lover, but their tendency to convey this to your children may not be deliberate. They have little to gain from sabotaging your new relationships. If, however, your ex harbors the hope that you'll reconcile or is intensely angry at having been rejected, the sabotage may be on purpose. If so, don't rush to your attorney. Try your best to change his or her mind. Tell your children that you feel bad that Daddy is upset but you plan to go ahead and reestablish a social life. You expect that your children will do their best to help you.

But you also need to listen very carefully to your children's objections. It may be that you're blind to unacceptable behavior on the part of your lover. I've heard too many stories from young adults about how their parents' lovers were very different with them when the parent was absent. Sexual advances between Mom's boyfriend and a teenage daughter happen more frequently than many people are willing to admit. Mothers can be so hurt at the thought that they deny their lover could ever approach their daughter—and in doing so leave the daughter unprotected.

If your partner leaves because he or she wasn't interested in being around your kids, it's very important that you don't turn on the children in your disappointment. They are not responsible for the disinterest in you. Or it may be that the conflict between your lover's children and your children was at the root of the problem. If they're old enough, you can talk to your own kids about what happened so you can build on that experience for the next time. Talk very straight. "I think John/Mary left because you didn't try hard enough to get along. I feel very bad about this because I had hopes our relationship would work out. Let's talk about what happened so you and I can take better care next time." Above all, don't let the lost relationship go unremarked by you. Every relationship merits respect and every loss will be noted by your children, whether they talk about it or not. It's better for you to take the initiative and talk with them. You're teaching them to respect love and friendship.

If, on the other hand, your love affair blossoms, as I hope it does, you may be heading for a second marriage and a totally new family life. Read on.

Chapter 28:   Remarriage

When you marry a second time, you stand on the threshold of a new partnership that you hope will last happily ever after. Having been handed a fresh start in life, you naturally push away any lingering doubts about the future—and why shouldn't you? You survived your divorce. You're well equipped to handle new problems that might arise.

While these feelings are human, they're not going to be enough to get your marriage off on the right foot. The good news is that you can do a lot at the beginning to anticipate the perils that lie in your path. As the years go by, you can develop methods to reduce friction and defuse the sorts of misunderstandings that wreck so many second marriages. We know a lot more about remarriage than we did thirty years ago. If you follow the advice I'm about to lay out, and if you've chosen reasonably well this time around—and made use of all that you learned from your earlier unhappy experience—the chances of your second marriage working out are high.

A second marriage is very different from a first marriage because children are around at the outset. It can be a wonderful experience, but it's not a new beginning. Rather it's a whole new life chapter for you and your children. You especially will have vivid memories of good times and bad times punctuated by the presence of ghosts from your failed marriage. If your spouse drank too much, was careless with money, or was unfaithful, these memories will haunt you in the early years of your new relationship. Much as you try to banish these fears, you'll worry that lightning can strike twice. Was your judgment better this time? Right from the beginning you have a fear that disaster, meaning divorce, might happen again. When she's late, will you worry about who she was with? Will his excuse sound pretty lame to your practiced ears? Of course you're hopeful, but you can't help but worry. Because you want to succeed this time around, you don't want to think about the doubts that sometimes haunt you.

Your children also struggle with fears and hopes, but being children their concerns are very different from yours. Moreover, their worries vary depending on their age and gender. Most children are happy and relieved if they see that you're happy. They've been worried about you. If they've come to like your new partner, they'll feel pleased with greater opportunities to do things together. Boys especially may welcome a man who can provide a reassuring male presence; if he can offer expertise in the skills that your boy is trying to acquire, he is especially welcome. The same can be true of girls and their stepmoms. One of the happiest girls I knew discovered that her father's fiancée played a great jazz piano and was willing to teach her.

At the same time children watch both of you carefully because they've seen things go so terribly wrong. They remember the fights they saw and often have powerful memories of you sobbing or being frantic. They keep their fingers crossed, breathing sighs of relief when you appear cheerful. And they have the special worries peculiar to children in divorced families. Will this new husband or wife draw your attention away from them? Will you love them less if you love your new spouse? And since time is always a scarce commodity, will your time with your new partner deprive them of their time with you? If they come to love their new parent, will they feel that they're betraying the outside parent? This fear of being a traitor is especially keen if the outside parent is not doing well. This is a very serious issue in remarriage because the child's sense of honor and integrity may be tied to loyalty to the outside parent. Children have many concerns. Daughters who become extremely close to their mothers after divorce often think of the new husband as a rival who will take their primary place as their mother's confidante. Of course, he probably will. Many of the children's concerns are grounded in a reality that will require adjustment from everyone.

GETTING STARTED ON THE RIGHT FOOT

As soon as you've decided to remarry, you alone should gather the children together and tell them. It's better if you do this without your new partner so the children will feel more at ease in asking their questions and expressing their feelings. Explain that you have good and important news and you want them to be the first to know. Tell them that you've been lonely since the divorce despite the many ways that they've cheered you and helped you. You would now like to share your life with a new partner. Say that you hope that they'll get to know her or him better and that you expect to have really good times together as a family. You hope very much that they'll become close friends and eventually love each other.

Allow lots of time for questions and reassurance. As you talk with your children try to keep in mind that your announcement has made them anxious. The older ones worry about what they will gain and what they will lose with the new family arrangement. The younger ones worry about how their life will change. Just as you did when you broke the news about the divorce, try to address their main concerns. The more facts you provide, the less room for worrisome fantasies. Where will you live? What about their outside biological parent? Does he know? Will anything change in that relationship? What shall we call the new step-parent? (Ask for suggestions but indicate that maybe they should ask the stepparent first.) Where will everyone sleep? Will they have a different home? A different school? The more you can reassure them about the stability of their world, the easier it will be for them and for you. If you're planning to move to your fiancé's home, make sure the children get familiar with it and with the neighborhood. If the children raise questions you can't yet answer, say so candidly, thank them for asking, and promise to find out. Also plan a small celebration with them and your new partner in honor of the forthcoming event. If the children are old enough, ask them how they would like to celebrate.

Make sure that the children know your plans well ahead and are included in the excitement of planning and participating in your wedding. I say this because many couples elope. Some people marry impulsively when they go away for a weekend together. Sometimes, since the partner has lived in the home a long time, they hardly mention it. One couple I know returned from a tennis tournament to announce to the children and their family that they had married. The children were stunned and distressed. One seventeen-year-old who learned of his father's marriage from his grandmother complained bitterly to me, "My dad got married and didn't even tell me." He concluded, "I guess I don't mean much to him."

It's much better for everyone if the children join in the celebration. It gives you a wonderful opportunity to help them feel included and, if possible, to give them an important role. It doesn't have to be an elaborate wedding for you to do this. A simple gathering of friends and family is very appropriate if that's your preference. Whether the wedding is small or large, get the children dressed up and make sure that you're attentive to them at the reception. Introduce them with pride to all of their new relatives. Thank them afterward and tell them later how pleased you were with their performance. If they're little, one of your relatives should be asked to keep a special eye on them to make sure that they're not lost in the throng and end up sitting in the corner or under a table.

There's a special reason to involve your children in the wedding. You want to educate them to appreciate the value you attach to marriage and family. You want to help them overcome their fear that relationships between men and women are doomed to fail. There's no better way to do this than by having them participate in the symbols and the festivities of your wedding.

On the other hand, don't take them on your honeymoon. Some people do. Tell them where you plan to go but leave them at home. You want to convey the very important message that you and your new spouse are a separate unit within the family. If your children were very young when you divorced, they may have no idea about how married families work. If you go on a trip, remember to call and to talk with all the children. And of course, come back with presents for all.

From the first day of your remarriage, two agendas appear on the table—one for you and one for your children. Your primary personal agenda in the first year is to strengthen your relationship with your new spouse, spend time together, build a happy sex life, and create an intimacy that will hold. To do this, you need time alone. Try to take a weekend a month to get away just by yourselves, just the two of you. If you can't afford a hotel, try a B and B or even just a day at the beach or a hike on a favorite trail. Take an evening out or whatever gives you both pleasure. Your new partner may adore your children, but his or her primary interest is in you. It's important to keep this attraction fresh in both your minds. You also need to be with adult friends to rebuild a social circle that includes you as a couple.

In a second marriage, you need to be aware of the other person's history and use this knowledge. You don't want to unwittingly trigger the fears that broke the first marriage. For example, Roger was devastated when his wife left him. He had no idea she was unhappy until she marched out. He was stunned. Why didn't she tell him? She remained silent. Roger was understandably worried that the same thing could happen in his second marriage. But Sue, his second wife, made it a rule to always tell him, in great detail, what she was thinking, what she planned to do, and how she was feeling. "I probably overdo it," Sue told me. "I'm a real blabbermouth. But Roger doesn't have to worry about my holding back important stuff."

If you know your new wife was left by an unfaithful husband, be sure to call her when you get delayed. You cannot say to her, as much as you may feel like it, "Why are you so suspicious?" You know the answer.

Your children have another agenda in the early months of the marriage, one that doesn't always mesh with yours. For starters, they worry that they'll lose your time and attention. They want to hold on to you as before, in fact more than before. Children don't understand your need to be alone with your lover. How could they? When you tell them to go away and play or find something to do, this confirms that they're not wanted. Your children are perfectly capable of devising strategies to regain your attention. If they make enough racket or get into trouble and start crying, you'll come running. What incentive do they have to keep the peace if their goal is to get your attention?

They also worry about who this new person is who's joining the family. Of course if they've known him for a year or more, this question will not be as sharp. Nevertheless, since he now occupies a new role in the family, they want to know more. Will he be strict or lenient? Mean or nice? Fair or selfish? Will he help with homework? Will he get mad and yell? Will she make me pick up my room? Will she let me have pierced ears? Will he sit in Daddy's place at dinner? Will she sleep in Daddy's bed? Does this mean Mom and Dad will never ever reconcile?

The first thing you need to do is to convince your children that they're not being squeezed out of your life. A few weeks into the remarriage, call everyone together and set up a regular time for talking about family activities, making suggestions, and airing complaints. Take a calendar and mark out the hours for each child's activities, for fun time together as a family, and for the time you and your spouse spend alone. Ask the children for their suggestions. If they say Disneyland and you can't afford it, say you don't have the money now but you'll take them as soon as you can. Make sure that everyone, including the littlest one, has a voice. The family meeting is symbolic in and of itself. It gives you both an opportunity to interact with all the children, to show how courteously you treat each other, and to demonstrate how kind and fair you are with each child. The meetings should be upbeat and fun. Laughter and good humor will help smooth the way. They should end with something really special for dinner. Pizza will do. But take these gatherings seriously. You're showcasing for your children how a good family functions—which is something they probably didn't see before.

I know that this may stretch you to the limit, but if you had a custom of spending private time with each child—say a weekend afternoon or an evening during the week with your daughter—keep doing this for the first year. Whatever you can do will help her. Tell her you want to hold on to that special mother-daughter time because it's so precious to you. Fathers, if you and your children have been used to spending some private time, hold on to it. You're not a blended family yet. These are the necessary steps that lead to blending. If you just get married and rely on your optimism to make things turn out right, you'll regret it. Hope is important, but it's not enough. Too many children have complained to me, "My step is great for my mom, but their marriage doesn't include me." Half of the children in my studies felt excluded from what they described as a happy remarriage for their parents. That's an unacceptable number that can be reversed if parents are aware of what their children need.

This balancing act—in which you hold on to your private time as an adult while you protect time with each child and time for the whole family—is incredibly difficult but imperative. The failure to work at such a balance can make or break your second marriage. How long do you need to do this? You'll know. Each child is different, but I would guess for at least a year and often until the youngest child leaves home. The full answer is that you do it until you've all learned to trust each other in the new family. When you've experienced a new history, shared holidays and crises, and built a store of good memories, you can sit back and breathe a sigh of relief. Until then be careful in what you expect of the children and your new partner. The new man or woman is not a parent in your children's eyes until he or she has won the right to carry that title. It's not conferred by your marriage certificate.

As the marriage gets under way, try to put yourself into the shoes of your new partner. Try to appreciate the newness of the situation and how hard it is to move into an already established family with habits, customs, and relationships in place. Your new partner may be outgoing or shy. He may know your children well or be a relative stranger. Either way, being an in situ member of the family is different. Try to help guide his or her entrance, not by staging it but by helping your partner get started on the right foot. Your new husband will probably sit in Daddy's old place at the table, and he should be prepared for the fact that your children may find this strange, even off-putting. Some children say, "Hey, that's Dad's place!" Your new husband should be prepared to handle this complaint as he sees fit. But you should be prepared to say to your child, "You're right. It was Daddy's place. But remember that Daddy and I divorced and Paul and I got married." Your job is to help your husband understand why the children might react this way. He should also be prepared for the fact that they may resent him. After all, they don't really know him that well, and anyway, like most kids, they've been hoping that you and your ex will get back together. Your spouse—a stepdad or stepmom— needs to be sensitive to each child's relationship with the absent biological parent. It's your job to provide as much information as you can about the current relationship between your ex and your children and how that relationship will affect your new family.

I think your new partner should tell your children directly that he or she has no intention of supplanting the biological parent. There are many ways to convey this message according to the child's age and understanding. A younger school-age child may respond to something like, "I know you have only one mommy and one daddy, and I thought that we could be very special friends." A teenager may respond to a frank conversation. "I know how complicated things can get in a stepfamily. Maybe you and I can work together to figure out ways to make things comfortable for everyone." In whatever way that works, your partner has to explain that he or she has not come to usurp anyone's place in the child's heart.

Once you've had these conversations and set new routines into place, hold on to your hat. As you'll read in the next chapter, finding harmony in a second marriage with children from a first marriage is a stupendous challenge. You'll need to summon all your courage and to develop new skills in conflict resolution.

A word of warning is in order: even with the best planning in the world, a second marriage has inherent potential for misunderstanding and conflict. For example, assuming you can't afford both, do you pay for your child's orthodontia or take your second wife on a promised vacation? Such decisions have a high potential to spin out of control and escalate into a family crisis. Faced with uncomfortable choices, many people in second marriages just close their eyes and hope matters will improve. But this is not a good idea. It's far better for you to bring conflicts and mis-understandings into the open and address them in broad daylight, im-mediately. If you learn how to do this, your marriage should grow stronger and happier.

Chapter 29:   Insiders and the Remarried Family

I f, as William Shakespeare said, "All the world's a stage and all the men and women merely players," your second marriage will have in it more players, more surprises, more fluctuations in parent and child relationships, more drama, and if you play the script right, more laughter, joy, and happy endings. From the day you remarry, your ex remarries, or both of you have found new partners, your child will be surrounded by an enlarged cast of characters, young and old, who may vie for his affection, love, and attention or, in other subplots, turn their backs on him with cold indifference.

I can easily name the players: you and your ex (the biological parents), a stepfather, a stepmother, and perhaps a few stepsisters, stepbrothers, or, with time, half brothers and half sisters. What I cannot do is predict how the human beings who play these roles will treat your child through the many years of living in a remarried family. On the other hand, I do know that where there are more parents per child, there's more room for confusion and conflict in everyone's mind. The relationships between all the adults may be friendly, fiercely competitive, or anywhere in between. The children may be best friends or archenemies or both, depending on the day you ask them. But even when everyone in a remarried family is friendly, there are currents and crosscurrents that don't exist in an intact family.

In this and the next two chapters, I'm going to explore the internal dynamics of the remarried family in terms of how all the players get along and what they can do to support one another. It's a complicated business, but let's start with the simplest arrangement, which is anything but simple. First, there's the biological parent who is outside the second marriage. Then there's the biological parent who is in the new marriage and who plays the lead role. Next is the stepparent, either a stepmom or stepdad. And, of course, there's the child or children of the first marriage. (For simplicity's sake, I'll refer to just one child in talking about this quartet. But obviously each child in a remarried family, depending on age and gender and temperament, will experience a different kind of quartet.)

To have a successful second marriage, all of the players in this quartet need to be in harmony. If just one of you creates dissonance or plays off-key, or is out of rhythm with the others, it can ruin the play and disrupt the child's life or even destroy the second marriage. But if you can learn to play together and give the quartet priority, you and your child have a better chance of enjoying the warmth of happy family life. The trick is to keep the emotional residues of your divorce from intruding into your new family life.

One such residue is the familiar human frailty called rivalry. Many parents get along for years after divorce, at least on the surface, until one decides to get remarried. Undercurrents of rivalry then become ignited, often between the outside parent and the stepparent, who compete for the child's loyalty. Or the outside parent and stepparent disapprove of each other, each wanting the other out of the way. Sometimes only one person is distrustful and difficult. But the result is the same. The quartet plays poorly. The child is in trouble because he feels torn.

This kind of rivalry happens far more often than most people realize and certainly more than they anticipate. Sometimes the outside parent says to the child, "Your step is a mess. He's only there to take advantage of your mom. Don't be fooled by his pleasantries." Or the step says, "Your dad has never done anything right. He's a loser. I certainly hope that you won't grow up like him." What quicker way is there to make a child miserable? He feels like a traitor whichever way he turns. Even when these two players don't set out to compete for a child's respect and affection, the child can feel torn because he's not sure he can love them both. He needs all the adults in his family to help him resolve his inner conflict.

The bottom line is that a second marriage only works well when all the players understand the importance of cooperating, of finding their own particular harmony. This plays out differently when each parent remarries, so let's start with the mother. She has found a new man to love and to cherish. She hopes to spend the rest of her life with him. She wants him to help her raise her children. What can each player expect?

PLAYER ONE: DAD IS OUTSIDE PARENT

My first words of advice go to the biological father who is outside the remarriage. When your ex-wife remarries, what you say to your children can help make or break the newly forming family. It's a serious matter. If you tell your child that it's fine with you if he befriends his stepdad, giving the new relationship your support, your child will have the freedom to make up his own mind about this person in his life. This is an important gift you can make your child. Indeed, you owe it to him.

But if your ex-wife's second marriage reignites your anger at her, and your anger leads you to block your child's relationship with his stepfather, you're asking for trouble. First, you may cause your child great emotional harm stemming from conflicted loyalty. Second, your child may lose respect for you when he gets older. After all, you're the one who instigated so much trouble in his mother's second marriage. You're the reason he hurt his mother's feelings when he turned on his stepdad.

In the early years of your wife's second marriage, you have an important opportunity. You're free to choose your own role, so why not focus on showing your child how adults treat each other with courtesy and mutual respect? Encourage your child to get to know his stepdad. He really needs your help. But don't think that by giving this encouragement, you weaken your own status as a father. Quite the opposite is true. No one can ever take your place in your child's life. You are his one and only biological dad and that can never change. Every child has the capacity for many important relationships in life. Love is not a zero-sum game. He can easily and happily love both of you if you let him know that this doesn't create any problems for you.

But now you may ask, exactly how does one father from the sidelines? What if your ideas about child-rearing differ from those prevailing in the remarried family? You need to exercise your judgment in this. You may not like certain rules that your ex-wife and her husband have laid down for your child. But ask yourself, is such and such a rule really a big deal? You can't micromanage your child's upbringing from the outside without causing serious disharmony. Your child needs to live peacefully in her new family and follow its mandates. If she objects to a rule or punishment laid down by her stepfather and mother and comes whining to you for help, stop and think before you act. Stay out of it as long as you believe no harm is being done. If, on the other hand, you do feel that your child is being treated unfairly—or is not being protected from inappropriate behavior by the stepfather—first let your anger cool. Then call your ex-wife and ask about the situation. On hearing all sides, you may agree with the way that the stepfather and mother handled the issue. If so, explain to your child why you agree with them. If you strongly disagree, talk to your ex-wife about your objections and suggest a compromise that may be acceptable to all of you. But keep this conversation among the adults. Your child should never be the messenger of your criticism about parenting skills in the remarried family.

As hard as this may be to hear, you don't have the right to change or run another man's family. You may think he's too lenient and indulgent. He puts you in a bad light with your child because you can't or won't follow suit. Or he's far stricter than you. You worry that your child will never be able to meet his rigid standards. Or he plays favorites with his children from a first marriage and your child gets the short end of the stick. In all these criticisms about his shortcomings, you may be right. But unless the stepfather is endangering or hurting your child, you need to keep your nose out of his family.

Of course, many fathers find the new stepfather to be a great guy. You genuinely like each other, especially with the passing years. If this happens to you, count your lucky stars. Your child will find life much easier. I know many families that invite outside fathers, especially those who haven't remarried or otherwise find themselves single again, to holiday gatherings. One father told me he was extremely happy when he got an invitation to Christmas dinner one year. "I felt really welcome in their home," he said. "They've done all the right things in their marriage and with the children." Needless to say, his children were pleased.

PLAYER ONE: MOM IS OUTSIDE PARENT

Now let's turn to the role of the biological mother as outside parent. Your ex-husband remarries. How can you keep the quartet harmonious? First, you need to recognize your power. While children can more or less accept the notion of having two fathers, it's much more difficult for them to have room in their hearts for two mothers. A biological mother yields her centrality to no one. This being the case, you play a critical role in helping your children accept their new stepmother as their father's wife and mistress of the household. You need to support her position in the eyes of your children so they can develop a healthy relationship with her. Should you become rivals, your children will suffer greatly. Imagine how angry your ex-husband will be if they attack his new wife. Think how unfair it is for a new wife to walk into a maelstrom of jealousy and unresolved anger.

If you find yourself in serious disagreement with your child's stepmother regarding discipline, there's not much you can do. If your child complains, all you can say is that you and the stepmother have different views. Then encourage your child to follow her rules in her home. If you feel your child is in danger, call your ex-husband to request a meeting, adults only. You may learn that your child is exaggerating or trying to please you by criticizing the stepmom. You may find that a candid discussion can improve matters. But please don't pick up the phone and call the stepmother to reprimand her for neglecting your child. And don't drag your child into the disagreement. If you don't seem to be getting anywhere and are still worried, invite a mediator to a family meeting to air the problem. If the stepmother slams the door in your face, so to speak, and won't hear of a mediator, you may have to step back and accept the fact that she has the right to run her house as she feels fit.

Many first wives feel that a second wife is a usurper. She's an intruder who is trying to take your rightful place and you see nothing good about her. If you feel this way—and many women do—you cannot lie to your children but you can refrain from mentioning her flaws. Your harsh criticism in fact can boomerang. An eight-year-old girl once told me, "My mom hates my stepmom because she's pretty. My mom wishes she had curly hair but her hair won't curl." This view of you as an envious woman who hates another is not one that you want your children to have. It demeans you in their eyes.

It is to be hoped your ex-husband has chosen well and his new wife brings components to the family that you admire. She may be a gentle, loving woman. She may be artistically talented. She may have special knowledge or skills. She may be direct and honest. Convey to your children whatever you find in her that's good. Encourage them to be kind and considerate toward her. This may be hard for you but do it anyway. We do many things for our children that are hard. In taking this stand, you're modeling the kind of good behavior you expect in your children. For example, you might say, "Your stepmom is a really great cook. Ask her to show you how she makes those scrumptious Christmas cookies." Or, "Your stepmother has very good taste. That dress she got you is perfect." I recall a nine-year-old girl who explained, "Mom tells me that it's my job to help my new stepmom understand me. She said I should tell all about myself. So I told her the colors I like and that I hate to wear my hair in a pony and that I love hot dogs but without ketchup. I'm drawing a picture of myself for my stepmom. Do you think she'll like that?" I assured the child that her stepmother would be very happy to have this important information and that her mother would also be very pleased. I thought to myself how lucky this child was to have such a wise and sensitive mother.

PLAYER TWO: MOM REMARRIES

Player two in the quartet is the newly married biological parent. Let's start with mothers. You're on the threshold of a great opportunity to create a really happy family. As you begin your second marriage, ask yourself what you can do to help your new husband and your children make this venture work. Think carefully about what lies ahead. What issues are you likely to encounter? How will life change for each of you and what can you do to smooth the way? Is your new husband more of a disciplinarian than you or is he more laid back? Will he be bothered by noisy children or will he find the household lively and exciting? Is he someone who takes easily to your children or will he need a lot of help from you in finding common interests? Is he an outgoing person who was raised in a large family? What about the children? How worried are they about losing your attention? Can you help to dispel their concerns or would it be better to say nothing until there's a problem? How is each one reacting? And, of course, what is the main attitude of your ex-husband? How cooperative is he?

What you can't do is sit back and let things take their course, hoping everything will work out with time. Time is not on your side. Second marriages with children break up sooner and more frequently than first marriages, but it doesn't have to be that way. You play an essential role in making this new marriage work. You're an essential bridge between your ex-husband, your children, and your new husband, so you have your work cut out for you.

Before the wedding, talk to your ex-husband about your plans and ask for his help. Reassure him that your child's affection for your new husband will not reduce the child's love for his daddy. Explain your plans for continued contact and that you don't expect your remarriage to interrupt his relationship with his child. Make it clear to everyone that your child is free to love both biological parents. If your ex-husband is angry or distressed about your remarriage, tell your child that from your point of view there is no competition. Be honest with your child. You're sorry that adults don't always get along, but she can be a daughter and friend to both men. Most of all, do not join the battle for your child's loyalty and don't take sides. Your child will someday choose her own values and will respect your forbearance.

As I suggested earlier, you need to help your new partner get to know your children and vice versa. Although it may sound strange, adults and children are often confused about how they get to know each other. Both are afraid of rejection. When everything is going well and you see a real relationship developing, be sure to speak up. Thank your husband and your children for their efforts. Reward them with praise. When things are not going well, don't get discouraged. Try to figure out what interests they genuinely have in common. Observe what went wrong. Ask each person separately what the trouble is. Maybe your husband was out of sorts or acting like a know-it-all and your child felt put down. I know one stepdad who bought his stepson an expensive airplane model. He made the mistake of assembling the parts and presented the completed model triumphantly to his stepson, who was speechless in his disappointment. Or perhaps your husband tried too hard. Or didn't listen to your child. Or maybe your child was determined not to let it work. A great deal can be right and a great deal can go wrong. The bottom line is that during the early years of the remarriage you're the one who needs to smooth the way and make things work for the people you love. You're the one who can help both your children and your partner to understand each other and to appreciate that their relationship takes time and patience to develop.

In talking to your child, explain that you hope she'll make friends with her new stepfather. If she balks, tell her that you expect her to give him a chance. That's the decent and fair thing to do. Tell her to take her time. Make sure that she understands you and she are still very close and your closeness is not threatened by the marriage. Tell her something about her stepdad that will make him sound interesting, to get her started. Suggest that they plan some activity that both of them enjoy. Above all, make it clear that you value her opinion. You want the new family to get started on the right foot, and she's a key figure in this venture. You may have to keep talking if you have an adolescent who's being negative. The first year is the hardest. After that, many teens come around and learn to value and love their stepdads. You need a lot of patience. Don't get discouraged if everything moves slowly.

I'm reminded of a sixteen-year-old named Jeff whose mom married an attorney who was in politics. Jeff was still angry about the divorce. He hardly said hello to his stepfather for six months. One day, after his mother gently urged him to give his stepdad a chance, Jeff decided that he would agree to have lunch, just once. The stepfather had suggested this many times. Well, it turned out that the step was an interesting and bright man who had a great idea. When Jeff finished his school term, he would arrange an internship for him in a congressman's office during the summer. The rest is history as they say, really good history. But it wouldn't have happened except for that lunch. Jeff had made it clear that he needed to wait until he was ready. He couldn't rush. Fortunately his mom and stepfather understood that and gave him the space that he needed. Just as important, Jeff discovered that his biological dad had no objection. So after taking his time, he was able to respond to the stepfather's overture. As it turned out, his relationship with his stepfather changed Jeff's life. Many years later, at age thirty, he said to me, "My stepfather is a great man and a really decent, honorable man. He has been the model for my career."

PLAYER TWO: DAD REMARRIES

If you're a biological dad in the role of player two, you also have your work cut out in getting your new marriage started and keeping it going. First, be sure to tell your ex-wife about your plans and ask for her co-operation on behalf of the children. She may be happy to help. But if you're marrying the woman who, from your ex-wife's viewpoint, broke up the marriage, your ex may feel bitter and unyielding. In that case, you should ask her forgiveness, but only if you really mean it. Hollow apologies will get you nowhere.

You need to prepare your children for life in the new family. Tell them that your new wife is not intended to replace their mother. No one could do that. But your new wife is your partner. She helps run your home, and it's very important to you that she feel comfortable. Your children need to see you as someone who respects both your new wife and their mother, someone who defends both women against any disrespectful remarks from any member of your family. This will help them bridge both relationships. Try not to leave your new wife in charge of your home while you go off on a business trip during the first year of your marriage. Your children might challenge her authority, especially if she's young. In these early months and years, your presence is very important in setting the tone of the household. It's better for you to be home for dinner with your wife and children as frequently as possible. Make it clear in a tactful and kindly way to your children that you will not brook any rudeness to your new wife.

Of course, you will need to help your new wife make contact with your children. You should tell her about each child, including all the likes and dislikes that you think will help her initiate a relationship with them. She will also need your support as she engages the children in joint activities. If she is a younger woman and you have an adolescent girl, you can encourage them to go out together to the ballet or theater, to go shopping, or to do whatever they find interesting that's within your budget. And you can, when appropriate, perhaps at dinner, ask about their shared activities and show your pleasure in their having a good time. If your wife spends time at your children's school and actively helps the kids with assignments or hobbies, it's very important for you to tell all of them—as a group and separately—how happy you are that they're spending time together. Consider yourself part of the glue that holds the new family together.

Of course, make sure that they do enjoy being together and it's not fakery. If you detect problems, which is not unusual, talk first to your wife to get her advice and perspective. The first step is for her to talk to the children without you to see if they can smooth over the difficulties. If not, you may want to institute a family council that meets regularly so everyone can have a say. This is especially useful in the early stages of the new family.

PLAYER THREE

The third member of the quartet is the child. Because children in second marriages tend to be older, I'm going to address my remarks to boys and girls who are age twelve or older. While this is an advice book for parents, you have a role to play in helping your family do well in the post-divorce years.

If your mom is getting remarried, you have a very important job right now and that is to help your mom. She wants you to get to know your stepdad and become friends. That's not going to happen unless you try and he tries. Whatever your hopes that your mom and dad would get back together, now is the time to put those dreams aside. Give this new person a fair chance. If you've been very close to your mom and you feel pushed out, be aware that she still loves you as much as before. And if she's a happier person, she may be a better mom, so do your best to help. You have a lot of power to make things go wrong and a lot of power to make things go right.

If your dad is getting remarried, the same advice holds. Give your new stepmom a chance. If you have complaints about her, go to your dad (not your mom) to say how you feel. Keep your concerns within the boundaries of the new family. Parents sometimes really need their children's help. They had a rough time with the divorce. This is a happy time for them and they really need you to help make it go well. Do your best. They will be very grateful. And if the marriage works out well, you'll benefit by knowing what you did to help.

Many kids worry that they'll get lost in the new family; they'll get less attention from their mom or dad. That can sometimes happen. You may know from friends that it does. But you prevent this from happening if you make sure that your mom or dad who's remarrying hears from you what you're feeling—including complaints. Of course, it helps a lot if you don't lose your temper when you speak up. But even if you do, it's better to say what you think and feel, not just to keep everything bottled up. If you keep your feelings to yourself or only tell your friends, nothing is going to improve. If you tell your folks, they can take actions to make things better for you. Your parent and your new stepparent would probably welcome realistic suggestions from you. So think seriously about what they can do to make your life more comfortable.

Keep in mind that even if you sometimes feel left out, you have high priority with your parent and stepmom or stepdad. They both want their marriage to work and be happy, so they could really use your advice. Be as honest and as open as you can.

Finally, your most important job is to learn all you can at school, to enjoy your friends, and to do what you can to help your brothers and sisters get used to your new stepparent. If you're the oldest, they'll look up to you and will probably follow your lead. Explain that your new stepdad or stepmom is probably not sure how you'll all get along. He or she is just as worried as you are, so let everyone pitch in to build a new family.

Chapter 30: **Stepparents**

Parent and child relationships evolve gradually. As the years pass by, family members discover what they enjoy about one another, what pushes their buttons, what interests they share, and where their interests diverge. In the intact family, the foundation for all of these relationships—whatever their later course—begins when a mother and father assume total responsibility for their helpless newborn infant. But in the remarried family, the stepparent-child relationship begins much later. It's rooted not in the child's birth but in the early days of the second marriage, which means it begins differently and runs a separate course. It's important that you understand this difference and shape your expectations to what you and your stepchild can create together. Because it's a relationship that starts midstream, it's more challenging for both of you. And it's a triumph for everyone in the family when you, the stepparent, become a really important person in your stepchild's inner world.

In other ways, however, you will always remain an outsider. Unless you legally adopt your stepchild, there is no legal bond between the two of you, even if you've been together for most of your stepchild's life. If your wife or husband dies or you get divorced, you have no legal rights or obligations to the child. So from the very start, your relationship is more fragile and less predictable than what you would have with your own flesh and blood. On the other hand the love between a stepparent and a child can be the most powerful influence in both their lives. It depends much on you and what transpires between you.

Let's begin with a general framework. If you're a stepparent embarking on this new role and if the child is very young, you'll have a great advantage. It should be easy for you to hold a toddler on your lap, play the many games that little children adore, read stories, sing songs, and altogether allow yourself to relax and enjoy the wonderfully appreciative audience of a small child. Inexpensive gifts at frequent intervals will also endear you to your young stepchildren. If you have children from a previous marriage, you'll find this role familiar. You'll know that children this age are often heartwarming. If they've been treated well, they're genuinely affectionate and will reward your attentiveness many times over. This doesn't mean they won't resent you for taking the place of the absent biological parent, but you have more opportunities to win a place in the heart of someone who is just beginning to lay down memories.

If your stepchild is older, starting in midstream poses new problems for both of you. Getting to know an adolescent is always a tricky business. If you have adolescent children of your own, you'll be familiar with the territory, including its joys and problems. It will be no surprise to find that since a teenager may be rebelling against adults in general, it's easy for you to get caught in that battle and to feel that the rebellion was triggered by your arrival on the scene. In this situation, it's better for you to stay in the background at the beginning and give the relationship lots of time to zig and zag, as it doubtless will. The chance that you'll be greeted warmly from the start is next to nil. Building a relationship with a child always takes time, so be prepared to give it plenty of time and patience.

PLAYER FOUR: STEPFATHERS

You're a lucky man. You're walking into a ready-made family that can bring you enormous pleasure. Undoubtedly your new wife is eager for love, companionship, and good sex. She may have had more than she could handle between her job and raising her children in joint or sole custody. Chances are she knows a lot about how to make you feel comfortable. But let me offer you some advice that will help you avoid making a common mistake. Like many men, you may be tempted, or even urged by your new wife, to move into the family wearing seven-league boots. Your goal is to rescue your new wife who is faced with an audacious son or daughter. You may offer to play this role out of kindness, especially if you think that your wife has lost control of her children. Or you may want to do it because you think this is a man's role. But if you move in and start to bark, hand out punishments, and assign extra chores, you may frighten the younger children and your teenage stepchildren are likely to say, "Who the hell gave you the right to give me orders?" This may get your back up even more. You may soon find yourself in a no-win situation with angry teenagers who refuse to listen to you or to their mother. When teenagers feel that their stepdad and mom are in league against them, they tend to feel unwelcome in their own home. Many leave at the first opportunity, long before they're ready to be on their own. National studies show that teens in stepfamilies leave home earlier than children in intact or divorced homes. To make new rules or to enforce old ones, you must first earn a child's love, allegiance, and respect. Until that happens—and with a rebellious teenager it can take years—avoid being the disciplinarian.

As far as setting rules for the household, your job in the early days of the new marriage is to support and encourage your wife in her role as the primary disciplinarian. She may be overwhelmed and her discipline may be lax, but your relationship with your stepchildren is better served if you let your wife be "the bad guy" and simply back her up when she needs you. You can certainly give her your best advice in the privacy of your bedroom and exert your influence indirectly. You can also play the role of the parent who can more freely sympathize with the child's side of the story. While you need to be careful not to undermine your wife, such sympathy can be an especially useful tactic with rebellious teenagers.

You can become a very important person in your child's life, a moral example he or she will seek to emulate. But being a good stepfather requires sacrifices on your part and humility, really trying to understand the inner conflicts of sons or daughters who feel that if they bond with you they will betray their tie to their biological father. Treating this with respect is the first principle of being a good stepdad.

Whether or not you have children of your own, you have a lot to catch up on with your new stepchildren. Try to get them to tell you about their history. Say that you're eager to get to know them, that you really feel deprived at never having had your own children, and that you would appreciate their help in filling you in on who they are and how they got there. Offer to talk about yourself if they're interested. But you should really try to understand their lives without prying. Which of their peers do they like and dislike? What kind of music do they love and what do they hate? What are their favorite sports and which teams do they root for? Ask about all the many things that go into the texture of their lives. If there are activities that you both really enjoy, see if you can do them together. But don't pretend to love baseball or rock music if you're bored to tears. The kids will find you out. On the other hand, you can keep an open mind and ask to hear a favorite CD. You might really like their taste in music. And if you don't, you'll at least know what they're interested in.

Stepfathers can make an especially huge contribution to the lives of their adolescent stepchildren. In some divorced homes, the biological dad drifts away, showing lukewarm interest in his teenage children. Stepfathers can move into this important fathering role and make a world of difference. If you have hobbies that might interest them, see if they want to join you. If your hobby is likely to attract your child's friends to join in, you'll gain points. One stepfather I know was a real wiz at math who helped all the kids in the neighborhood, including his stepchildren. He helped them with tough homework assignments and rewarded them with math puzzles that the children found fun and fascinating. Another stepfather was a nature photographer whose skill and darkroom were a source of great interest to the stepchildren and their friends. As a special treat he would take the youngsters out at dawn to photograph birds and other wildlife. Gradually they shared a serious interest in the environment and the need to work to protect it.

If you have a preteen or teenage stepdaughter, you have an important opportunity to offer a relationship that may shape her view of men and what she expects from men as she matures. The extent to which you show respect for her opinions and encourage her to take on new intellectual, artistic, or athletic challenges will be very influential as she grows up. Your pride in her has very special meaning. I have heard from many young women about the importance of their stepfathers and how they revolutionized their lives.

I do, however, want to offer you a gentle warning. Remarried families have what psychologists call a lack of biological incest taboos. They are not referring to actual incest but rather to the unconscious temptations that emerge in families without a shared psychological history that represses incest. Look at it this way. In an intact family where father and daughter have known each other since the girl was in messy diapers, the father builds up an immunity to viewing his daughter as sexually attractive. When she enters puberty many years later, this immunity protects the adolescent girl and her father. Dad may be aware of the changes in her body and her exciting presence, but he's wearing blinders that a newly arrived stepfather rarely has.

But you are not her biological dad and her presence can be unpleasantly erotic. I suggest that you and your wife together take extra precautions regarding the behavior of your teenage stepdaughter around the house. If she likes to parade around in the thinnest of underclothing or in very short shorts that show off her figure, her mom needs to tell her to dress appropriately. She should say, "I don't want you walking around the house without a robe. Your body is changing, honey. You can't do

that." Her mother (and not you) needs to take the initiative before anyone feels uncomfortable. If your stepdaughter wails that all the girls wear
short shorts and halter tops to school, you and your wife are going to
have to use your judgment. If your daughter is like most girls her age,
her Lolita-like seductiveness may be hardly conscious. Much of her co-
quette behavior is entirely harmless, and you don't want to create problems that aren't there. Moreover, if you take on the world of peer
pressure, you may lose. If short shorts are the current costume, there's
not much you can do, but in your house you can make sure that nothing
more comes off. Her mom, with your quiet backing, can alert her daughter to your expectations, but you don't need to tell her why. Quite im-
personally, these are your standards.

PLAYER FOUR: STEPMOTHERS

If you're a stepmother—whether or not you've been married before—of
course you have high expectations. You love this guy and you're looking
forward to getting along with his children. My first advice is, slow down
and temper your expectations. Be forewarned that the presence of these
children can interfere with your feeling of being a bride. Your husband's
full attention will not be entirely on you. No matter how lovely and nice
you are and no matter how well behaved the children are, they're in the
way. Given this reality, you're caught. When you marry a man with
children, you can't wake up the next morning and say, as one stepmother
did, "I wanted the man but not the kids." You can't say that out loud to
your husband or the kids. If you suggest that you want the children to
go back to their mom for a period of time, or that you two should take
more trips together, you're paving the way to bruised feelings. You can't
say to your husband, whenever his kids visit, "I feel like they're invading
my house." You've entered the life of an ongoing family. They have ways
of doing things and you have only partial influence in changing their
lifestyles and habits. You don't have the freedom you would have in a

first marriage to set the total tone and climate of your home. So face it. You may love the man and your decision to marry him may have been the best decision of your life, but your wish to be a bride on a year's honeymoon will be frustrated from the start. One compensation is that your husband, having sustained one divorce, is likely to go out of his way to please you. So you can be a happy wife and a good stepmother, but you forgo the privacy of just the two of you.

You need to think from the start about what you can do to overcome the young children's fears that you'll be the kind of stepmother they've read about in the fairy tales. Children worry that their stepmothers will block their relationship with their dad. They fear that you have all the trumps in sharing his bed and his company. They worry that they'll lose their access to him. You'll have to bend over backward to show that you are not standing between them and their dad.

You have a great deal to offer the children if your help comes without strings attached. You can offer them a wonderful and nurturing friendship, a sympathetic ear, and if they're little, a warm and loving lap. You know that you're not their mother. You're not there to occupy the mother's role, but you can be a role model and a major influence on their growing up. If you treat your stepchildren with kindness and affection and give the relationship time to grow, they'll learn to love and admire you. They'll be grateful that you make their father happy.

If you have teenage stepchildren and you're much younger than your husband, they may find it difficult to think of you as a parent or to willingly accept your authority. Since you're closer in age, they may actually envy you. They may resent your youthfulness and attractiveness compared to their own mother, who is aging. Keep in mind that the children are likely to maintain their prime loyalty to their mom, especially if she has not remarried, and to treat you, at least in the beginning, as an unwelcome intruder. If these feelings emerge, it's especially important for your husband to maintain his prior role in the household. You shouldn't be asked to parent teenagers under these circumstances. While you may want to try to take on this role, it's probably impossible to carry off. On the other hand, you can be especially helpful to your stepdaughter if you play the role of an older sister or confidante. Your stepson is another matter. If you try too hard to embrace a teenage boy, he may find his physical contact with you sexually stimulating and he may find your innocent friendliness seductive. Keep in mind he's an adolescent struggling with powerful sexual feeings. To avoid the misunderstanding inherent in these situations, it's important to be tactful and to keep your physical distance when you befriend the boy.

FLUCTUATING AFFECTIONS

Keep in mind that your child's affections—for biological parents and stepparents alike—can fluctuate wildly. For example, suppose you're a stepmom who feels secure that your stepdaughter loves you and reciprocates your love in full. Then, wham, she slams the door in your face to make room for her mom, who hardly raised a finger to help raise her. One woman told me how she put her all energy and even her own funds into bringing up her stepdaughter, who on winning a prestigious academic honor, gave the two tickets to the awards ceremony to her estranged biological mother and father. The girl seemed unaware of her stepmother's enormous pain at being excluded. On the other side of the coin, there are biological mothers who make great sacrifices for their children only to find that their children openly prefer the stepmother. One devoted mother was hurt deeply when her twelve-year-old daughter sent a loving Mother's Day card to her stepmom and not to her mom.

But affection directed at one parent as opposed to the other may or may not last. The twelve-year-old girl who hurt her mother's feelings on Mother's Day sent a passionate card plus an apology to her mom two years later. The young woman who graduated with academic distinction later turned to her stepmother for advice about whether to accept a marriage proposal. Asked whether she had consulted her mother, the young woman said, "Of course not. She knows nothing about my love life. You're the person I trust most in this world." Such flip-flops are common in second marriages, especially among stepmothers and children. They reflect the child's bewilderment with the remarried family and the conflict between loyalty to a biological parent and appreciation of a step-parent. Who to credit for achievements? Who to honor in the ceremonies of growing up? Who should be invited to graduation, the stepmother who raised me or the mother who bores me? Who will give me away at the wedding, my father or my stepfather?

It would be very helpful of course if the two mothers could acknowledge that each has an important role in the child's life. That way the contribution of both could be properly acknowledged. Unfortunately, our society is still built on the notion of the intact two-parent family. Graduation ceremonies and other public events sometimes allow only two tickets to the occasion. Whichever way the child turns, she's sure to hurt someone who is close and dear. The bottom line: all parents in remarried families need to be flexible and to help the children not have to make such hard choices.

NEW BABY

The arrival of a new baby in a second marriage brings new joys and fresh challenges. If the marriage is going well, you as parents have an opportunity to show children from the first marriage how welcome an infant is to a family. But the baby's arrival inevitably also gives rise to worries. The older child asks, Will I have to take a backseat to this new person? Will my mom or my dad love me less or need me less now that the baby is here? While children in intact families worry about being usurped by the new baby, the fear is compounded in a second marriage.

You need to go out of your way to include your children in planning for the baby's arrival, choosing a name, and decorating the nursery. Make sure that your children understand that the baby is being added to your family circle and is not displacing them. Older children will probably enjoy taking care of the infant, helping you bathe and feed her. But younger children need time on your knee. Their fear of being displaced is more realistic and more threatening.

If your remarried family is well established, your children should have no trouble treating each other as full siblings, as long as you treat them that way. But if you treat the new baby like an heir—the little prince or princess who alone carries the father's name—you're asking for trouble. Stepmothers who have their first child within a second marriage may push the other children away. And if the new child is indeed prettier, smarter, or more talented than the older children, parents need to do backflips to keep things fair.

"I was very upset when my stepmother had her baby," said Allison. "I figured that we would be less wanted as stepchildren. I also didn't like it when she said that my sister and I were chubby. I think she was jealous because my mom is known for her beauty."

If you take care to include all your children in the orbit of warmth around the baby, the children will thrive. When your friends bring presents for the baby, suggest that they bring something for the other children as well. If they forget, have some special something in your closet. Everything depends on your consideration of the children's fears and feelings. Ask the older children for help, but be very, very careful not to let them overdo it. And be sure to express your appreciation for their generosity and skill. If an older child wants to hold the baby and this terrifies you, let him do it in a protected area while you sit close by. You face a great opportunity to provide a warm and loving ready-made family for your new child if you keep in mind the double and triple need of all the children to be included and loved and appreciated.

WHO GETS WHAT

When you marry an older man, you may also have to deal with uncomfortable questions of family legacy. In plain words, will you get the money, property, and heirlooms, or will his children from his first marriage be entitled to part or all of the estate? Will your children from an earlier marriage of your own share in the wealth? Will they receive the lion's share because they spent more time with your husband compared to his biological children? Financial issues are very serious, even if there is not much money involved. But when there's a fortune at stake, anger and litigation can go on for many years over how to divide the estate. Everyone in a remarried family with children should leave clear instructions about the division of property. Family treasures like valuable art, jewelry, Great-Granddad's portrait, or Grandma's rocker can be sought after by many family members.

Passions are aroused at this time and can wipe out years of friendliness. Make sure that you're scrupulously fair. Consider your stepchild's emotional and financial wishes to inherit his father's beloved possession. Put yourself in his shoes. As the stepmother, you can become the tabula rasa for all grievances that the children have held against their father over the years. Quite irrationally, you may be blamed by your husband's adult children for having your eyes on their dad's money and for having replaced their mother unfairly. And of course, they assume you were a potent influence when their father wrote his will.

If you're a stepmother in this position, I suggest that you lower your expectations of being appreciated by the adult children whom you did not raise. This way you avoid disappointment and hurt. I also suggest that you familiarize yourself with the law, with your rights, and with the rights of your children and stepchildren during your husband's life and after his death. Your husband's children may never realize how much you loved and helped their dad. On the other hand, your stepchildren may be exceptional. They may express their deep appreciation for all that you have done for their dad and perhaps also for them. If so, consider yourself very lucky.

All of the problems that come up in the remarried family seem bigger than life because you feel so unprepared. As with divorce, there's no dress rehearsal. You may be thrown curves that no one can anticipate. My best advice is don't panic. Don't conclude that your marriage is on the rocks. Too many people give up on second marriages at the first sign of trouble. Give it time. Reread this chapter. Talk together. Sit down with a skilled mental health counselor. Before you put yourself and your children through a second divorce, wait a few months for things to cool down. A second divorce may feel familiar, but one and one adds up to a lot more than two for your children. Try your darnedest to keep your marriage together for them and for you.

And remember. Perhaps the most important gift that a second marriage bestows on children is a good example of a loving relationship between man and woman. Your behavior as husband and wife can supplant their jaundiced view of marriage. Children whose parents create happy second marriages have a much easier time when they become adults. They can draw on good images in selecting a life partner and in creating a good marriage of their own. They learn from you both that marriages can work and that two people can create an orbit of love and harmony that protects everyone in the family.

Chapter 31:   Blending Two Families

I f your new spouse has children who join your household, you face all the challenges I've discussed about how to create a good remarriage and then some. Your children have the opportunity for rich, rewarding friendships with their half siblings. But sharp rivalries may also be in the cards. While you can't predict the course of these relationships, you and your new partner can help shape their direction. Of course, a lot depends on how many children there are and how close they are in age. If the children of one parent are very young and the others are adolescents, all the children may be very happy with their opportunity to mix. Older children often like to help take care of and play with younger children, all of whom who bask in mutual admiration. Younger children are more likely to welcome older half siblings in their lives.

Problems arise when children who are close in age require the same kinds of parenting from you both. Gender is important. One seven-year-old girl I knew well was the only girl and the youngest child among four older male siblings and half siblings. She grew up feeling very special. Her brother and three half brothers, who were quite rough on one another, were very gentle with her. On the other hand, girls or boys close in age can compete with cruelty, fighting verbally and physically for years. Their conflict can continue into adulthood. Or they can become fast friends whose devotion to each other lasts a lifetime. Although much depends on what you do to help them, a lot depends on the children themselves and on the unpredictable chemistry of human relationships.

One rarely mentioned parental nightmare is when teenage half siblings are sexually attracted to each other and share the close quarters of the family home or apartment. This is often handled by separating the two and sending one to live with another parent or relative. Some parents have made the mistake of dealing with an innocent love affair or attraction as if it were an incestuous relationship, which it is not. It's better to treat the two youngsters with consideration and respect for their feelings toward each other but to try to keep them apart without embarrassing or humiliating them. You can't control behavior but you can think ahead and avoid tricky situations that might arise by how you allocate sleeping arrangements and how much supervision you provide.

In Chapter 28, I talked about the need to sit down separately with each child before the wedding to talk over feelings. The same thing holds for two sets of children in a soon-to-be blended family. Each of you should meet separately with each child from both families. This sets the stage for your future relationship and immediately declares your interest in each child. But don't line them up and assign fifteen minutes to each. You need to treat them as individuals. These conversations enable you to take your first step toward the new children and to reassure your own that you love them as much as ever. Tell your new stepchild how pleased you are that you will all be members of one family. If you don't know her well already, ask her to tell you about herself, where she is in school, her interests, and her concerns. Invite her to come talk with you whenever she pleases or has something on her mind. Promise each of them that you'll try your best to make them happy and to be fair. You know they'll have to make adjustments, but you're looking forward to being a really happy family. If you can win the confidence of all the children, I promise you that you'll be rewarded many times over. Moreover, these conversations will greatly enhance your understanding of what lies ahead and what you and your new partner will need to do.

Very soon after the wedding you'll need to clarify a whole lot of issues in daily living. Start by convening another family meeting but this time with everyone present. Big changes are afoot and you all need to help each other. Change is not always easy, but it's an adventure that can be fun. Confess that creating a blended family is new for you and for them. You can learn together how to help one another. You'll need to talk about sleeping arrangements, school transportation, and all the mundane details of family life. Be prepared for disagreement or argument right there, especially about sharing rooms and giving up space. Don't squelch it. On the contrary, be open to and even welcome dissent. You can assure everyone that you'll be fair and forthcoming but be advised that they'll watch what you do and draw their own conclusions about whether you really are trustworthy. From your individual conversations you'll be able to build your personal agenda about each child's concerns.

What do children worry about most when they enter the newly blended family? In a word, fairness. On the surface, they worry about the fairness in assigning chores, about who gets to decide which television shows get watched, about how you will decide on activities like sports and movies. They worry that the other kids will get more goodies or better presents on birthdays or other special occasions. They're anxious about sharing their moms. On a deeper level, they worry about favoritism. Will my step favor his or her kids over me? Will my own parent favor me over my half sibs? Or will I always come second or last or first? They worry especially about losing time or closeness with their biological parent.

Such worries are not misplaced. It's sad but true that some parents in blended families favor their own children over those of their partner. Others bend over backward to give their partner's children the lion's share to avoid accusations of favoritism. For your own peace of mind, try to be extremely fair. Whatever the perk, split it down the middle. Rotate the unpleasant chores. But however well you do in this regard, be prepared to hear complaints that you're not being fair. Keep a calendar for who gets to use the car and other privileges dear to adolescents. See if you can find an extra-large one that you can read from across the room or a marker board so everything is out in the open. You may have to become a scheduling genius to avoid feelings of unfairness among all your children. Be sure to reward special cooperation. In all these aspects of daily life, the burden of the blended family is much higher than in the intact family because the children are watching for signs of inequality. Until each parent passes this test successfully, the sense of loyalty and trust in the family cannot take root.

There are other tests. Some children get into trouble soon after your wedding, including minor or serious problems at school and delinquency. These will tax your maturity and your patience. Don't let your anger get the better of you. By all means have a set of rules that the children know about, like curfew and bedtime. Try to enforce these calmly and fairly. Consider any early acting out behaviors as testing the limits of what you'll let them get away with. Then call them on it. Also be aware that delinquent behavior may reflect the child's effort to turn back the clock and restore the family that existed before your remarriage. A child may feel lost in the shuffle of so many other children. He may feel shunted to the margin. He may be acutely unhappy and have no other way to show his frustration except through misbehavior. And of course, his behavior may reflect a wish to live with the outside mom or dad. Consider all these possibilities seriously. You and the errant youngster can benefit from an extended conversation that tries to locate what's distressing him. If the opportunity to live with the other parent is a real possibility, it's fair to let the child explore it. The outside parent may be able to deliver or may be spinning an unrealistic hope. In either case, that parent remains influential in your child's life. Sometimes a child will simply need extra time with you. Blended families are bigger, noisier, more chaotic. Some children can deal with this and others find it overwhelming. Every child needs some quiet time alone with you. If you're wise, you'll find a way to provide it even if it means making sacrifices. Discuss this with your partner so he can understand. And do it.

Anna was five when her mother remarried a man with three bois-terous children. Anna was a shy little girl who was frightened by the new noise in the house. She missed being her mother's only child. Her mother noticed very soon that Anna was looking listless and was hardly playing with her toys. One evening at dinner, without any apparent reason, Anna slid under the table and sucked her finger vigorously, refusing to emerge. When the family finished dinner, the mother got under the table and said that she was looking for a little girl. Could Anna help her? The mother continued that the little girl she was looking for had been a very happy child but now she was sad and lonesome. Anna climbed into her mother's arms and said, "That's me!" The mother said, "Let's pretend we're still at our old house." Anna took her mother to her bedroom, climbed into her lap, and ordered, "Story." Then she ordered, "Sing." After that, Anna went peacefully to sleep. This routine, so charmingly dictated by Anna, continued for six days. By the end of the week, Anna said that she wanted to see what the other children were doing. When her mom asked her if she was ready to join the family, Anna nodded her head happily. Later her mother assured her that if she wanted special time again she should tell her. With this help, Anna was able to move into the remarried family.

RIVALRIES GALORE

Does a blended family ever get to be like a regular family? Probably not. For starters, they are livelier. There will always be more compromises and more tensions because there are more conflicting claims. Tensions among the children will spill into your relationship with your spouse. You'll all have more room for tears and more opportunity for laughter. You'll have to work closely together to avoid taking sides. Your children will form coalitions based on shared interests and on excluding others from being part of their little club. You need to help the child who is out of the loop. In the blended family prepare to play mediator, umpire, coach, and nursemaid. You may witness malicious behavior at times that absolutely requires your tactful intervention, and you will surely witness generosity.

If the children from both families are all boys or all girls, you can expect shifting alliances and friendships. Some will get along very well and others will compete ferociously. If this competition becomes chronic, you'll need to put time and effort into helping these kids get along, to finding interests in common, and to keeping them active. If you can create unity under some banner of common interest, it's easier. If one child plays the flute and another plays drums, you can make a family band. You can go camping or skiing together. Action-oriented families build tight bonds if you make sure everyone is included, including the child who can't run fast or catch the ball. When you do things together, make sure each child gets rewarded by each of you with praise.

If you have a child in one family who is gifted in some sphere, he or she may feel especially admired. He's used to enjoying the recognition and praise that goes with the achievement and limelight. Then along comes another child gifted in the same sphere. This can create enormous tension between the two children and between the two parents, since each of you is invested in your child. Anticipate this. Talk to the kids together after they've gotten to know each other a bit. Tell them you are enormously lucky, you have two champions, two great musicians, two dancers, whatever. You feel very fortunate. You hope they can help each other, but that's not as important as your hope that they won't collide. Of course they'll compete. There's no way they won't in American society.

If you have an academically gifted child, praise him but also reward him for helping his siblings. Don't let him lord it over the others. In brief, you have lots to look out for and lots to do. Talk over your observations with your partner and try to agree on a united front for handling conflict. Remember what happened in the Old Testament to Joseph, whose brothers hated him and sold him into slavery because his father had given him a many-colored coat—and because he was his father's favorite. Joseph was also the son of his father's beloved second wife. His brothers were the children of the less favored first wife.

This kind of jealousy is a long-standing issue in family life. So if you see these kinds of frictions arising, quickly bring the children together and explain that each child is different and you love each of them unconditionally. One may be gifted in learning while the other is generous and kind. You do not favor one over the other.

Also make sure that the academically gifted child recognizes that you're proud of all the siblings for different reasons. When it's time to apply for colleges, you may need to revisit the issue and have repeated talks with each child, showcasing each one's abilities. You can do this at family meetings or informally in the day-to-day course of family life.

If one child is having trouble at school, give that child special attention but be careful not to overdo it. Don't let any child get pushed into the shadows. Again, in a remarried family, each child is acutely aware of how everyone is treated. Can you be fair?

Many people don't pay attention to problems like the ones I've mentioned until things have gotten beyond repair. For example, Jean had a very gifted child and her new husband, Cliff, had a child who was in serious trouble academically. This broke the marriage. Cliff felt humiliated. Instead of being able to help his son, he shared his son's pain and overidentified with the boy. When there's competition between the children, as inevitably occurs in all families, there's greater potential for parents to line up on opposite sides of a fence, only to end up back in the divorce lawyer's office. I believe that a large number of failed second marriages could be saved if parents could empathize with all the children.

Actually, many failing second marriages could be saved if the parent with the gorgeous, talented, or overachieving child could better empathize with the parent whose child is in trouble—and reach out to undo the hurt. For example, I know a woman who rescued her marriage after her son won a scholarship to a prestigious private high school the same year that her stepson flunked the tenth grade. Her husband was devastated. Realizing his hurt, she invited her husband to Hawaii where they had honeymooned. After recapturing some of their early romantic connections, she told him frankly that she was worried about their marriage because of his son's failure and her son's success. She said that she loved him and that their marriage was more important than who won what race in high school. Their job as parents, she said, was to prevent the successful son from becoming obnoxious and to encourage the failing son to keep trying and learn to lean on his strengths. As they planned what to do when they got home, the husband's anxiety diminished and the marriage was saved by a savvy lady and smart strategy that is easily learned.

SPECTACULAR PARENTS REQUIRED

More than in intact families, mothers and fathers in blended families need to stick together as a team because of the complex dynamics under one roof. You need to anticipate problems and to stay in close communication. You need to plan ahead for each year and sometimes each season. In short, you need to be super parents. Nightly pillow talk is essential to keep the blended family afloat. Life is never dull. Maybe that's why television shows about blended families are so popular.

But don't forget to spend time alone. To enjoy your marriage and keep from being overwhelmed, you'll need a close bond and time just for you. Don't skimp on that. In one blended family the father and mother took several short vacations each year. Several weekends alone, meaning without a spouse, two weekends together as a couple, and one or two weeks with all the kids. They said that they needed this for their mental health and I believe them. Whatever works for your peace of mind is best.

If you pass all these tests, you can expect to see loving friendships develop among some of your children and with each of you. Blended families bring their own kind of blessings. When they work well, they offer the opportunity for lasting friendships among stepchildren that last into adult life and include extended families. Reunions are boisterous and fun. On the other hand, bringing it all off is exhausting. How can you keep your relationship fresh and alive with all the chaos around you? This may be the hardest part. This will tax your imagination, your inventiveness, and your energy. Whatever revives your courtship days, do it. If it's an adventure, pursue it; if it's just doing nothing in a beautiful setting, do that; if it's retracing your honeymoon, do that. Whatever it is, don't forget to give it your full attention and the budget that it needs. Paris is expensive but you deserve it, just the two of you.

Chapter 32:   Holidays and Special Occasions

I n a blended family or remarried family where adults have different upbringings, you have to put together the different traditions of the two families at Christmas, Chanukah, birthdays, and other family occasions. This can be a big job because typically each family is like a small civilization in its customs, especially those that include the children. Over the years these traditions come to have great symbolic significance. Even food—apple or pumpkin pie, sweet potatoes or plain white potatoes, turkey or duck at Thanksgiving and Christmas—can induce fighting words. Are gifts distributed on Christmas Eve or in the morning? Do you or don't you celebrate Chanukah? Do you buy new clothes and go to church on Easter? Do you hold a large seder with friends or a smaller one with family at Passover? All these decisions have their roots in traditions that people are reluctant to change because they are symbols of family life.

The practical arrangements are not difficult to manage. Many combinations are possible. All work some of the time and fail at other times. But thorny problems can only be solved if people plan ahead and decide on general principles. There is no royal solution, no better or best for everyone. Traditions can be changed yearly or customs can be alternated. One guiding principle is to choose traditions that work for most people and cause the least hurt and inconvenience. Another is to make sure that those involved know ahead of time what the plans are. Since in most holidays the children play a key role, you should keep an eye on how to provide them with a maximum of pleasure and the opportunity to be with as many members of their family as possible and to minimize their disappointment and fatigue.

Symbolic meanings are harder to manage. How do you change traditions without offending one or more family members? Some children cling to traditions. They feel lost with even a small change. Others couldn't care less. All that matters is whether the food is tasty and the gifts are right. Most of what matters to adults and to children is that they be consulted about changes in their tradition and told ahead. Otherwise the holiday can bring tears and hurt feelings. Sadness is always very close to the joyful surface during the holiday festivities.

You should be thinking about Thanksgiving and Christmas holidays by early November if not sooner. A perennial question after divorce with or without remarriage is where each child is going to spend each holiday. I'm often asked if the parents should get together for the holiday celebration. Actually, I see no harm if the parents can do it. Often, however, especially in the years immediately following the divorce, relationships are too tense. In addition, you don't want your children to get the idea that you're going to reconcile. More often than not, it's better to work out some fair division. Thanksgiving to one parent, Christmas to another on alternating years. Or if parents live close to each other, Christmas Eve in one home and Christmas morning in the other, with the assortments of grandparents, uncles, aunts, and cousins divided accordingly. Chanukah planning is much easier because there are eight days for celebration. But the Passover seder needs to be negotiated, alternating homes each year or in some families the tradition is two seders, which makes planning easier. However, if the children are twelve or older I would recommend that you consult them about their preferences for how the holiday celebration should be divided. Once you've decided, be sure to let everyone know the plan.

Gifts require special thought in all families at holiday time but especially so in the blended family. Parents after divorce should always try to equalize their gifts within reasonable bounds. In blended families, equalizing the gifts takes on special significance as the children watch carefully for what each of them receives because of the message that the gift conveys. That's why this is the time when you need to be especially fair and kind. Sadly, many parents fail the test. I recall vividly the suffering of one boy who saw his father give his binoculars to his stepson and not to the boy. The boy had watched his father use the binoculars for bird-watching for many years and had his heart set on inheriting them. When they went to the other child, his heart was broken. I've talked to children who recount with grief how a stepsibling their same age was given a cherished item—a locket handed down from a grandmother or a pocketknife from a favorite uncle—when they were given nothing equivalent. You need to keep in mind that gifts to children are important in and of themselves, but they also carry enormous and lasting symbolic significance. Save family heirlooms or handed-down gifts for birthdays or graduations, when children are not competing for your affection. And, of course, don't give one child a bicycle and the other wool mittens. Gifts are loaded with feelings, and in divorced and blended families they come with that crucial question, Do you love me as much as the others? Adults understand the concept of intent over material goods, but children do not. In a blended family the girl will watch what her stepsister gets no matter what you say.

Finally, be aware that you and your children may feel sad over the holiday celebrations. You all may remember the intact family and look back nostalgically, weeping anew for the warmth and tenderness of family that was lost. Offer some quiet time to a child who looks unhappy. Sit quietly or hold her hand and recall the past together. Offer a loving hug and a lap to a young child. These are important times for sharing. Kiss away her tears but don't try to suppress her memories or to cheer her up by dismissing her sadness. Memories are important and they merit your respectful attention.

INTERRACIAL INTERFAITH

Many parents ask me how interfaith or interracial divorces will affect their children. Will they feel half Japanese, half Catholic, half Jewish, half Hispanic? Will it shake their identity? Will my children have to choose, the way we have to choose custody? Will children in joint custody hold on to both heritages? This is a very serious issue since there are millions of intermarriages and divorces in America today.

The differences that arise in the two traditions are only rarely the root cause of divorce. But these differences feed into divorce when the extended family gets involved or when there's a great deal of anger between the parents. Families can act like tribes fighting for the allegiance of a child. This only increases conflict between the parents and hurts the children. Nevertheless, this tribal warfare is not uncommon when people divorce.

Mia had a different take. A charming eighteen-year-old with a Japanese father and a Jewish mother, she explained it all: "I'm not half Japanese. I'm one hundred percent Japanese. I'm not half Jewish. I'm one hundred percent Jewish. I hate it when people refer to me that way. I'm not a half person. I'm a whole person. I meet new friends at my dorm and I say I'm Jewish and they don't believe me. Their litmus test is, have you had a bat mitzvah? You bet I have. I went to Israel with my classmates. Then my father took me to Kyoto and Tokyo." I was very impressed with her healthy integration of the two traditions and her ability to hold on to both parents despite the divorce. It obviously helped Mia that her parents continued to respect the traditions of the other parent during the marriage and the divorce.

If your marriage held two traditions, I caution you to be aware of the schism you can create in your children's hearts and minds. Each child is a whole person. To expect loyalty to one tradition can involve disloyalty to the other. That would be like cutting your child in half. She'll suffer, feel like a traitor, and have problems with her self-image. Ultimately she may deal with your pressure by rejecting you both.

I asked Mia who she wanted to marry. She laughed. "I have no limits of how I marry. I was brought up on diversity. I believe in it and I'm not setting limits ahead of time."

Sometimes you have to choose. You can't be a practicing Catholic and an observant Jew at the same time. However you resolved these conflicts for your children during your marriage, continue your chosen tradition after the divorce. If you were raised a Mormon and you wanted to be married in the church, you probably agreed to raise your children as Mormons. Let's assume that your husband accepted it at the time. After your divorce, there's no reason to reverse this decision as long as your children are content with your religion. If, on the other hand, your children's religious training was a major source of marital conflict, you need to deal with the conflict. I know a family that split up because the father converted to the Jehovah's Witnesses and the mother remained a Lutheran. They fought over their three children for years, until the children grew up and left home. All of them turned their backs on all religion, which is hardly what the parents wanted.

To their credit, children can live with two different sets of values. A child has no problem saying that each parent worships at a separate altar. They feel little conflict in saying my dad keeps the Sabbath on Saturday and my mother goes to church on Sunday. But when parents insist there is only one way of worshiping, then they do have a problem. Children don't become serious about religion until adolescence. At that time you should invite them to explore and choose what they find most helpful for their own needs. They may, in dealing with ethnic difference, embrace both. Or they may decide to postpone their choices. In our society, it is their right.

PART FIVE

*

CONVERSATIONS FOR A LIFETIME

Chapter 33: How to Protect Children of Divorce in Young Adulthood

Y ou may not be comfortable with my final piece of advice on raising children after divorce. What I'm about to describe is not advice you've heard before and frankly it may be difficult for you to do. It draws on what I learned from talking to young adults whose parents divorced twenty-five years ago and who have been describing their thoughts, feelings, and experiences to me at regular intervals through all these years. Based on what they have told me, I am recommending that as your children go through adolescence and enter young adulthood, you need to carry on an open-ended conversation about what caused your divorce and what you have learned about how to avoid the mistakes you made. Your goal in these conversations is to convey your hopes for their happier future and your confidence in their ability to succeed in love and in creating a committed relationship.

Why do this? Why not simply bury the past and get on with life? Won't dredging up past hurts just make things worse? My answer is an emphatic no. Your children need to know what went wrong in your marriage so they'll have a better chance of creating a lasting, happy marriage of their own. Moreover, they need your loving encouragement to feel hopeful that they will succeed where you failed.

One of the things I have learned from adult children of divorce is that parents often fail to explain the breakup. From the child's point of view, the divorce struck like lightning from a clear blue sky. It was an unforgettable shock that blew the family to pieces, even though the parents may have known it was coming for years. And even when an initial explanation for the divorce was offered, no one talked much more about it as the years passed. And then, according to these now grown children, came other losses that reinforced their conclusion that relationships between men and women are fragile and often unreliable. Dad's new girlfriend moved in but a year later moved out. Mom remarried but after three years that, too, didn't work out. Now Dad has a pretty good second marriage and Mom is dating a new guy who may last, but may not. Many children grew up feeling that one parent was a lot happier while the other was still struggling to build a happier life after the divorce.

So where does this leave the children? If you put yourself in their shoes, you can imagine that it's pretty hard to think seriously about commitment and marriage when you feel from the get-go that relationships can't be trusted to last. Sure you can fall in love, but how can you trust your heart to a relationship that's likely to fail? How can you plan on having children when marriage is so chancy? Face it, the people you love can disappear without warning. Adult children of divorce tell me, "I'm always waiting for that second shoe to drop." They say, "If I go to bed happy with a guy I love, I'm always afraid when I fall asleep that he'll be gone by morning." They're amazed to learn that their friends who grew up in well-functioning intact families don't feel the same way. And since their parents never really talked about why they divorced, the children figure the reasons must have been just too awful or shameful to describe.

You may be thinking to yourself, how can that be? We explained the divorce to our kids years ago. We sat them down and carefully went over the reasons. We didn't hide anything that they were old enough to understand.

But that is exactly the point. When you explained the divorce to your children, they were just that—children. The explanation you provide a five-year-old is different from what you tell a ten-year-old and different still from what you say to a fifteen-year-old. One of the striking things about children of divorce is that they continue to work on understanding your divorce all through their childhood and beyond. This may be hard for you to believe, but they don't forget about it or take it for granted. As a matter of fact, at each developmental stage they replay the story using their increasingly sophisticated ability to comprehend complex human relationships. Children of bereavement do the same. They replay their loss again and again as they grow up. If they lost their mom when they were very young, they miss her when they're old enough to go to school and they miss her again, differently, when they reach adolescence. Children of divorce miss their original family when the breakup occurs and they miss it again when they get older and rework the experience. By the time the children reach adulthood, they've thought about the divorce and added up what they gained and lost a thousand times. You need to appreciate the fact that by the time they reach adulthood, they're truly ready to understand what you experienced. But they need your help to reach this understanding so they can finally put your divorce behind them and get on with their own lives. They also need your permission and encouragement to talk to you to get the facts straight.

I suggest that you carry on a continuing conversation with your child about the divorce and that you get more candid as he or she gets older. It can begin whenever your child opens a door to the topic. For example, you'll be folding laundry when your twelve-year-old turns to you and says, "My teacher said that people should never divorce. He thinks that they should work things out."

You've been playing tennis with your fifteen-year-old. On the way home he says, "My friend Johnny thinks his parents are going to divorce. He's worried about moving away and that we'll never see each other again."

One thirteen-year-old found an old button that read "Make Love

Not War." He brought it to his dad. "That's not what you and Mom did," he said with a cold stare.

Think for a moment about what your child is asking. Yes, he's curious about what people say about divorce and what they think of him and you both. But he's also curious about your divorce, about your family history, and what it means to him today. Mostly he is concerned about himself and his own future chances at the brass or gold ring. Perhaps your son was three when you divorced. But now that he's fourteen he wants a new explanation, one befitting his greater maturity. He is right.

So to begin, I suggest you answer the opening question. You can correct the teacher's view—which reflects your child's questioning—by saying, "Yes, people have different ideas about divorce. Some people think it's very wrong and that everybody should stay married. Your dad [or mom] and I feel differently. We divorced because living together made us unhappy. We thought about it a long time before we decided. It was not a rushed decision. But your teacher may be saying that he thinks it was too hard on you kids." Your son has a right to remain silent while he's thinking about what you said. Or he may say, "You bet it was hard." Or he may assure you, "Naw, it was fine. Don't worry, Mom." No matter what his response, you have left the door open to continue the conversation when he's ready.

You can talk about moving: "Sometimes that happens because people don't have enough money after divorce to live nearby. It did [or did not] happen to us. How can we help your friend? Would it help him by telling him what happened to you? Do you want to invite him to spend the weekend? Maybe, in time, we can figure out with his folks a plan for visiting so you guys can continue your friendship even if his family has to move." This response is calculated to support the youngster's concern about his friend and to say to your boy that his experience might be helpful to someone else and by implication to himself as well.

It's very useful to counter an accusation with a question. "Did it feel like war to you?" Get your child to tell you his experience. Chances are, you'll be startled at what he recalls. He may have completely misunderstood or he may have gotten it straight, but in either case he has a right to know what happened. And you surely owe him the observation, "You must have been really scared." However you phrase your reply, you have an opportunity to repeat your explanation of what led to your divorce in a language appropriate to your child's age and new level of understanding. You have a chance to clarify what happened to your family and why. It should always be an open dialogue, not a secret that no one can talk about. And you can remind him that after the war you made a peace treaty.

This is important because your child needs your help to create a continuing life story for himself. Some parents try to erase the past, as if the family before the divorce never existed. In starting over, they assiduously avoid talking about the old neighborhood and what life used to be like. It's too painful. Better to get on with the future.

This kind of censorship can impair your child's sense of who he is by eradicating a portion of his life from memory—and I mean that literally. I was shocked to discover in my work that some young adults can't remember anything about family life before the divorce. It's as if their early years were erased from the planet. I've talked to people who assured me that they have no memory before age twelve, which was when the divorce occurred. This is a serious gap in their identity that scares them. Your children need to understand that their pre- and post-divorce lives are chapters in a family history in which they're leading characters. Remember, they didn't ask for the divorce. They didn't ask to change their family or to have parents who live in separate households. Their wish as they get older is to make sense out of what happened then and what's happening now—the whole story without deleted chapters.

Thus you can help your adolescent a great deal by integrating life before and after divorce into an ongoing narrative. It's useful to say, when it comes up in conversation, "Remember when we lived on Oak Street and we used to walk to the little park down the street?" Such early memories are part of your child's life experience and should be respected. The family they knew before your divorce doesn't have to disappear. Not everything in it was awful, especially for them. Some experiences were probably good. Try to keep some of their good memories alive by retelling funny episodes or important milestones in the child's life. "That was when you learned how to swim" or, "That was our home when you were born. I remember how excited your dad and I both were." One mother made a point of returning once a year to the community where the children had been raised before the divorce so they could refresh their early friendships. Her children had a sense of continuity in relationships that they valued and held on to until they left for college. Her son said approvingly, "My mom was one smart lady. I still have my friends from when I was nine years old."

You can also help by explaining what happened in the early days after your divorce from your point of view. Tell your children why you had to move, how you chose their custody plan, why you've had to work so hard, and so on. If serious financial pressures kept you away from them for long hours, explain why you had no choice. Your goal is to help them understand you in a more mature way by explaining what led you to the decisions that shaped their lives.

MORAL ISSUES

Children raised in divorced families also need to clarify a host of moral issues. They are understandably unclear about the rights and wrongs of married life. In a number of families I know, the siblings argued for years about whether their dad or mom was having an affair before the divorce. This was an especially hot issue if a parent remarried very quickly after the divorce. In one family the siblings argued whenever the children got together. Yes, he did! No, he didn't! This went on throughout their adult lives until the father died suddenly. Going through his desk, the children found old letters that confirmed his infidelity. Two of the sisters were crushed and very angry. This was still a live issue for them years after the divorce when they were adults with children of their own. I do think it would have been better for them if, when they were older, their dad had said, "I'm not proud of it, but I was very lonely with your mom and Carol helped me survive."

What if your child asks, "Is my father a good man?" "Is my mother a good woman?" I've heard these questions often. The first time it came from a fifteen-year-old who marched into my office and, before he sat down, demanded, "Tell me, is my mother a good person?"

"What makes you doubt it?" I asked.

"She's not like any other mom. She rides a motorcycle. She wears strange clothes. What is she like with you?"

"She's pretty direct with me."

"But why did she divorce my dad?"

"John," I said, "you're a lucky boy. You have the kind of mom who, if you ask her anything, will tell you honestly like it is. You can trust her. Then ask your dad what he thinks. That way you can begin to answer your own question. It's one of the most important questions you can ask. Talk with them and then let's talk about you and what you want for yourself."

Every child needs to believe that he or she has a father and mother worthy of respect. But the divorce and often a parent's behavior before and after divorce can shake this belief. Children have a strong moral sensibility. They judge us every day. Are we fair? Are we honest? Are we moral people? If your child asks you this question, you need to answer it. But you need to help him make up his own mind. If you just tell him what to believe, you will fail. You can say, "I can't answer for you, but I can tell you what I think. This is something you will have to answer for yourself." Then speak honestly, "I don't think either of us was very good. When people are unhappy, they can make mistakes that they later regret." Or, if it is relevant, you can say, "Your dad has been a much better husband and father in his second marriage, but he was not a good husband for me. I think you should talk with him. You may get a different version." Or you can honestly say, "When I married your mom, I thought she would be a good wife for me. I think she tried to be a good wife but I don't think she succeeded. But check it out with your mom. It's very important for you to figure out your own ideas and standards."

Praise your child for asking questions about right and wrong. Treat it as something he or she will be struggling with for some time to come. When your son or daughter reaches later adolescence, you can answer in greater detail: "Now that you're seventeen, I really want you to know more about what happened so you can learn from our experience. You should talk with your mom, but I don't think she behaved well and I would feel very bad if you behaved like she did in your future marriage. But you have to make up your own mind about her and about me." Or you say, "I really want you to know that I made a mistake when I married your dad after knowing him only six months. I found out after the marriage all the things that I should have found out before. I don't want you to make the same kind of mistake. So take my experience to heart."

Don't rush to close off your child's concern with moral issues. Encourage these questions, as painful as they are for you both. This is an important stage of growing up. Your child's doubts about both of you are very good. He's developing a conscience separate from yours. Children of divorce need to figure out for themselves a lot of troubling issues. But an important part of the struggle is reaching a conclusion about how honest and trustworthy you are with them. Can they expect an honest answer from you? If they learn to trust your honesty, they'll have an easier time when they're attracted to someone and realize they need to ask important questions: How trustworthy is he? How well do I know her? How does he treat other people? What do I know about her background and history? My strong recommendation is that you try your best to help them so that they will be grounded in reality in their search for a life partner.

If your family belongs to a church or a synagogue and your youngster has a good relationship with the minister or rabbi, suggest that they talk. But don't duck out of your own role in answering. They're asking about what is right and wrong, good and bad for themselves, and they are asking about you. Those are exactly the kind of questions that a parent should welcome.

ABOVE ALL, BE HONEST

It's become a mantra to tell divorced parents one overarching rule: do not fight. Don't tell the children about your anger or true feelings. Never say anything negative about the other person. The logic is simple—by refraining from criticizing your partner you will not upset your children. You'll set a good example. But I have a different take on this "don't fight" rule. I don't go along with the advice that like Bambi, you should only say nice things about people. There's a middle road to expressing your feelings that is far more honest.

So what should you say? What is appropriate? Children after divorce are intensely observant of their parents. If you say nothing, they notice. If you hurl insults at each other, they notice. Somewhere in between you need to speak calmly and honestly. As your children grow up in a divorced family, they should have some ongoing understanding of the serious issues that led you to divorce.

There's a real advantage in saying to your children, "I'm angry at your father," or, "I'm annoyed at your mother." Or, "Your dad disappointed me," or, "Your mom hurt my feelings." Or, "I wish your father had better judgment," or, "I wish your mother thought before she acted." With these words, you don't deny feelings and you don't magnify feelings. You walk a thin line, I grant you, but that's the legacy of divorce. Use your judgment. Say things more softly than you feel, but don't deceive your children. Your very important job as a parent is to help them to understand their family. If you know your ex-husband is always late, don't get your child ready at exactly six o'clock so you can confront your ex one more time with vituperous complaints about his tardiness. Tell your child, "Daddy often forgets to look at his watch. That makes it hard for both of us." If you know your ex-wife makes promises she's not going to keep, you can mute your child's disappointment and protect him from a let-down or you can reinforce his pain. It's better to say, "Sometimes Mom forgets things that she said, so we'll wait and see what happens" than it is to say, "Your mom doesn't care about your feelings." If you know that your ex-husband has been picking on your son for little things, you can soothe the boy by saying, "Your dad has always been like this. He takes little details so seriously. It used to drive me crazy, but don't let it get to you." If you know your ex-wife tells your daughter that she's fat and not the pretty little girl she always wanted, tell your daughter, "To me you look lovely." You can surely add, "One of the problems with your mom is that she doesn't understand how much things she says can hurt you."

I'm sure you can think of examples in your own post-divorce life where you can say what you feel without burdening your child. This is a modified "don't fight" rule that I think makes more sense. Don't rage, but don't deny your perceptions. Don't deny your child some understanding that the divorce had real causes or refrain from helping her deal with difficulties related to your ex's behavior. In the end, you'll respect yourself and your child will respect you for telling the truth. What's more, you will teach your child to trust her perceptions and her feelings.

ANXIETY ABOUT LOVE AND MARRIAGE

When your child goes off to college or begins living independently, you can be sure that his or her relationships with the opposite sex are moving center stage. The search for someone to love takes on an entirely different, more serious quality. Graduated from puppy love, the young adult asks: What am I looking for? What kind of person would make a life mate? How will I know if I'm in love? At the same time they're thinking about mature life goals. What are my values? What will be my major in college? What kind of job do I want? How important is money? How important is marriage? Do I want children? A career? Both? If I have children, can I count on their father's help? These are the questions that young women sit up late into the night talking about in college dorms.

Young men, too, are thinking about their future in serious ways, although they're less likely to devote bull sessions to their concerns. Both sexes struggle with "What's in the cards for me? What can I expect?"

For the child of divorce these universal questions arise with special poignancy. It's a hard time for them because the ghosts of your failed marriage loom into view as they enter adulthood. Memories of the divorce rise from the depths of long ago and become more powerful as your daughter thinks about love and marriage in her own life. In thinking about trust and commitment, she'll recall your failure and her own fear of loss. She'll think about both of you and what happened between you when she begins to sort out her relationships. She'll be frightened, but she won't tell you about her worries or ask you troubled questions about the past. She won't ask because she loves you and she doesn't want to upset you. Everyone colludes in the silence.

"My parents divorced after twenty years of marriage, when I was in the fifth grade," said Greta, a twenty-five-year-old high school teacher in Portland, Oregon. "Although I graduated with a master's degree in education and have a great job, I'm suffering a lot. I'm always worried about many things I should not have to worry about. One major fear is that if my parents were together for twenty years and it was fine, what can I possibly see down the road for my own life? So I get scared and don't want to marry at all, even though I desire marriage more than anything. I'm always afraid that any man I love could be gone the next day. Every relationship I've ever been in ended because I was so clingy. I was so afraid that the guy would not like me tomorrow. As a result, my clinginess made them do just that. They left. I try to control it, but it's really hard because I get so scared. I watch each guy from my window as he walks down the street at the end of the evening and I just know that I will never see him again. Please help me if you can."

Children of divorce often experience what I call a "sleeper effect"—the effect of something that happened long ago, went underground, and only comes up when issues that draw on those past experiences move to the center of the stage. Your child's experience of your divorce remains alive as memories. Those memories, which may be partly forgotten during childhood, rise to the surface when searching for love and establishing sexual intimacy are the key agendas of her life. That's why children in late adolescence and early adulthood begin to fear they're doomed to follow in your footsteps. They feel unprepared for how to create a lasting, happy relationship. They say, "No one ever taught me about relationships" and, "I've never seen a man and woman on the same beam" or, "I'm not prepared" or, as a twenty-one-year-old said, "Sometimes I think I have been raised on a desert island. It's not sex that scares me. It's getting close. Combining sexual intimacy with love is a strange idea to me."

To understand what your children are missing when they stand on this important gateway to adulthood, you need to think about the countless small exchanges that occur within a reasonably functioning intact family. Children watch how their father treats their mother and their mother responds in kind. They observe their parents kissing, fighting, arguing, yelling, apologizing, and helping each other get up when one stumbles. They see how a man and woman every day hold on to love and friendship, how they survive economic and social difficulties, and how they try to solve crises in ways that safeguard their children and themselves. At the other end of the spectrum, they can watch parents hurt and humiliate each other in exchanges that most of us can't imagine. Cruelty and vicious behavior can rule the male-female relationship, leaving children open to a lifetime of suffering and pain. Whatever they have observed in how parents treat each other and how parents treat children are the images they bring to young adulthood and work on as they mature.

WHAT YOU CAN DO

You need to understand that your child is probably not going to confide in you about her concerns unless the channels of communication have been kept open over the years. But even then nineteen-year-olds rarely turn to their parents for advice about their relationships. Your daughter is not likely to call you up from college to tell you that she's having problems because every time she gets into a relationship that makes her happy she's afraid it will be gone the next day. Your son won't confess that he gets discouraged and feels he'll never be able to have the family that he wants. In contrast, studies show that compared to children of divorce, college students from intact families have an easier time asking their parents for advice. They are, I submit, less worried about upsetting their parents with their confidences and likely more hopeful about getting useful advice.

You're probably going to have to make the first move. This will take tact and courage on your part. If your daughter tells you that she and her boyfriend have broken up and she seems discouraged or even depressed about her relationships, you can ask gently whether she's worried about the effects of your divorce on her life. Of course, your first efforts might be rejected. But make your love and concern clear. Tell her that if any part of your experience can be helpful, you are happy to share it.

If your son says that he really doesn't feel that he and his girlfriend have much in common—she drinks too much or is interested in subjects that bore him but insists that she loves him and needs him whenever she's feeling down—tell him that it's sometimes hard to know the difference between love and dependency. It's very good of him to want to take care of her, but she doesn't sound like the kind of person who will fill his needs. Tell him, if it's true, that he seems to be acting like he did with you and your ex in wanting to be the good son who pleased everyone and took care of everyone. Perhaps he could see one of the counselors at the health center to talk about this pattern of behavior. Commend him for telling you about his concerns and that you want to help him avoid making a decision he may regret.

Having made yourself available to continue the conversation, try to keep it going without being intrusive. You're laying a groundwork that says, How are things going? Is there something you want to confide in me? Is there something you want to tell me? If your son or daughter provides you with an opening, you can help by saying, "Don't be discouraged. Building a relationship takes time. It's rare to find the right person the first time you try. In fact, if you find somebody too soon, you should probably beware." You can say, "Take your time. It takes a long time to know what you really want and maybe even longer to find the right fit with another person. First you need to know what you really want."

It may ease your task to know that children of divorce at this age frequently seek counseling services at college. So what you are talking about may be a subject she has thought a lot about. If your daughter tells you that she's seeing a counselor, by all means support this. Say you were sorry you did not have anyone to go to when you were in a quandary. Or you found therapy helpful in understanding yourself and deciding what to do. However you carry on this dialogue, you want to express confidence that your child will find a worthy person to love. That person is worth waiting for. Marrying too soon can be a disaster. Tell your child to get to know himself first and then choose a life partner.

If your children keep repeating that they're afraid to trust anyone, you can agree that knowing whom to trust and whom to reject is one of the hardest tasks there is. But it doesn't mean you can't trust anybody. Trust may be something you learn slowly but you can learn it. Tell them to take time to listen to the other person, to look at that person's values and plans for the future, to check out carefully how they are treated and how the person they are considering deals with his family and friends.

LEARN FROM MY MISTAKES

I suggest you try to talk about yourself and the mistakes you made, knowing this may be the hardest thing in the world to admit. Nevertheless, at this particular time in your child's life, anything you say about why you think your marriage failed can be tremendously helpful. It will be especially helpful if you can admit your own errors that caught in time might have protected you from heartbreak.

For example, if you married a violent man and you think back on your courtship, I suspect you'll find that there were subtle (and sometimes not so subtle) clues about how explosive he was. If you chose to ignore these signs, you may have reasoned that your love would be more powerful than his violent tendencies. You said to yourself, if I love him enough, he'll become the loving husband I want him to be. Now is the time to tell your daughter that nothing could be further from the truth. Love is powerful but it cannot transform a violent person into a pussycat. Love cannot help a person develop self-control. This is terribly important for your daughter to understand, because so often young women raised in violent families seek out violent men to love and rescue. Like you, she may figure that her love will overcome his rages. Your warning may not be sufficient to change her, but it will surely strengthen her own doubts and may steer her toward getting therapy in order to avoid a bad marriage.

If you married your wife knowing that she drank too much or you found out about her problem early on and turned a blind eye, tell your child you made a mistake. Tell her that you could have saved everyone a lot of suffering had you intervened and gotten your spouse into treatment early in your relationship. After all, you had your greatest leverage in those early years. "I should have taken your mother by the hand and insisted that she go into AA instead of expecting that her drinking problem would go away over the years."

If you married when you were both very young and decided you were so in love that you had to elope, tell your daughter or son to learn to always wait 'til morning. If a man is lovable after six months, it's better to wait to see how he'll be at a year. The characteristics that impress you at the beginning of a relationship are not necessarily those that endure. If it's love, it will endure and even deepen if she can wait.

Tell your children to treat this major decision of their lives with respect, to give it time and not be carried away by impulse. Your message should be: Don't do as I did, learn from my mistakes and from what I have learned. We were kids when we got married. Neither of us knew what we wanted. Later when we grew up we discovered we had nothing in common. You can avoid this happening to you.

If infidelity broke your marriage and you're comfortable discussing it, you can be especially honest with your adolescent or college-age child. What did you contribute? Did you ignore the growing distance between you? Did you take her for granted? Did you return from work and hide in your study all evening and consider that a good marriage? Did you figure he'd always be there no matter what you did? Were there gaps in some important part of the relationship? Did you spend all your time taking care of the baby? Did you give up on sex? Did you stay at the office instead of coming home? Did you talk with your mom or your women friends all evening? Such are the many signs that can be an overture to infidelity. People often don't see the warnings until it's too late and another relationship has formed.

Tell your children to talk about serious matters before they get married. Do you both want children? If only one wants children, what will you do? If they have different religions, how will they raise children? Most of all, tell them that a marriage needs love, care, and tending. It's not only the union of two people, it's a new creation that needs to be nurtured regularly. Tell your child to look especially hard in a partner for integrity, capacity for loyalty, and a sense of morality. This can be evaluated during courtship if they know how to look.

Finally, you can say that there are no sure things in life. Every relationship has some element of gamble. But your children can improve their odds by drawing on your knowledge, learning from your mistakes, and getting to know themselves well before they decide on a life partner.

NEVER TOO LATE

It's never too late to have the conversation I'm talking about. For example, Julia is an attractive thirty-four-year-old who lives in San Francisco. Not long ago she got an e-mail from her dad, who lives in Portland.

"How is it you don't have a boyfriend?" he asked. "You're such an attractive, intelligent woman. What's going on?" Julia was touched by her dad's interest and when they met in person a month later, decided to have a heart-to-heart with her dad. I was present. Julia said, with tears welling, "Dad, you need to know something about me. When you left home, Mom instructed us to always look good and pretend that we weren't hurting. I remember I wanted to cry and throw my arms around you and beg you to stay, but instead I obeyed Mom. I sat quietly as you walked out the door. And do you know, Dad, I've kept up the pretense of never needing a man to this day."

Julia's dad was dumbfounded by her confession. He said, "You played that part so well. I had no idea that you even missed me. So I stayed away." With that, they embraced, crying, laughing, and crying some more. Julia later told me that it was the best thing she could have done for herself and her father. She felt relieved of a burden that she'd carried since childhood, of muting her own feelings and pretending she was so independent she didn't need anyone. A few months later Julia e-mailed me (and her dad) to say that she'd met someone. They were dating and she hadn't been so happy in years.

With a parent's help, adult children of divorce can let go of long held patterns of behavior that block their relationships. It's as if they're all tied up, waiting to be set free, waiting for permission from their parents to move forward in life. A mother's encouragement is especially important to young women who may feel that they dare not have for themselves what their mothers had lost. "I was so tied to my mother," said thirty-year-old Brenda, "that I really lost track of where I began and she ended. Finally I broke free." I asked her what happened.

"She helped me," replied Brenda. "She gave me the permission to have what she had never had. That was holding me back more than I realized. She told me that her most important desire was for me to have a happier life than she had and she wanted to see me with a loving man."

Sons need a different kind of advice, especially from fathers. Too many dads try to be just pals with their young adult sons. They discuss sports or the weather or they tell jokes. There's nothing wrong with that as long as the father realizes that his son needs a father, not another buddy. Sons in divorced homes especially need to feel that their father has confidence in them as they venture into the adult world. It would mean a lot to your boy to know that you're interested in his plans and in what he wants out of life. What kind of husband or father does he expect to be? How does that tie into his career plans? He will welcome your encouragement and feel empowered as he matures. Tell him honestly the problems you ran into on your first job. How did you overcome your own anxieties about marriage, about having children? How long did it take before you felt secure in any of your adult roles? These questions are certainly not easy to review, but your experiences, including your successes and failures, will help your son.

What you should never do is minimize your adult children's distress by telling them that these problems will go away or aren't serious. Heartbreak and discouragement about relationships are the most serious problems a young adult can have. Depression is common when young men and women feel rejected. After being betrayed, some young men have a hard time trying again. Even being turned down for a casual date seems too much for them to surmount.

If you keep your eyes open, you can find all sorts of opportunities to help your adult children change their outlook on the past. For example, not long ago a divorced friend from Chicago told me about a visit from her thirty-five-year-old son who was happily married and launched in a good career. While they were in a restaurant with friends, the son saw his estranged father across the room and became so anxious that he left the scene and fled to his mother's apartment. A little while later, the mom found him and asked what happened. He was distraught.

"I just panicked when I saw Dad."

"What were you afraid of?"

"I was afraid he'd make fun of me like he used to."

This episode gave mother and son an opportunity to review what had happened and to talk about his fears. It enabled her to say that he was an admirable adult in every other part of his life. How come the sight of his father across the room could reduce him to being a child again? Emboldened, the son called his father a few days later. They hadn't spoken for twenty years. When they finally met, the son realized that his father was a paper tiger who had no intention of being cruel and no power even if he wanted to. The moral of this story is don't ever give up on your kids or on your capacity to influence their decisions. Realize that it takes children of divorce longer to grow up because they have a lot to learn in adulthood that they did not learn as children.

I have many examples of men and women who were headed nowhere, when at age twenty-seven or twenty-eight, help from a parent turned their lives around. I think of a gifted young woman who flitted from one cocktail waitress job to another and one man to another who got an unexpected call one day from her father, who after many years had gained control over his drinking problem. "You're wasting your life," he said. "I think you should go to college. I'll pay for it." She nearly fell over with surprise. But he was delighted when a few years later she graduated with honors. By the time she was thirty-five, she had a career in science and he had two grandchildren.

Indeed, you have many chances to improve your relationship with your children when they become adults. Perhaps through no fault of your own or because of something you've done, your children may have been angry at you for a long time. Whatever the roots of their anger, justified or not, when they're in their twenties and floundering, you can help, big time. Along with your renewed interest and counsel, you can provide resources—money for school, for drug and alcohol rehabilitation, or for whatever they truly need. If you give this help along with a demonstration of interest and affection, you will find that there's real potential for your relationship, which has been in trouble for years, to turn around, and real potential for your child to change his life.

MAKE TIME FOR CONVERSATIONS

It also wouldn't hurt as these conversations arise to spend a weekend somewhere nice with your son or daughter, just the two of you—at your expense, of course. Do something you enjoy doing together. Go hiking, visit a museum, eat at a great restaurant. And be sure to lace your advice with humor. Pomposity will alienate your children. You can have the conversation tactfully. I know one father who kept giving funny names to his daughter's suitors, and as she giggled, he had a chance to say exactly what he thought. Another said, "I know you like biology, but you gotta know that divorce is not in your genes. If there's any divorce DNA it stopped in my generation."

If your second marriage is working well, it's worth talking about. Sit down with your son or daughter and analyze what you did differently that made this marriage work. Were you more considerate? Did you learn not to take offense at an argument? Are you better at reading the body language of your partner? You have learned tricks to make a successful marriage that children in post-divorce families don't have in their bones. If your children are fortunate enough to have been raised in a good second marriage, they won't be so different from children raised in good first marriages. But most divorces happen when children are younger and second marriages come along when they're older. The norm is for children to spend their formative years with single parents. They need to know that people who love each other get angry and that it's safe to fight. A conflict-free marriage is an oxymoron. Tell them.

If you and your ex-partner have mellowed over the years and treat each other with a new kindness and understanding, tell your children. If therapy helped you better understand yourself and make a better choice in your second marriage, I suggest that you say that to your son or daughter. They, too, may find therapy helpful in understanding what they didn't have while growing up.

BECOMING A GOOD GRANDPARENT

The arrival of a baby and your becoming a grandparent always heralds a new beginning. If you can take advantage of this opportunity, you can recast your relationship with your adult child. Babies offer an extraordinary chance to improve relationships and resolve long-standing estrangement. After a new baby arrives, your son and your daughter will be more open than ever to reshaping their relationship with you. New parents undergo a developmental spurt. They begin to understand a lot of things they never understood before. And, if I may say, so do you. It's as if both generations realize that they're united in their responsibility and love for the new child.

One young mom said to me, "Now I understand why my mom was so frantic. It wasn't that she didn't care about us. A child takes so much out of you. I see myself in her every day."

Another young mother said, "I told my dad, I can't forgive you for the past for not being there when I really needed a father, but I love you now and my son loves you and that's what counts the most."

If you can reach out and grasp this opportunity, you can play a very important, helpful, and loving role in your child's and grandchild's life. This is a time for reconciliation, forgiveness, and new growth. Good luck!

The message I hope you can convey is not unlike the one given to immigrant children by their parents, who say, "We want you to make a fresh start and build a new, different, and happier life in this land, and in this you have our blessings." Let your adult children know how much you hope they can make better marriages and succeed where you stumbled.

EPILOGUE

After you finish reading this book, I'd like you to lean back, close your eyes, relax your shoulders, and consider the broad outlines of what I've said. Put my advice, including the many suggestions on what to do and what to say to help your children, on hold for a moment as you bring to mind the larger picture. This is what you need to understand as you approach the many crossroads that lie ahead.

I have tried to show you that divorce has the power to transform your life, for better or worse. It's not a time-limited crisis, as some people still like to argue, but an ongoing chain of shifting family relationships and changed expectations that you and your children will deal with well into their adulthood.

Divorce is not just a flight from an unhappy marriage. The legal divorce is only the first step. Although the divorce itself is never easy for a parent, the hardest part begins after you walk down the courthouse steps and embark on building your new life and meeting the challenges that await you. Divorce leaves an unexpected legacy for a family with children. Unless you're able to meet these new circumstances head-on with knowledge and courage, you may find that you've only substituted new problems for old ones.

People can fail at divorce as they have failed at marriage. A successful divorce requires that you rebuild your life and broaden your relationship with your children in the many ways that I've suggested. In this rebuilding, you become a stronger, different person. You also become a different, stronger, and wiser parent. The experience of being a mother or a father is transformed in the divorced family—not better or worse, but different, more challenging, and certainly harder than being a parent in a reasonably functioning intact family. Your experience of being a coparent outside a supportive family structure will also tax you. Unless you're able to overcome its vexations, it, too, may be as difficult as being locked in an unhappy marriage.

During and after your divorce, your children will observe you carefully. They're looking to you for guidance because they've been shaken by the divorce and are worried that love is fleeting and close relationships are fragile or even doomed to fail. They look to you for clues to guide their own lives and for encouragement that love can be strong and lasting. They need to believe that parents are faithful forever in caring for their children. My hope is that they'll learn from you that people have the courage to start over and correct their mistakes. Human beings who have hurt each other can forgive and go on to treat each other with civility. I have no doubt that someday they'll appreciate the sacrifices that you made and how hard you fought to protect their childhood.

While all children need their parents as role models, a divorced parent sets an example with added potency. As your children grow up, they need your active encouragement in learning how to trust and to believe that their own relationships will endure. They need to understand from you that an unsuccessful marriage is not a random natural disaster but the result of human error that you and others can help them avoid. They need a vote of confidence from you.

My goal throughout this book has been to restore your hope and your high expectations for your future and your children's futures. I have sought to give you the knowledge that you need to go forward with faith in your abilities as a loving parent. Then and only then will you make good use of the second chance that divorce has the power to bestow.

INDEX

Abandonment
    fear of, 55, 56, 58–61, 88
    past, 207
    preschool children feel, 254
Abortion, 250
Absent father(s), 261
Accidents, 69
Acting out, 32, 67, 326
    by adolescents, 103, 109, 250
    in anger, 81
    in delayed reaction, 225
    at home, 70
Activities, 12
    after-school, 94, 136, 152
    and custody choice, 218
    family, 85, 281
    loss of participation in, 198–99
    planning, 133, 146
    six-, seven-, eight-year-olds, 67, 68, 71–72
Adolescence, xiv, xvii, 75, 82, 83, 86, 93, 248,
        258, 267, 341, 348
    early, 98, 129
    girls, 263, 264
    growth in, 248
    hazardous time, 88
    moving into, before ready, 33, 88, 249
    in post-divorce family, 247
    relationships with parents in, 243
    stormy, 248–49
    vulnerability of children entering, 130
Adolescents
    anger in, 100, 102, 254
    help from, 103, 105–6, 112
    leaning on, for emotional support, 232–33
    life narrative, 345
    and moving away, 201–2
    older, 117
    reaction to divorce, 87, 99
    sexual feelings, 250, 284, 318
    and stepfathers, 307, 314–15
    and stepparents, 312, 313
    taking sides, 110
    telling about divorce, 21
    see also Teenagers
Adult children of divorce, 20, 68, 179
    divorcing, 40–41
    and inheritance, 321
    father's role and, 268
    memories of learning about divorce, 20, 23–
        24
Adult relationships
    children do not understand, 270
    children of divorce, 236–37
Adult roles
    for teenagers, 257
Adversarial representation, 166–67
    alternatives to, 167–69
Affections (children), fluctuating, 318–19
After school, 70–71
    activities/programs, 94, 136, 152
    activities/programs: parents attending, 106
    informing children about arrangements, 135
    structure for, 94
Age of child
    and alignments with parents, 242–43
    in blended families, 324
    and changes in custody arrangements, 183, 184
    and custody choice, 193, 216
    and reaction to divorce, 31, 33, 35, 88
    and remarriage, 290
    and telling about infidelity, 27
    and time to divorce, 127, 130

Aggressive impulses, 83, 98
Alcohol, 98, 103, 128, 250
Alcohol treatment programs, 253
Alliances, child-parent, 76, 239–46
Anger, 27, 40
  controlling, 213
  and courts, 204
  and development, 32
  after divorce, 14–18, 160–61
  enjoying, 15
  escalating, 128
  at ex-spouse, 241, 242, 301, 302
  family and, 145
  in high-conflict divorce, 205, 211, 212, 214
  involving child in, 245
  and joint physical custody, 196
  letting go of, 128
  in nine- and ten-year-olds, 75–77, 78, 79–81, 85, 86
  at parents, 359
  between parents, 239
  in remarriage, 306
  in teenagers/adolescents, 100, 102, 254
  using, 15
  and violating agreements, 182
Anxiety
  in college-age children, 114
  about love and marriage, 350–52
  in nine- and ten-year-olds, 75, 79–80
  in preadolescents, 94
Apologizing, 161, 162
Assets, dividing, 171
Attachment
  and custody arrangement, 193
  with ex-spouse, 8–9
  to family, 120
Attention deficit disorders, 227
Attorneys, xv, 19, 164, 165, 166–67, 168, 171, 172, 173, 172, 191, 207, 208, 243, 244, 262
  and collaborative law, 170
  and custody, 184, 186, 209
  in high-conflict divorce, 210, 212, 213
  and moving away, 200, 202
  in parallel parenting, 181, 182
  and parenting plan, 176, 177
  reviewing mediation agreement, 169
  selecting, 165
Aunts, 145

Babies, 31, 43–46, 319–20, 361
Bedtime, 69, 133, 134–35
  in joint physical custody, 196

Bedtime routines/rituals, 56–57, 135, 217
Bed-wetting, 64, 217, 218, 223
Behavior
  expectations of, 84
  home/school difference, 37–39
  motives for bad, 251–52
  risky, 88, 98
  standards of, 96, 98, 103
  unacceptable, 109
Behavior change, 36
Biological father(s)
  drifting away, 314
  outside remarriage, 301–3
  remarriage, 308–9
Biological incest taboos, 315–16
Biological mother(s)
  and child's preference for stepmother, 318
  as outside parent, 303–5
Biological parent
  loyalty to, 317, 319
  and remarried family, 299, 300
Birth control, 98
Birthdays, 72, 333
Blame/blaming, 15, 25, 84
  children blame themselves, 54, 65–66, 124
  by college-age children, 115–16
  mothers, 273
Blended family, 282, 295, 323–31
  equalizing gifts in, 335
  traditions in, 333
Boys
  aggression, 206
  assuming father's role, 70
  delinquent behavior, 249
  helping parent(s), 105–6
  learning difficulties, 33
  need for fathers, 108
  preadolescent, 90, 92–93
  and remarriage, 290
Brazelton, T. Berry, xi
Breakup, xv, xvi, 3, 202, 343
  behaviors in, 35–37
  reasons for, 110

Calendar(s), 61, 133, 179, 294, 326
California, 191, 193
Caregiver(s), 57–58, 124
  hiring, 47
CASA (Court Appointed Special Advocates), 210
Cause and effect, 54, 63, 66
Cell phones, 95, 137

Center for the Family in Transition, xiii
Changes, xiii, 325
  children coping with, 199
  as children grow, 170, 262
  children understanding, 58
  in/and custody arrangement, 175, 183–84
  in divorce, 99–100
  in/and divorce negotiations, 170–71
  flexibility in adapting to, 193
  in parent-child relationship, xv, 4
  in parents' lives, 220
  vulnerable children and, 123, 124
Chanukah, 333, 334
Child abuse, 128, 205, 211
Child alienation syndrome, 243
Child-rearing, 186, 302
  after divorce, 12–14
  by men, 11–12
Child support, 158, 160, 167, 171, 192
  custody arrangements and, 179, 193, 220
  paying, 191
Childhood, loss of, 102
Children, xii–xiii, xiv, xvii, 10, 29
  adult relationships, 236–37
  as allies in upsetting ex-spouse, 241–43
  assessing condition of, 138–39
  assurances to, 53
  blame themselves for divorce, 54, 65–66, 124
  in blended families, 323–30
  caregiving role, 233
  changes over time, 170, 262
  considering wishes of, 29
  custody form in psychological adjustment, 192
  in divorce negotiations, 170–71
  effect of parental conflict on, 204–5
  effects of divorce on, xvi, 19–20
  entering adolescence early and persisting
    longer, 247
  father's new role with, 263–68
  fear of change in parents, 9
  fear of parents' leaving, 52–53
  fluctuating affections in second marriage,
    318–19
  flying alone, 202
  as friends of parents, 105, 231
  growing up, 359
  help from, 84–85
  hiding feelings, 26
  in high-conflict divorce, 205, 206, 213–14
  and holidays, 334
  hopes to restore marriage/family, 20, 241,
    242, 281, 296, 326

  including with new baby, 319–20
  input from, in family meetings, 134
  and interracial/interfaith divorce, 336–37
  involving in setting up two-home space, 194–
    95
  involving in wedding, 292–93
  in joint physical custody, 197–200, 206
  leaning on, for emotional support, 232–34, 235
  leaving home, 272–73
  listening to, regarding new lover(s), 286–87
  looking for guidance, 364
  loving both parents, 173
  mental health consultation, 39–40
  of new lover/partner, 277, 282, 287
  not responsible for divorce, 26
  and parent's dating, 278–83
  and parents' sex life, 283–87
  participating in making plans, 180
  perception of family, 35–36
  private time with, 295
  protecting in young adulthood, 341–61
  protective role of, 26, 28, 232, 235
  psychological evaluation, 208–9
  in remarried family, 299–301, 309–10
  sabotaging new relationships, 286–87
  and second marriage, 289–93, 294–97, 318–
    19
  several years after divorce, 223–29
  in sole custody, 187–88
  and stepparents, 311–22
  telling about divorce, 19–30
  telling about divorce: what to tell, 23–30
  understanding of divorce, 20, 27–29, 35–36,
    54, 343–46
  and unhappy marriage, 130, 131
  when to tell about divorce, 21–22
  see also Older children; Reaction to divorce;
    Vulnerable children; Young children
Children from previous marriage, 300
  inheritance, 321
  in second marriage, 312
Chores, assigning, 135, 147
Christmas, 333, 334
Church, 152–53, 348
Class reunions, 151
Clinical social work, 228
Collaborative law, 164, 169–70
College-age children, 113–20
  what to do, 117–20
College education, 178
  plans for, 100, 107–8
  protecting, 119

College tuition payment, 165, 254
  in divorce agreement, 171–72
Comfort(ing), 53, 55, 78
Commitment, 283, 342, 351
Communication
  in coparenting, 180–82
  with ex-spouse, 14, 49, 77
  with preadolescents, 98
Community Centers, 152
Community resources/supports, 12, 141–42,
  151–53
Compassion, 78–79, 233
Competition between children
  in blended family, 328, 329
Compromise resolution, 166–67
Confidante, child as, 105, 231, 232
Conflict
  child(ren) in, 241
  among children in blended families, 324
  and divorce, 66
  handling, between siblings, 136
  low, 128–29, 360
  potential for, in second marriage, 297
  over religious training, 337
  see also High-conflict marriage
Conflict resolution, 176
Conscience, 78, 91
  in adolescents, 103, 104
  developing, 255, 267, 348
Consistency, baby's need for, 50
Consultations with children, 11–12, 105
  regarding parenting plan, 179–80
  about schedule(s), 67
  in setting up two-home space, 194–95
Continuity, 176, 346
  children in sole custody, 187
  in child's life, 59
  grandparents in, 142, 144
  loss of, 198–99
Control
  over children, 137, 138
  lack of, with more responsibility, 12–14
  loss of, 271
  of your life, xii, xiii, 4, 141
Conversations
  with preadolescents, 92, 96–98
  with young adult children about what caused
    divorce and what you learned, 341–46,
    353–59, 360
Cooperation, 6, 22
  in second marriage, 301, 308

Coparenting, xiii, 6, 9, 13, 158–59, 167, 283, 364
  arrangement for, 177
  communicating and trusting in, 180–82
  foundation for, 175–84
  relationship in, 160, 162
Counseling services, 354
Courts, 152, 158, 163, 202, 203–4, 211
  custody forms, 215
  family fights in, 240
  move away policies, 201–2
  and schedules, 181, 182
  see also Going to court
Courtship, 282, 331, 355, 356
Cousins, 145, 147
Crisis, xvi, xvii, 253
  family meeting in handling, 254
Crying, 4, 100
Cultural change
  and father's role, 267–68
Custody, xvii, 6, 157, 158, 185–202
  choosing right, 215–20
  fighting over, 203–5, 207, 210–14
  foundation for, 175–84
  law and, 163
  losing to other parent, 201
  schedule of, 67
Custody agreement/arrangements, xiii, 12, 28–
  29, 172, 175–76, 177, 182, 346
  adolescents, 107
  changing, 175–76, 183–84
  conflicts caused by, 71
  detrimental to children, 202
  lawyers and, 165
  and moving away, 200–1, 202
  psychological evaluation in, 208
  views on, 48
Custody issues, reexamining, 183–84

Dating, 95, 277–87
Daughters
  adolescent, 285–86
  and fathers, 105, 106, 263, 264, 267
  and mother's lover, 287
  and remarriage, 291
  see also Girls
Day care, 47, 216
Decisions, 206
  regarding custody, 215–17
  reviewing, 228
  sharing, 190–91
  to divorce, xii, xiii, xviii, 4, 5, 21–22, 76

Delinquency, 91, 109, 249, 326
Denial, 66, 88–89, 139
Dependency, emotional, 235
Depression, 116, 227, 228
  and acting out, 67
  in adolescence, 254, 255–56
  and babies, 44–45
  in child, 67, 218–19, 225
  in college-age children, 114
  in vulnerable child, 125
  in young adults, 358
Development, 33, 98, 129, 158, 227
  activities in, 71
  in adolescence, 247
  college-age children, 113
  and custody issues, 183, 216
  delays in, 45
  effect of violence on, 127
  effects of divorce on, 19, 91
  interrupted by divorce, 32
  lawyers and, 165
  in new parents, 361
  problems in, 204
Developmental ladder, 31–41, 223
  baby, 44
  nine- and ten-year-olds, 73–74, 75, 81–82
  six-, seven-, and eight-year-olds, 64, 68,
    70
Developmental stage(s), 239
  adolescence, 101–2, 108
  and father-child relationship, 263, 264, 266,
    267
  and understanding of divorce, 343
  vulnerable children, 123, 125
Dinner, eating together, 136
Disabilities, 121, 123, 178
Disappointment, 8, 14, 131
Discipline, 97, 101
  disagreement with stepmother about,
    303–4
  lack of, 103, 249
  by older siblings, 135–36
  in remarried family, 313–14
Distrust, 45
Divorce, xi–xii
  "best" time for, 127–31
  cause of, 26
  challenges in, xii–xiii, 4, 10–12
  choice to, 130
  completing, 159–60, 203
  consequences of, xv–xvi

  conversation about cause of, 341–46, 349–
    50, 353–59, 360
  decision to, xii, xiii, xviii, 4, 5, 21–22, 76
  delaying, 46, 93, 114, 124, 129
  effect on sibling relationships, 146
  effects on children, xvi, 19–20
  emotional residues of, 300–1
  first years after, 15–16, 138–39
  issues in negotiating, 170–72
  legacy of, 349, 363
  is life-transforming, 363
  looking at self several years after, 223–29
  is process, xvi, 224
  recovery from, 207, 212
  recovery of children, 224, 227
  second, 322
  as second chance, 41, 138, 364
  successful, 6, 363–64
  taking care of yourself in, 3–18
  telling children about, 19–30
  telling children about: what to tell, 23–30
  see also High-conflict divorce; Explanation of
    divorce; Reaction to divorce
Divorce agreement
  review mechanism, 171
Divorce revolution, 192
Divorced families, xv
  alignments in, 239–40
  development in, 33–34
  father role in, 260–68
  parenthood transformed in, 364
  playing parents off against other, 76–77
Dr. Spock's Baby and Child Care (Spock),
    xi
Don't fight rule, 349, 350
Drug abuse, 103, 128
Drug treatment programs, 253
Drugs, 98, 253
Dual residence
  see Joint physical custody

Early childhood, 88
  see also Young children
Eating disorder, 256
Education, 177, 187
  continuing, 11, 116, 153
  special needs in, 178
  see also School
Educational programs, 152
Elementary school years, development in, 31–
    32

Eleven-, twelve-, and thirteen-year-olds, 87–98
    early adolescence, 249
    what to do, 93–95
    what to say, 95–98
Emergencies, 69, 137, 234
Emotional maturity
    in adolescents, 103
Emotional support
    leaning on children for, 232–34, 235
Emotions, gaining control of, 9
    see also Feelings
Empathy, 136, 329–30
Empty nest syndrome, 273
Estate, 321
Exercise, 49
Explanation of divorce, xvii, 84, 109,
        342–43
    to college-age children, 117–18
    to vulnerable child, 124–25
    see also Talk(ing) to children
Ex-spouse, 299
    and adolescents, 251, 252–53, 254, 257
    attachment with, 8–9
    and changing schedules, 220
    child as ally in upsetting, 241–43
    child in role of parent to, 235–37
    children with, 270–71
    civility toward, 95
    and college-age children, 117, 118–19
    and college plans, 107
    commitment to be good parent, 180–81
    communication with, 14, 49, 77
    connection with, 158–59
    cooperation from, 308
    danger from, 162, 205, 210
    in family conference, 109
    fighting with, 147
    financial support from, 11, 49, 226
    in high-conflict divorce, 212, 213
    and joint physical custody, 195–96, 211
    and moving away, 200–1
    and new lover(s), 286
    and parenting plan, 176–79
    playing the field, 98
    psychological evaluation of, 207–8
    relationship with, xiii, 12–13, 60–61, 87–83,
        110, 160–2, 360
    and second marriage, 306
    threat from, 213
    and vulnerable child, 125
    and working, 176

Extended family
    and adolescents, 112
    support from, 145
Extramarital affairs, 131
    see also Love affairs

Failure, divorce as, 100–1
Fairness, 241
    blended families, 325–26, 335
Family(ies), 4, 17, 84, 85, 86, 248
    advice from, 166
    attachment to, 120
    child's hopes to restore, 241, 242, 281, 296,
        326
    in divorce, 27
    fear of losing, 79
    help from, 47, 130
    loss of, 136
    sense of, 85
    stable, 90, 107
    weakened, 98
    see also Blended family; Divorced families;
        Intact family(ies); Post-divorce family;
        Remarried family
Family, new
    supporting, 141–53
Family agencies, 152, 226, 256
Family court, 173
Family history, 344, 345
Family law cases, 166–67
Family legacy, 320–21
Family life, issues in, 325
Family meetings, 109, 285
    in blended families, 325, 329
    regarding college plans, 107–8
    regarding rules, 133–34
    in second marriage, 294–95, 304, 309
    with teens in trouble, 254
    for telling children about divorce, 19, 29–30
Family members, 178
    in family meeting for teens, 254
    and high-conflict divorce, 207
    support from, 141, 142, 145
Fantasies, 33, 53–54, 65, 81, 82, 92
    of reconciliation, 139–40
    sharing, 147
Fantasy, role of, 139
Fantasy play, 81
Father-child contact, 66–67
Father-child relationship, 46, 47, 172, 260, 261–
        62

Father-son relationship, 97, 268
Fathering
  from outside second marriage, 302
  in post-divorce family, 260–68
Fathering role
  in sole custody, 189
  stepfathers, 314–15
Fathers
  and adolescents, 108, 252–53
  child support, 193
  custody, 154
  and daughters, 105, 106, 263, 264, 267
  disappearing, 158
  fear of being marginalized, 266
  importance of, to children, 270
  living arrangements for children, 11–12
  and moving away, 200–1, 202
  new, 50
  new home, 59, 66–67
  new kind of, 259–68
  as outside parent, 301–3
  paying college tuition, 171, 172
  private time with child(ren), 295
  raising children, 11–12, 186, 187, 192
  remarriage, 308–9, 310
  responsibility for children, 13
  and sole custody, 186–87, 188–89
  visiting, 185, 186, 187, 188
  and young men, 357–59
  see also Biological father(s); Stepfathers
Fathers' groups, 152
Fathers' movement, 158
Fault, 6, 161–62
Favoritism, 329, 303, 325–26
Fear(s), 41
  of abandonment, 55, 56, 58–61, 88
  in child's reaction to divorce, 51–52, 55
  of happiness, 23
  in high conflict, 128
  letting go of, 128
  of losing family, 79
  of loss, 351
  of ex-spouse, 205
  in six-, seven-, and eight-year-olds, 64
  in teenagers, 100, 101
  of violence, 127, 128
  years after divorce, 226
Feeding children before school, 136–37
Feelings, 349
  acknowledging child's, 84
  control of, 9

  expressing, 310
  hiding, 26, 36, 38, 87, 100
  suppression of, 204, 211–12
  unresolved, and joint physical custody, 196
Financial arrangements
  custody and, 220
Financial consultant, 166
Financial help/support
  with baby, 49
  from grandparents, 144
Financial implications/issues, 118, 166, 179,
    346
  in divorce negotiations, 171–72
  estate settlement, 321
  of joint physical custody, 193
Financial obligations
  of fathers, 13
  with vulnerable child, 125
Financial settlement, 118
Forgiveness, 161, 162
Forgiving yourself, 274
Fourteen-, fifteen-, sixteen-, and seventeen-year-
    olds, 99–112
  what to do, 104–9
  what to say, 109–12
Fourteen-year-old
  custody choice (example), 218–19, 220
Friend(s), 17, 71, 72, 293
  advice from, 166
  help/support from, 130, 142, 148–50
  treating children as, 105, 231
Friends/friendship (children), 68, 85, 102, 223,
    310
  adolescents, 107
  confiding in, 147
  including, 84, 85, 94, 189, 245
  lack of, 255–56
  need for, 147–48
  new, 72, 152, 224
  teenagers, 106–7
  in two neighborhoods, 197, 198–99
Fun, 138, 139

Gender
  and blended families, 323
  in parent-child alignments, 240
  and preadolescent changes, 90
  and reaction to divorce, 31, 33–34, 35
  and remarriage, 290
Gifted children, 328, 329
Gifts, equalizing, 335

Girls
  adolescent, 250
  and fathers, 108, 263–64
  helping parent(s), 106
  preadolescent, 90, 92
  and remarriage, 290
  seductive behavior, 206
  sexual behavior, 103, 249, 255, 263
Going out alone, 150–51
Going to court, 166–67, 172–73, 182, 236
  over custody, 176, 186
  fathers, 266
  to prevent moving away, 201
Gonzales, Elian, 207
Grandparents, 49, 178
  becoming good, 361
  in family meeting for teens, 254
  help from, 112, 226
  support from, 142–44
Gratitude, 142
Grief/grieving, 8, 273
Groups
  for divorced parents, 151–52
  joining, 153
Guilt, 77, 80, 162
  in mothers, 255, 256, 273–74

Half siblings, 299, 323
  sexual attraction, 324
Healing process, 7–8
Help
  acknowledging child's efforts, 84–85
  from adolescents, 103, 105–6, 112
  with babies/toddlers, 47–48
  from college-age children, 118
  from family and friends, 130
  see also Support
High-conflict divorce, 203–14, 227
High-conflict marrige, 127–28
Holidays, 72, 303, 333–37
Home, 119
  children leaving, 272–73
  loss of, 101–2
  lover moving into, 284–85
  moving out of, 223–24
Home/school transitions, 71
Homosexuality, 110–11
Honesty, 26, 27, 83–84, 85, 146, 348, 349–50
  in talking to adolescents, 112
Honeymoon, 293

Hormonal shifts, 90, 92
House, selling, 102, 116
Humor, 80–81, 96, 151, 360

Identity
  change in, xii, 3, 4, 7–10
  gap in, 345
  transition to new, 17–18
Incest taboos, 315–16
Independence, 179, 180, 197, 267
  adolescents, 101
Infants and Mothers (Brazelton), xi
Infidelity, 100, 346–47
  adolescents and, 110
  discussing with young adults, 356
  explaining to children, 27, 79
Inheritance issues, 118, 119, 320–21
In-laws, 49, 57
  support from, 141, 143
Insiders
  and remarried family, 299–310
Insurance, 177, 226
Intact family(ies), xv, 20, 48, 76, 192, 220, 224, 257, 319, 342, 364
  alliances in, 239
  changes in, 183
  children speaking their minds in, 179–80
  and children's activities, 71
  and development, 33, 34
  dialogue about children in, 262–63
  exchanges in, 352
  family history, 24
  father role in, 108, 261
  father-son relationship in, 268
  parent-child relationship in, 311
  parent-child resemblances in, 240
  parenting in, 48
  planning for college in, 107
  siblings in, 136
  social life in, 280
  spending time with, 149–50
  unhappy, 241
  young adults from, 353
Intact marriages
  empty nest syndrome, 273
Internalized images
  of aggressor/victim, 211
Interracial/interfaith divorces, 336–37
Interracial/interfaith marriages, 178, 207
Irreconcilable differences, 128–29

Jealousy, 17, 119, 196, 329
Jewish tradition, 274
Joint custody, xv, 13, 60, 158, 179, 185, 188, 208, 215, 217, 220, 223
court-ordered, 205
Joint legal custody, 190–91
Joint physical custody, 48, 186, 191–200, 210, 218
advantages/disadvantages of, 197–99
court-ordered, 205, 211–12
Journal of Attachment and Human Development, 48–49
Judges, 163–64, 166, 168, 172–73, 185, 191, 204, 240, 243, 244, 270
joint physical custody, 205, 210
move away policies, 201
Judgment
in adolescents, 104, 250
in preadolescents, 90, 97

Kidnapping, 210

Law (the), 163–73
Lawyers
see Attorneys
Learning difficulties, 33, 227
Legal advice, 200
Legal agreements
regarding schedules, 181–82
Legal custody, 185, 190–91, 200
Legal implications/issues, 166, 179, 202
Legal rights/obligations
in second marriage, 311–12
Legal system, 9, 163–64, 243
Letting go, 8
of anger, 16–17
in divorce, 160
of fear and anger, 128
of memories, 8
of youngest child, 273
Life story, 345
Limits, 79, 91, 101, 249
Listlessness, 68, 261
Litigation, 207
regarding inheritance, 321
Loneliness, 40, 76, 128, 271
breaking out of, 277
Loneliness (child), 36–37, 53, 65
siblings counteracting, 146
Losing one's temper, 80, 272

Loss(es), xv, 58, 59, 342
of family, 136
in father role, 262–64
fear of, 351
of feeling in control, 271
of home, 116
of lover, 285–86, 287
past, 207
replaying, 343
for vulnerable child, 123
Love
anxiety about, 350–52
cannot stop violence, 355
college-age children, 113
is unreliable, 114, 364
young adults succeeding in, 341
Love affairs, 83, 97, 272
Love-hate relationship, 159
Lovers, 17, 248, 253, 283
children driving away, 286–87
loss of, 285–86, 287
moving into home, 284–85
Loyalty, 306
to biological parent, 317, 319
conflicting, 301, 319

Madam Butterfly fantasies, 65
Male-female relationships, 96, 128
children's worries about, 293
examples of good, 322
fragile and unreliable, 342
issue in adolescence, 248–49
stability of, 283–84
young adults and, 352
Manipulation, 77, 251
Marginalization, fathers' fear of, 266
Marital problems, 100, 131
Marriage
advising young adults about, 355–56
anxiety about, 350–52
baby threat to, 43–44
disappointment in, 131
child's hope of restoring, 20, 241, 242, 281, 296, 326
failed, 4, 8, 25–26, 138, 161, 228, 290, 351, 354
good, 270, 271–72
unhappy, 20, 131, 272, 283
unhappy: staying in, 130, 131
violent, 273–74
Marriage and family counselors, 228

Meals, eating together, 136
Mediation, xv, 164, 167–69, 202
Mediation agreement, 169
 review mechanism, 171
Mediator(s), 164, 167–69, 171, 181, 202, 206, 220
 and custody arrangement, 184
 in family meeting(s), 304
 in high-conflict divorce, 212
 and parenting plan, 177
Meditation, 49
Meeting new people, 151
Memories, 9, 335–36, 345, 346
 adult children of divorce, 20, 23–24
 child's experience of divorce in, 351–52
 letting go of, 8
 resurfacing, 40
Men
 challenges in divorce, 10–12
 see also Fathers
Mental health consultation, 39–40
Mental health experts/professionals, xv, 82, 158, 172, 176, 184, 200, 211, 243, 256
 advice from, 166
 background and training, 208
 hiring, 166–67
 for psychological evaluation, 207–9
Mental illness, 128
Middle/high school years
 development in, 32
Mistakes
 correcting, 364
 learning from, 110, 354–56
 talking about, 96–97
 young adults avoiding, 341–42, 348
Modern American culture, 91, 158, 251, 267–68
Modern divorce culture, values clash in, 201
Money
 borrowing, 10–11, 49, 145
 and college plans, 107
 in divorce settlement, 165
 need to work for, 134
 for treatment, 256
 for young adults, 359
Moral issues, 346–48
 adolescents and, 102, 103
 discussing, 96, 97
 nine- and ten-year-olds, 74
Moral judgment, 27, 109–10, 244
Moral justice
 courts and, 172, 203–4

Moral standards, 104, 106, 257
Morality, 164, 255
 ex-spouse, 213
 nine- and ten-year-olds and, 78–79, 82–83
Mother-child bond, 157
Mother-child relationship, 172
Mother-daughter relationship, 97
Mother-infant bond, 45–46
Motherhood role
 changed by divorce, 270–74
 men in, 264
Mothers, 267
 changes in, and child's reaction to divorce, 51–52
 custody, 157
 go-between between young children and fathers, 263
 guilt feelings, 255, 256, 273–74
 new, 50
 new kind of, 269–74
 as outside parent, 303–5
 private time with child(ren), 295
 remarriage, 305–7, 309
 responsibilities for children, 13–14
 sending teenagers to live with fathers, 252–53
 sole custody, 190
 working, 10–11, 49, 57, 124, 129, 134, 158
 and young women, 357
 see also Biological mother(s); Stepmothers
Mourning, 8, 160
 loss of home, 116
Move away policies, 200–1
Moving away, 14, 72, 100, 161, 176, 190, 200–2, 346
 adolescents and, 106
 and parenting plan, 178–79

Negotiation
 continuing, 183–84
Neighborhood(s)
 friends in, 198–99
 unfamiliar, 195
Never married (custody agreement), 200
New husbands, 305, 306
New partner, 296
 introducing children to, 280–81
 see also Lovers
New wife, 308–9, 313
Nine- and ten-year-olds, 73–86
 alignments with parents, 242–43

tellling about infidelity, 27
what to do, 79–84
what to say, 84–86
Nine-year-old
custody choice (example), 218, 219–20
No-fault divorce, 54, 162
Nursery school, 216

Older children
as babysitters, 237
in blended families, 323
coming to terms with divorce, 223
helping with younger, 135–36
and new baby, 319, 320
and remarriage, 291
school contacts, 39
and stepparents, 312
too much responsibility, 147
Older men/women, opportunities for, 116
Once married and divorced (custody
agreement), 200
Only child(ren), 147–48
Outside parent, 290–91, 300–1, 311–23,
326
father as, 301–3
mother as, 303–5
Overburdened child, 231–37
what to do/say, 234–37
Overnights with father, 188
court-ordered, 48–49

Pain, getting stuck in, 5
Parallel parenting, 181–82, 206
Parent alienation syndrome, 243
Parent-child alignments, 239–46
Parent-child bond, 46, 173
broken, 259
Parent-child relationship, 96, 138, 192
adolescents, 108
after baby arrives, 361
changed by divorce, 231–34, 239
changes in, xv, 4, 105
changes in adolescence, 243
contract in, 35
and custody choice, 217
evolving, 311
in second marriage, 299
in young adulthood, 359
Parent role, 92
with adolescents, 107
child assuming, 70, 234, 235–37
in transition, 18

Parenthood, shared, 191
Parenting, xiv–xv, 52, 217
adolescents, 257
aggressive, 250
in blended families, 323–24
nature of, changed, 259
partner in, 271–72
in post-divorce families, 48–49
and relationship with ex-spouse, 13
roles blurred, 186
shared, 6
transformed by divorce, 231
Parenting plan, 191
how to make, 176–77
questions, 177–80
Parents
in blended families, 330–31
changes in lives of, 220
college-age children rescuing, 114–15, 120
dependence on child, 207
fighting, 35, 82
help from, 57
new kind of, 3, 4, 5–7, 157–62
playing off against other, 76–77
same-sex, 97
spending time alone, 330, 331
teenagers think are sexless, 284
of vulnerable children, 123
weekend off, 86
see also Biological parent; Stepparents
Passover, 334–35
Pediatrician, 45, 82, 125, 226, 227
advice from, 166
Peers, 92, 104
sharing problems with, 147
Pensions, dividing, 165
Perspective, 212, 258
loss of, 233
regarding teenagers, 247–48
restoring, 8, 112
Pets, 30, 194–95
Petty theft, 76, 84, 225, 252
Phone numbers, 68–69, 234
Physical custody, 185
Physical custody agreement, 200
Physical joint custody
see Joint physical custody
Play, 55–56, 85
Playground, 64, 70
anger manifest at, 76
rules, 63
Playmates, 68, 195, 216, 223

Pleasure, 138, 139
Popular culture, 255
Post-divorce family, xii, xiii, xiv, xvi, xvii, 37, 129, 141, 182, 215
  adolescence in, 247
  challenges of, 224
  children's preferences in, 204–5
  creating, 153
  custody changes in, 219
  custody plan, 183–84
  fathering in, 260–68
  foundation for, 22, 165
  lack of supervision in, 249
  life arrangements, 30
  overburdened child in, 234
  parent role in, 259
  parenting in, 48–49
  parents leaning on children for advice in, 232
  planning, 106, 179
  sense of, 85
  sibling conflict in, 136
  social change and, 158
  stability in, 86
Postpartum depression, 45
Praise, 31, 67, 306
  for helping, 135
  teenagers, 106
Preadolescents, 89–92
  adolescent behavior in, 33
  in trouble, 129
  see also Eleven-, twelve-, and thirteen-year-olds
Pregnancy, 43, 103, 250
Preschoolers, 129, 194
  with absent fathers, 261
  activities for, 11
  feel abandonment, 254
Private school, 144, 178
Privileges, earning, 256
Professional help, 17, 81, 82, 179
  in abuse cases, 211
  in developmental delay, 32
  in high-conflict divorce, 212
  see also Therapist(s)
Property, division of, 163, 321
Protecting your child, xiii, 20, 86, 129, 202, 203, 245
  from doing too much, 237
  in high-conflict divorce, 211
  in parenting plan, 176–77, 181
  in sole custody, 190

  in violent marriages, 128
  vulnerable child, 124
  in young adulthood, 341–61
Psychiatry, 228
Psychoanalysis, 157
Psychological advice, 179, 200
Psychological changes, 7–10
  in parenting role, 259
Psychological evaluation, 207–10
Psychological health of child, 192, 199–200, 206
Psychological understanding, 66
Psychology, 157, 228

Rage, 5, 80, 128
Reaction to divorce, 28, 35–37, 223, 224–25
  absent fathers in, 261
  age and gender in, 21, 31, 33–34, 35, 88
  college-age children, 113–20
  delayed, 225
  eleven-, twelve-, and thirteen-year-olds, 87–98
  fourteen-, fifteen-, sixteen-, and seventeen-year-olds, 99–112
  lack of, 89
  nine- and ten-year-olds, 73–86
  six-, seven-, and eight-year-olds, 63–72
  temperament in, 34–35
  three-, four-, and five-year-olds, 51–61
Real estate approach to divorce, 24
Rebuilding your life, 117, 203, 363–64
  moving away in, 201
Reconciliation fantasies, 139–40
Regression, 64, 218, 223
Rejection, 207, 241, 267, 358
  fear of, 306
Relationships
  advising young adults about, 353–54, 356, 357, 358
  boy-and-girl, 99
  fragility of, 23, 364
  new, 17
  right and wrong in, 83
  teaching children about, 285–86
  uncommitted, 283
  unreliable, 114, 118
  young adults succeeding in, 341
  see also Adult relationships; Male-female relationships
Religion, 278, 337, 356
Religious training, 177, 187
  source of conflict, 337

Remarriage, 14, 178, 180, 183, 188, 189, 190, 261, 289–97
  agendas in, 293–94
  and custody, 201
  father, 308–9, 310
  getting started on right foot, 291–97
  mother, 305–7, 309
  see also Second marriage
Remarried family, xv, xvi
  flexibility in, 319
  insiders and, 299–310
  problems in, 321–22
  stepparent-child relationship, 311–12
  traditions in, 333
Representation, 164–65
  self, 164–65
  see also Adversarial representation
Resemblances between parent and child, 240
Residence, 177
  changing, in adolescence, 252–53
Resilient children, 57, 224
Respect, 85, 97
Responsibility
  in adolescents, 103
  with less control, 12–14
  sense of, in child, 180
  teaching by example, 95
Responsibility for divorce
  child and, 54, 76
Restraining order, 210
Rewarding children for helping, 58, 85, 106, 135
Right and wrong, 248
  children's judgments regarding, 83
  questions about, 346, 348
  standards of, 255
Rituals, 135, 159
Rivalry, 300–1
  in blended families, 323, 327–30
Role models
  fathering, 265
  parents as, 82–83, 95, 104, 131, 364
  stepmother as, 312
Role reversal, 231–32, 233–34
Routines, 55, 93, 206
  bedtime, 56, 217
  new partner and, 284–85
  setting, 133–40
Rules, 63, 77, 79, 84, 85, 86, 96, 101, 137–38, 147, 182
  in blended families, 326
  changing, 13

  enforcing, 93, 251
  family meeting regarding, 134
  of fathers, 265
  in high-conflict divorce, 206
  lack of, 138
  in post-divorce family, 249
  in second marriage, 302
  of stepfather, 313–14
  of stepmother, 304
  teenagers, 253, 255, 256, 257
  in joint physical custody, 196
Run away, impulse to, 87–88

Sadness
  in children, 36
  in holiday celebrations, 335–36
Schedule
  changing, for children, 264
  mother's, 52, 70
Schedule (child), 34, 85, 133
  activities, 67
  changing, 183–84, 186, 219
  and custody choice, 216
  in high-conflict divorce, 206
  in joint physical custody, 195–96
  legal agreements regarding, 181–82
  parents' responsibility for, 193
  reevaluating, 220
  renegotiating, 184
  in sole custody, 187–88
School, 69, 106, 223, 310
  anger manifest at, 76
  behavior problems, 67
  changing, 100
  child's behavior at, 37–39
  education about drugs, smoking, alcohol, 98
  missing, 253
  new, 224
  in parenting plan, 178
  problems, 219, 326
  six-, seven-, and eight-year-olds, 63, 64–65, 70, 71
  teenagers, 257
  withdrawal from, 81
School counselor, 39, 225, 226, 256
Second marriage, xvii, 129, 220, 251, 260, 287, 289–91
  balancing time in, 295
  breakup rate, 183
  child's fluctuating affections in, 318–19
  failed, 329

Second marriage (*continued*)
finding harmony in, 297
giving up on, 322
mother, 301–2, 305–7
new baby in, 319–20
players in, 299–310, 313–18
potential for misunderstanding and conflict in, 297
stepparent-child relationship in, 311–12
talking to young adults about, 360
see also Remarriage
Secure attachment, 44
Self-centeredness, 75, 103
Self-comforting, 53
Self-esteem, 17, 84, 242, 283
in adolescents, 108
in girls, 92
protecting, 24
work and, 10
Self-image, 4, 7–8
in adolescents, 101
in girls, 92
protecting, 24
Self-pity, 17
Self-sufficiency, 233
Sense of humor, 258
Separation, 56, 90, 117, 123, 223, 227
difficulty with, 244
from youngest child, 272–73
Sex, 283–87
adolescent girls, 255
college-age children, 113
teenagers, 250
Sex education, 98
Sex issues in adolescence, 248–49
Sexual attraction
half siblings, 324
Sexual behavior of parents, 43, 110
and preadolescents, 95–96, 97–98
protecting children from, 27
Sexual deprivation, 76, 128, 283
Sexual drives/impulses, 83
girls struggling with, 263
in preadolescents, 88, 90, 98
in teenagers, 284, 318
Sexual loneliness, 150
Sexual stimulation, 255
Sexually transmitted diseases, 98, 250
Sibling rivalry, 147
Siblings, 36–37, 76, 80, 136, 184, 239
caring for, 94

child care by, 58
in family meeting for teens, 254
fighting, 146–47
moral issues, 346–47
overburdened child and, 234
in remarried family, 320
and stepparents, 310
support from, 146–48
Siblings of parent(s), support from, 145
Single men/women, 142, 150–51
head of family, 269
as threat, 148–49
Single parents, 5–6, 157–58, 187, 360
Sitters, 30, 147, 197
older child as, 237
sharing, 195
Six-, seven-, and eight-year-olds, 63–72
what to do, 66–69
what to say, 69–72
Sleep, 69
parent with child, 56–57
Sleep disturbances, 224
Sleeper effect, 351–52
Sleeping around, 253, 255
Smoking, 98
Social adaptability, 193
Social change, 158
Social contact, avoiding, 256
Social life, 277, 280
Sole custody, 158, 179, 186–90, 208, 218, 219, 220
fathers, 263–64
Solomon, Judith, 48–49
Sons
and fathers, 267, 268
see also Boys
Sorrow, 65
Special needs (children), 123, 178, 179
Special occasions, 333–37
Spiritual groups, 152–53
Spock, Benjamin, xi
Springer relationships, 17–18
Stability, 29, 130, 176, 220
grandparents in, 142
of home, 190
of post-divorce family, 183
in remarriage, 292
from routines, 140
Staying in community, 176
Stepbrothers, 299
Stepchildren, friendships among, 330–31

Stepdaughters
  preteen/teenager, 315–16
  stepmother(s) and, 317–18
Stepfathers, 188, 265, 279, 296, 299, 300, 301,
  302–3, 307, 309, 310, 313–16
Stepmothers, 279, 296, 299, 300, 303–5, 310,
  316–18, 319
  and inheritance, 321
  new baby, 320
Stepparents, xvii, 142, 251, 311–22
Stepsibling, 218
Stepsisters, 299
Stepsons
  stepmothers and, 318
Structure, 86
  post-divorce family, 249
  after school, 94
  setting, 133–40
Substance abuse, 208
Supervision, 137, 257
  lack of, 249
  need for, 219
Support, xii, 125
  lacking, for fathers, 260
  in mothering, 272
  for new family, 141–53
  from peers, 104
Support groups, 153
Symbolic legacy, 119
Symbolic significance
  of gifts, 335
  of traditions, 333, 334
Synagogue, 152–53, 348

Taking care of yourself, 3–18
Taking sides, 118
  adolescents, 110
  grandparents, 143, 144
Talk(ing) to children, xvi–xvii, 21, 39, 40–41,
  166
  adolescents, 102, 109, 110–11, 250–51
  about blended family, 324–25
  college-age children, 117–18
  about college plans, 107–8
  about custody arrangements, 195, 218
  about dating, 280–81
  in delayed reactions to divorce, 225–26
  in divorce negotiations, 170
  about loss of love, 287
  about remarriage, 291–92, 307, 309
  about school problems, 67

  about visiting, 245–46
  see also Conversations
Teachers, 32, 55, 69, 74, 125, 197, 227
  advice from, 166
  complaints from, 67
  conference with, 82, 225
  talking with, 12, 37–40, 68
Teenagers
  and custody arrangements, 184
  getting into trouble, 251–52, 253–54, 326
  helping, 249–50
  new kind of, 247–58
  sent to live with fathers, 220
  sexual impulses, 284
  staying in touch with, 249–50
  and stepmothers, 317–18
  think parents sexless, 284
  two homes, 199
  years after divorce, 223
  see also Adolescents; Fourteen-, fifteen-,
    sixteen-, and seventeen-year-olds
Temper tantrums, 53, 224
Temperament, 35
  in babies, 45, 47–48
  and custody arrangement, 193, 216
  in reaction to divorce, 34–35
  and time to divorce, 127
Thanksgiving, 334
Therapist(s), 19, 82, 181, 209
  in cases of abuse, 211
  child's relationship with, 218–19
  in collaborative law, 169–70
  and high-conflict divorce, 207, 212
  selecting, 212, 226–27, 228–29
Therapy, 8, 45, 128, 211–12, 228–29, 354,
  355, 360
  grandparents paying for, 144
  in high-conflict divorce, 214
Thinking in children, 52–53, 54, 65
Three-, four-, and five-year olds, 51–61
  sleep problems, 88
  telling about divorce, 21
  telling about infidelity, 27
  what to do, 55–58
  what to say, 58–61
three-year-old
  custody choice (example), 217–18, 219
  fretfulness, 88
Thumb-sucking, 64
Time alone with child(ren), 138
Time-outs for parent(s), 112

Toddlers, 44–45, 46–47
  development, 31
  overnight visits, 49
Traditions
  interracial/interfaith, 336–37
  symbolic significance, 333, 334
Transportation, 71, 216, 217
  in joint physical custody, 194
Traumatic events, 129–30
Truancy, 76, 84, 103, 219, 225
Trust, 61, 351, 364
  in babies, 44, 50
  in coparenting, 180–82
  learning, 354
  loss of capacity to, 128
Truth-telling, 97, 110
  see also Honesty
Turning points, xiii
  divorce as, xv, 19
Two homes, 5, 29, 48, 59–61, 219
  disabled child and, 190
  in joint physical custody, 193–94
  shuttling back and forth between, 133, 191,
    197, 198, 200, 206, 216–17, 263
  similarities/differences, 181, 198, 216
  teenagers in, 199
  vulnerable child and, 124
  what child needs in, 194

Uncles, 145
Unhappiness, 130, 131

Values, 201, 250, 337
Violence, 17, 35, 100, 127, 128, 130, 227, 255,
    273–74, 355
  and mediation, 169
  seriousness of, 210, 211
  threat of, 80
Visitation/visiting, xvii, 28–29, 59–60, 157–58,
    200, 223
  adolescents, 107
  back-and-forth, 59–61
  children refusing, 243–45
  conflicts caused by, 71
  forcing, 245
  and moving away, 200–1
  schedule of, 67, 163
  supervised, 210

Vulnerable children, 121–26
  and sole custody, 190

Weddings, 159, 292–93
Withdrawal, 81–82, 153
Women
  challenges in divorce, 10–12
  working, 10–11, 49, 57, 124, 129, 134,
    158
  see also Mothers
Work
  for children, 94
  and custody arrangements, 176, 193
  delaying/reducing, 57
  and parenting plan, 178
  returning to, and vulnerable child, 124
  women, 10–11, 49, 57, 124, 129, 134,
    158
Worries (children), 64, 65, 68
  in blended families, 325–26
  about new baby, 319
  about parents, 78, 85, 135
  in remarriage, 290–91, 294

Young adulthood, xiv, xvii
  protecting children of divorce in, 341–61
Young adults, 114, 117
  anxiety about love and marriage, 350–52
  continuing conversation with, 341–46, 353–
    59, 360
  what you can do, 352–54
Young children, 129
  in blended families, 323
  change in, 183
  need for care, 129
  and new baby, 320
  and remarriage, 291
  stability of care, 130
  and stepparents, 312, 313
  two homes, 198
Young men
  fathers and, 357–59
Young women
  mothers and, 357
Y's, 152

Zero to three years of age, 43–50
  what you say and do, 46–50

JUDITH S. WALLERSTEIN is the founder and executive director of the Center for the Family in Transition. She is senior lecturer emerita at the School of Social Welfare at the University of California at Berkeley, where she has taught for twenty-six years. She has spoken with more divorced families than anyone in the nation, and lectured to thousands of family court judges, attorneys, mental health professionals, mediators, and educators. She has appeared on *Oprah*, the *Today* show, and *Good Morning America*, among others. She is the author, with Sandra Blakeslee, of the national bestsellers *The Good Marriage: How and Why Love Lasts* and *Second Chances: Men, Women, and Children a Decade After Divorce*; with Blakeslee and Julia M. Lewis of the bestseller *The Unexpected Legacy of Divorce: A 25 Year Landmark Study*; and, with Dr. Joan Berlin Kelly, of *Surviving the Breakup: How Children and Parents Cope with Divorce*. She lives in Belvedere, California.

SANDRA BLAKESLEE is an award-winning science writer who contributes regularly to the *New York Times*. She lives in Santa Fe, New Mexico.